Educational Leadership and Children's Rights?

Kinderrechte als Führungsaufgabe?

Collaborative School Development / Gemeinsam Schule gestalten

edited by / herausgegeben von
Jonas Scharfenberg & Julia Hugo

Volume / Band 6

Julia Hugo, Charlotte Assmann,
Andreas Schmidt (Eds.)
with the assistance of David Sehmisch

Educational Leadership and Children's Rights?

Kinderrechte als Führungsaufgabe?

Waxmann 2025
Münster · New York

Bibliographic information published by the Deutsche Nationalbibliothek
The Deutsche Nationalbibliothek lists this publication in
the Deutsche Nationalbibliografie; detailed bibliographic data
are available in the Internet at http://dnb.dnb.de

Collaborative School Development, Volume 6 /
Gemeinsam Schule Gestalten, Band 6

ISSN 2512-8612
Print-ISBN 978-3-8309-4825-4
E-Book-ISBN 978-3-8309-9825-9
https://doi.org/10.31244/9783830998259

Steinfurter Straße 555, 48159 Münster

www.waxmann.com
info@waxmann.com

Cover design: Anne Breitenbach, Münster
Typesetting: Roger Stoddart, Münster
Print: CPI Books GmbH, Leck

Printed on age-resistant paper,
acid-free as per ISO 9706

MIX
Papier aus verantwortungsvollen Quellen
FSC® C083411

Klimaschutz-Beitrag
First Climate
2025
CO₂-Zertifikate

Printed in Germany

Content

Focal point

Children's Rights – and Educational Leadership?

Focal points

Julia Hugo, Charlotte Assmann, Andreas Schmidt (Eds.)
Educational Leadership and Children's Rights?/
Kinderrechte als Führungsaufgabe?

Preface – Series Editors

Vorwort der Reihenherausgebenden

In the academic discourse on school development and leadership, the idea of considering the children's perspective in theoretical considerations, in the design of empirical research projects, and the linking of research results to educational practices has repeatedly come into focus. It is argued that children are to be seen as subjects, rather than objects of educational programs. As such, they are entitled to rights. The necessity to bring together the discourse on children's rights and the role of leadership in the educational system marks a gap that the sixth volume of the series *Collaborative School Development*, entitled *Educational Leadership and Children's Rights?*, explores. As children's rights are also an international topic, the volume is – for the first time – primarily written in English.

The basic conception of this volume once again corresponds to the general principles of the series: The volume sees itself as a link between academic theory and professional practice and as a nexus between discourses that often take place in parallel and sometimes isolated areas. It combines theoretical and empirical contributions from the leadership discourse and enriches these with guest contributions that discuss the implications of children's rights for specific pedagogical areas.

We are delighted that this diversity is also reflected in the editorial board, which adds to the series editors' expertise. While Charlotte Assmann, with her expertise at the interface of school supervision and law, represents the current academic discourse on leadership at the level of educational administration, Andreas Schmidt contributes his methodological profile from his empirical work on meta-reflexivity and teacher professionalism.

We would like to thank the Alumni Association of the Foundation of German Economy (Stiftung der Deutschen Wirtschaft, sdw) as well as the foundation itself for financing this volume, and Waxmann Publishing House for their creative and constructive support at every stage. We would also like to thank the authors who have enriched the volume with their contributions and the reviewers for their support in the review process. Finally, the work of David Sehmisch, which was crucial to the formal completion of the volume, cannot be sufficiently recognized.

Given the wide range of topics covered by the articles, we hope you find the volume inspiring and that it can serve as an incentive for the continued exploration of intersections between leadership and children's rights.

Jonas Scharfenberg & Julia Hugo

Preface – sdw Alumni e.V.

Vorwort des sdw Alumni e.V.

Education plays a pivotal role in promoting children's rights. As Nelson Mandela said: "Education is the most powerful weapon which you can use to change the world."

The sdw Alumni e.V. of former scholarship holders of the *Foundation of German Economy* (Stiftung der Deutschen Wirtschaft, sdw) is especially concerned with this challenge. We are an impactful, interdisciplinary, and entrepreneurial community that has grown to approximately 3.000 members since its inception in 1999. In 2024, we celebrated our 25th anniversary under the motto "25 Years of Courage & Doing". Entrepreneurial thinking and acting are vital for cultivating an open and progressive society. In this society human rights form the foundation of a self-determined life, enabling people to develop their full potential and take responsibility for their actions. Thus, especially the recognition and protection of children's rights is crucial. Therefore, we are delighted that this year's volume addresses a topic central to the pursuit of a just and equitable society, namely children's rights as human rights.

The sdw Alumni e.V. aims to make meaningful contributions to society. Future generations must grow up in environments that foster physical, emotional, and intellectual development. By prioritizing entrepreneurial values and educational leadership, we want to contribute to ensuring that every child – and, finally, every human being – can reach their full potential and become an active, informed citizen, who listens to understand, challenges the status quo, sees more opportunities than fears, treats everyone else (including and especially competitors and competing views) with respect. The future of our society depends on the investments we make in our children today.

With this in mind, we wish you an inspiring reading,

Carena Scheunemann
Board Member
sdw Alumni e.V.
www.sdw-alumni.de

Julia Hugo, Charlotte Assmann, Andreas Schmidt (Eds.)
Educational Leadership and Children's Rights?/
Kinderrechte als Führungsaufgabe?
 https://doi.org/10.31244/9783830998259_1

Julia Hugo, Charlotte Assmann, Andreas Schmidt & David Sehmisch

Educational Leadership and Children's Rights? Two Disparate Strands United

Führung und Kinderrechte im Kontext: eine interdisziplinäre Perspektive

The discourse and the research on leadership in education have been established internationally since at least the late 1980s (see e.g., Fullan, 1998; overview in Gumus et al., 2018) and continue to be a focus of attention (for an overview: English, 2011; Waite & Bogotch, 2017; English, 2020). Over the same period, children's rights became increasingly important in politics and society. Since 1989, this development has been promoted by the ratification of the United Nations Convention on the Rights of the Child (UN CRC) in almost all countries around the globe. However, the scientific discourse, for the most part, neglects to consider the interrelationship between the two topics (exc.: Theoharis, 2024).

On a theoretical and empirical level, central strands of the *discourse on leadership* include different models of educational leadership (overview in Grootenboer, 2018), ranging from leadership theory in general (e.g., Spillane, Halverson & Diamond, 2004) to specific leadership models such as new public management (Dubs, 1996), distributed leadership (Harris, 2004; Tian, Risku & Collin, 2016; Phillips et al., 2023) and its efficacy (Pietsch & Tulowitzki, 2022), co-constructive forms of leading from the middle (Grootenboer et al., 2017; at district level: Hargreaves, 2024; as teacher leadership: Strauss & Anderegg, 2020), and – from a perspective of change – transformational leadership (fundamentally Bass, 1999; Sun & Leithwood, 2012). Regarding individual leaders, the (subjectively perceived) roles and task profiles of educational leaders, as well as their interactions, are of interest (Warwas, 2015; Fossland & Sandvoll, 2021; Veletić & Olsen, 2021). In view of educational governance, the social, structural, organizational, and individual factors determining the probability of (non-) successful leadership are analyzed (Gallagher, 2021). Finally, at the professionalization level, the leaders' needs for specific competencies and resources are researched, to derive implications and content for further training (Schratz et al., 2013; Bush, 2018). These concepts are also related to children and young people in the sense of leadership for learning (Leithwood & Jantzi, 2008; Townsend & McBeath, 2011; Anderegg et al., 2023). The effects of leadership on students' outcomes are, therefore, of great interest (Robinson, Lloyd & Rowe, 2008; Day, Gu & Sammons, 2016).

The international academic debate on *children's rights* is divided into a legal and an educational strand. The legal part covers the discussion about inclusion (UN CRPD; Liefaard & Sloth-Nielsen, 2017; Tobin, 2019) and other specific children's rights, primarily participation (Correia et al., 2019) as well as the relevant transnational case law before the European (ECHR) or the International Court of Human Rights (ICHR) – all at an international level. At the level of individual states, questions of the validity, scope, and implications of international law for the state law and, thus, the respective education systems (Lundy, Kilkelly & Byrne, 2013; Kilkelli, 2019) are discussed, as well as the validity of national fundamental rights (e.g. the right to education, McCowan, 2013). In *educational science*, the discourse on inclusion and children's rights as a school subject dominates. The former regularly refers to the UN CRPD, but without considering the legal implications (e.g. Cornett & Knackstedt, 2020). The latter culminates in children's rights education as a concept (Covell, Howe & McNeil, 2010; Quennerstedt, 2011, 2019; Jerome et al., 2015). Furthermore, the debate about leadership addressing social justice and equity (Brown, 2004; Shields, 2010; for an overview: Tillman & Scheurich, 2013) as well as the aforementioned learning of children and young people (Southworth, 2011; Anderegg et al., 2023) touches (fundamental) legal issues. Apart from only a few studies (for Art. 12 UN CRC see Lundy, 2007; Lundy & Templeton, 2022), the question of a connection between leadership and the promotion of children's rights is critical.

However, if educational leadership is understood as "the quality and competence of exerting leading influence on educational organization members, teachers and faculty, students, and diverse stakeholders within and beyond certain educational organizations and settings towards the achievement of educational visions and goals" (Yan & Han, 2018, n.p.), then children and young people, as the addressees of these "visions" and "goals", are influenced by leadership in the educational context. Accordingly, children's rights become visions and goals of educational leadership.

This ties in with the overarching goals of schools and education in a modern, progressive society. The (social) goal of education is to enable children and young people to participate in society, provide them with the necessary skills and competencies (in the sense of education), and ultimately support them in their personal development so that they can lead a self-determined life. Conversely, leadership in schools is legitimized by the educational mandate of the respective state, usually regulated legally at the constitutional level (e.g., in Germany, France, India, South Africa, etc.) or the statutory level (e.g., in the USA, United Kingdom, Canada, etc.). Despite the respective state's responsibility for education on the one hand and the importance of children's rights for leadership on the other, what is missing is a united discourse on educational leadership and children's rights.

Against this background, this volume interweaves the discourse on children's rights and leadership from different theoretical, conceptual, and empirical perspectives. The compiled articles are situated in one or both areas, always considering the implications for the other. They either focus on leadership and discuss impacts on children's rights, or they focus on children's rights and their implications for educational leadership. In this way, the volume is divided into two sections.

Educational Leadership – and Children's Rights?

The section on *Educational Leadership – and Children's Rights?* includes contributions addressing specific aspects of school leadership and discussing them in relation to children's rights.

In the first article – *Leading with an Equity Vision as a Driver of Instructional Change at Schools Serving Marginalized Communities? Evidence from Four German Schools* – the authors, *Hanna Luise Bronnert-Härle* and *Esther Dominique Klein*, explore a specific concept of leadership – transformational leadership. They ask how educational leadership focused on equity can enhance teaching in schools facing adversity. Using a transformational leadership framework, the study analyzes four German schools, and emphasizes the importance of a clear vision of equity to overcome challenges such as teacher pessimism and student marginalization. A commitment to children's rights, including equitable access to education and recognizing every child's potential, underpins the successful implementation of school instructional strategies. By contrast, schools lacking a unified equity-focused vision struggle with low teacher morale and ineffective teaching practices. The research suggests that leadership anchored in social justice, equity, and children's rights can inspire teachers and promote sustainable instructional improvement, urging leaders to establish inclusive goals that counteract negative beliefs and ensure educational opportunities for all students.

The second article focuses on teachers and their training. *Andreas Schmidt, Ruth Luzmore,* and *Colin Cramer* discuss the role of *Teachers as Educational Change Agents for Children's Rights. Implications and Challenges for Meta-Reflexive Teacher Education,* particularly in upholding children's rights as outlined in Articles 28 and 29 UN CRC. The article highlights the concept of meta-reflexivity in teacher education, which encourages teachers to reflect critically on their roles and navigate complex educational goals. They argue that by adopting ten principles of meta-reflexivity, teachers can better handle the challenges of promoting children's rights. Ultimately, teachers are seen as pivotal change agents, requiring professional development that prepares them to implement these ideals in diverse classroom settings.

Complementary to these articles focusing on leadership actors, the following two contributions examine the structural conditions of the education system in general: In the article *Academic Tracking in Germany as a Challenge to Children's Rights. Implications for School Leadership,* the authors *Robert Pham Xuan* and *Dong Nguyen* analyze Germany's academic tracking system. They raise concerns that tracking, i.e. dividing students into different secondary school paths based on ability, can deepen social inequalities, especially for students from low socio-economic backgrounds – which can be an issue regarding children's right to school education. The article notes limited evidence on whether mobility between tracks can alleviate these issues and emphasizes the role of school leadership in promoting fairness through equitable teacher recommendations and informed parental involvement to ensure tracking decisions benefit all students.

Another contribution addressing the structural level is authored by *Philipp Schubert, Melanie Hochmuth, Julia Hufnagl,* and *Silvia Annen.* Their article about *Recogni-*

tion Authorities as Gatekeepers? Immigrants' Legal Opportunities to Utilize their Qualifications Acquired Abroad explores the role of authorities in facilitating or hindering immigrants' ability to use foreign qualifications in Germany. They highlight that only a moderate number of immigrants manage recognition procedures and that political, social, and economic factors often influence the process. Leadership is essential in ensuring that recognition procedures are transparent and fair, promoting professional integration and social participation for immigrants, as well as their children. The study emphasizes the need for structured management approaches to reduce barriers and inequalities in labor market access through recognition processes.

The section on educational leadership concludes with a contribution drawn from pedagogical practice in early childhood education. *Antonia Bongen's* article *Diversity Management for Discrimination Prevention. A Leadership Task in Daycare Centers* explores the potential of implementing diversity management to prevent discrimination in early education settings. She emphasizes that children's educational success is often linked to their social background, making early education vital for addressing these inequalities. Adapted from business models, diversity management aims to create inclusivity at the leadership level; promoting equal opportunities and reducing discrimination – an objective that corresponds to the prohibition of discrimination in Art. 2 Para. 1 UN CRC. Bongen points out that effective leadership in early childhood settings is essential for embedding diversity awareness and fostering inclusive practices.

Children's Rights – and Educational Leadership?

The section *Children's Rights – and Educational Leadership?* includes contributions addressing specific aspects of children's rights and discussing them with regard to leadership.

In the first article, *School Principals and the Obligation to Act Under a Zero-Tolerance Policy Against Bullying in Schools, Carolina Dahle* and *Tine Sophie Prøitz* give an insight into Norwegian education law and the perspective of one of the countries that has long incorporated children's rights into national legislation. As there is remarkable legal regulation in Norway, by which actors in schools can be criminally charged if pupils do not feel included, they examine the legal obligations under the Norwegian Education Act. The Act mandates principals to ensure a safe and inclusive school environment but places them in a dilemma when conflicting regulations and possible personal sanctions arise. Through content analysis of national regulations and a school leaders' magazine, the authors highlight the growing burden on principals, as well as the need for enhanced competencies and support to effectively manage these responsibilities amidst pressures from policy requirements and practical constraints.

The second article, *Talent Development in the Context of Children's Rights. The Goal of School Design and Leadership,* focuses on a specific child's right: Namely on Article 29 Paragraph 1a of the UN CRC, which grants every child the right to develop their talents. *Mirjam Maier-Röseler, Enkeleta Shtërbani,* and *Gabriele Weigand* argue that schools should support all children in nurturing their unique abilities, tying this to educational equity. Achieving this goal requires significant changes in school structures, teaching approaches, and educator training, transforming individual and group practices. The article reviews vital research on giftedness and the need for educational support, underscoring the importance of a talent-promoting school environment and highlighting the essential role of school leadership in driving these changes with guidance from current theories and research findings.

A concept to practically implement children's rights on a school level is provided by *The UNICEF Child Rights Schools Program. Evaluation from the Perspectives of Teachers, Pupils, and Parents.* The authors *Margit Stein, Benjamin Möbus,* and *Fabio Wensing* examine the UNICEF Child Rights Schools Program, which seeks to empower children and adolescents to be actively involved in their educational environments. They evaluate the program's effectiveness, focusing on the perspectives of various stakeholders – 25 teachers, 39 students, and 33 parents – from a certified UNICEF Child Rights primary school. Their research explores the acceptance and support of the program, the implementation of children's rights, and the perceived opportunities and challenges faced during implementation. The findings indicate that teachers understand the program better than students and parents. While protection rights related to bullying and discrimination are well established, provision and participation rights, such as equitable educational opportunities and student engagement, are less effectively realized. The authors emphasize the need to address information gaps and enhance participatory structures to better integrate children's rights within the school context.

The second part of this volume concludes with two focus articles, both discussing implications for pedagogical practice. First, *Linn Behrendt* analyzes the *Normative Demands of Art. 12 UN CRC on Educational Institutions and their Leaders* for early childhood education. Article 12 guarantees children the right to express their opinions on matters affecting them and to have their views given appropriate weight. Educational institutions are tasked with developing participatory structures to ensure children's rights are respected, requiring educators to adopt a participative approach. Leadership plays a crucial role in fostering environments that support children's involvement. The article highlights how early childhood education can instil participatory rights, emphasizing that leadership must actively promote children's rights and participation.

Second, *Thea Jenner* contributes a paper on *A Children's Rights Approach to All-day Schooling. Implications of the Convention on the Rights of the Child for All-day Education and Care Programs,* where she examines the implications of the UN CRC concerning the shared responsibilities of the school system and child welfare system in organizing all-day education and care programs under the German "Ganztagsförderungsgesetz" (GaFöG). Jenner argues that the broadly defined children's rights – protection, care, academic support, and participation – must be translated into specific recommendations to enhance the quality of all-day programs. This focus on actionable steps aims to ensure that children's rights are effectively integrated into educational practices, ultimately fostering better support and development for children in these settings.

In conclusion, this volume brings together contributions, that show examples for bridging the gap between the fields of educational leadership and children's rights, offering insights into their interplay and mutual impact. The articles presented tackle essential issues such as educational equity, talent development, anti-bullying policies, and inclusion, emphasizing the critical role of leadership in fostering environments that uphold children's rights. Through diverse theoretical, empirical, and conceptual lenses, each contribution highlights how leadership in educational settings can support or hinder children's rights and explores actionable strategies to address this. The debate on this highly relevant issue does not stop here. While the volume aims to inspire further dialogue and research by uniting these strands, underscoring the importance of leadership that actively integrates children's rights into educational practices for meaningful and equitable educational experiences, each article remains focussed on one strand. Further work, that genuinely integrates both educational leadership and children's rights, is needed. This volume serves as a first step in this direction.

References

Anderegg, N., Nies, A., Jesacher-Rößler, L., & Breitschaft, J. (Eds.). (2023). *Leadership for Learning – Shaping Schools for Effective Learning Together.* hep. https://doi.org/10.36933/9783035523010

Bass, B. M. (1999). Two Decades of Research and Development in Transformational Leadership. *European Journal of Work and Organizational Psychology, 8*(1), 9–32. https://doi.org/10.1080/135943299398410

Brown, K. M. (2004). Leadership for Social Justice and Equity. Weaving a Transformative Framework and Pedagogy. *Educational Administration Quarterly, 40*(1), 77–108. https://doi.org/10.1177/0013161X03259147

Bush, T. (2018). Preparation and Induction for School Principals: Global Perspectives. *Management in Education, 32*(2), 66–71.

Cornett, J., & Knackstedt, K. M. (2020). Original Sin(s): Lessons from the US Model of Special Education and an Opportunity for Leaders. *Journal of Educational Administration, 58*(5), 507–520. https://doi.org/10.1108/JEA-10-2019-0175

Correia, N. Camilo, C. Aguiar, C., & Amaro, F. (2019). Children's Right to Participate in Early Childhood Education Settings: A Systematic Review. *Children and Youth Services Review, 100*, 76–88. https://doi.org/10.1016/j.childyouth.2019.02.031

Covell, K., Howe, R. B., & McNeil, J. K. (2010). Implementing Children's Human Rights Education in Schools. *Improving Schools, 13*(2), 117–132.

Day, C., Gu, Q., & Sammons, P. (2016). The Impact of Leadership on Student Outcomes: How Successful School Leaders Use Transformational and Instructional Strategies to Make a Difference. *Educational Administration Quarterly, 52*(2), 221–258.

Dubs, R. (1996). School and New Public Management. *Contributions to Teacher Education, 14*(3), 330–337. https://doi.org/10.36950/bzl.14.3.1996.10477

English, F. W. (2011). *The SAGE Handbook of Educational Leadership. Advances in Theory, Research, and Practice* (2nd ed.). SAGE.

English, F. W. (2020). *The Palgrave Handbook of Educational Leadership and Management Discourse.* Palgrave Macmillan. https://doi.org/10.1007/978-3-030-39666-4

Fossland, T., & Sandvoll, R. (2021). Drivers for Educational Change? Educational Leaders' Perceptions of Academic Developers as Change Agents. *International Journal for Academic Development, 28*(3), 305–318. https://doi.org/10.1080/1360144X.2021.1941034

Fullan, M. (1998). Leadership for the 21st Century: Breaking the Bonds of Dependency. *Educational Leadership, 55*(7), 1–4.

Gallagher, T. (2021). Governance and Leadership in Education Policy Making and School Development in a Divided Society. *School Leadership & Management, 41*(1–2), 132–151. https://doi.org/10.1080/13632434.2021.1887116

Grootenboer, P. (2018). Theories and Models of Educational Leadership. In P. Grootenboer (Ed.), *The Practices of School Middle Leadership* (pp. 21–41). Springer. https://doi.org/10.1007/978-981-13-0768-3_2

Grootenboer, P., Rönnerman, K., & Edwards-Groves, C. (2017). Leading from the Middle: A Praxis-Oriented Practice. In P. Grootenboer, C. Edwards-Groves & S. Choy (Eds.), *Practice Theory Perspectives on Pedagogy and Education* (pp. 243–263). Springer. https://doi.org/10.1007/978-981-10-3130-4_13

Gumus, S., Bellibas, M. S., Esen, M., & Gumus, E. (2018). A Systematic Review of Studies on Leadership Models in Educational Research from 1980 to 2014. *Educational Management Administration & Leadership, 46*(1), 25–48. https://doi.org/10.1177/1741143216659296

Hargreaves, A. (2024). *Leadership From the Middle. The Beating Heart of Educational Transformation*. Routledge.

Harris, A. (2004). Distributed Leadership and School Improvement: Leading or Misleading? *Educational Management Administration & Leadership, 32*(1), 11–24. https://doi.org/10.1177/1741143204039297

Jerome, L., Emerson, L., Lundy, L., & Orr, K. (2015). *Teaching and Learning about Child Rights: A Study of Implementation in 26 Countries*. UNICEF.

Kilkelly, U. (2019). The UN Convention on the Rights of the Child: Incremental and Transformative Approaches to Legal Implementation. *The International Journal of Human Rights, 23*(3), 323–337.

Leithwood, K., & Jantzi, D. (2008). Linking Leadership to Student Learning: The Contributions of Leader Efficacy. *Educational Administration Quarterly, 44*(4), 496–528.

Liefaard, T., & Sloth-Nielsen, J. (Eds.). (2017). *The United Nations Convention on the Rights of the Child: Taking Stock After 25 Years and Looking Ahead*. Brill Nijhoff.

Lundy, L. (2007). 'Voice' is not Enough: Conceptualising Article 12 of the United Nations Convention on the Rights of the Child. *British Educational Research Journal, 33*(6), 927–942.

Lundy, L., Kilkelly, U., & Byrne, B. (2013). Incorporation of the United Nations Convention on the Rights of the Child in Law: A Comparative Review. *The International Journal of Children's Rights, 21*(3), 442–463.

Lundy, L., & Templeton, M. (2022). Children's rights and School Leadership: An International Perspective. *International Journal of Educational Research, 114*, 101980.

McCowan, T. (2013). *Education as a Human Right: Principles for a Universal Entitlement to Learning*. Bloomsbury Academic.

Phillips, D., Stewart-Fox, T., Phillips, S., Griffith, M., & Bhojedat, J. (2023). Distributed Leadership in Education: A Systematic Review of its Role in Fostering Innovative Practices and Enhancing School Performance. *International Journal of Science and Research (IJSR), 12*(11), 2083–2089. https://doi.org/10.21275/SR231128014118

Pietsch, M., & Tulowitzki, P. (2022). Effects of Distributed Leadership on Teachers' Job Satisfaction, Organizational Commitment and Organizational Citizenship Behaviour: a Systematic Review and Meta-Analysis. *Educational Management Administration & Leadership*, *50*(5), 764–781.

Quennerstedt, A. (2011). The Construction of Children's Rights in Education – a Research Synthesis. *International Journal of Children's Rights*, *19*(4), 661–678.

Quennerstedt, A. (2019). Language Use in the Human Rights Education of Children. *Human Rights Education Review*, *2*(1), 25–46.

Robinson, V. M., Lloyd, C. A., & Rowe, K. J. (2008). The Impact of Leadership on Student Outcomes: An Analysis of the Differential Effects of Leadership Types. *Educational Administration Quarterly*, *44*(5), 635–674.

Schratz, M., Laiminger, A., MacKay, F. K. P., Křižková, E., Kirkham, G. A., Baráth, T., Cseh, G., Kigyós, T., Chrappán, M., Kovács, E., Révai, N., Hašková, A., Laššák, V., Bitterová, M., Erčulj, J., Peček, P., Malmberg, K., & Söderberg, T. (Eds.). (2013). *The Art and Science of Leading a School – Central5: A Central European View on Competencies for School Leaders.* Tempus Public Foundation.

Shields, C. M. (2010). Transformative Leadership: Working for Equity in Diverse Contexts. *Educational Administration Quarterly, 46*(4), 558–589. https://doi.org/10.1177/0013161X10375609

Southworth, G. (2011). Connecting Leadership and Learning. In J. Robertson & H. Timperley (Eds.), *Leadership and Learning* (pp. 71–85). SAGE. https://doi.org/10.4135/9781446288931.n6

Spillane, J. P., Halverson, R., & Diamond, J. B. (2004). Towards a Theory of Leadership Practice: A Distributed Perspective. *Journal of Curriculum Studies, 36*(1), 3–34. https://doi.org/10.1080/0022027032000106726

Strauss, N.-C., & Anderegg, N. (Eds.). (2020). *Teacher Leadership – Leading Schools Collectively*. Hep.

Sun, J., & Leithwood, K. (2012). Transformational School Leadership Effects on Student Achievement. *Leadership and Policy in Schools*, *11*(4), 418–451.

Theoharis, G. (2024). *The School Leaders Our Children Deserve*. Teachers College.

Tian, M., Risku, M., & Collin, K. (2016). A Meta-Analysis of Distributed Leadership from 2002 to 2013: Theory Development, Empirical Evidence and Future Research Focus. *Educational Management Administration & Leadership*, *44*(1), 146–164. https://doi.org/10.1177/1741143214558576

Tillman, L. C., & Scheurich, J. J. (Eds.). (2013). *Handbook of Research on Educational Leadership for Equity and Diversity*. Routledge.

Tobin, J. (2019). *The UN Convention on the Rights of the Child: A Commentary*. Oxford University.

Townsend, T., & MacBeath, J. (Eds.). (2011). *International Handbook of Leadership for Learning*. Springer.

Veletić, J., & Olsen, R. V. (2021). Exploring School Leadership Profiles Across the World: A Cluster Analysis Approach to TALIS 2018. *International Journal of Leadership in Education*, *27*(5), 1090–1116. https://doi.org/10.1080/13603124.2021.1953612

Waite, D., & Bogotch, I. (Eds.). (2017). *The Wiley International Handbook of Educational Leadership*. Wiley. https://doi.org/10.1002/9781118956717

Warwas, J. (2015). Principals' Leadership Behaviour: Values-based, Contingent or Both? *Journal of Educational Administration, 53*(3), 310–334.

Yan, W., & Han, Y. (2018). Educational Leadership. In A. Farazmand (Ed.), *Global Encyclopedia of Public Administration, Public Policy, and Governance* (pp. 1581–1586). Springer. https://doi.org/10.1007/978-3-319-20928-9_2236

Educational Leadership – and Children's Rights?

Julia Hugo, Charlotte Assmann, Andreas Schmidt (Eds.)
Educational Leadership and Children's Rights?/
Kinderrechte als Führungsaufgabe?
 https://doi.org/10.31244/9783830998259_2

Hanna Luise Bronnert-Härle & Esther Dominique Klein[1]

Leading with an Equity Vision as a Driver of Instructional Change at Schools Serving Marginalized Communities?

Evidence from Four German Schools

Abstract

Despite challenges, some schools serving marginalized communities (SSMC) pursue a vision centered on educational equity, yet few studies systematically examine how this vision focused on equity aids instructional improvement in schools with such contexts. This paper argues that leading with an equity vision is crucial in less successful SSMC, where teachers, facing repeated experiences of failure, need a clear vision and supportive structures to counteract pessimistic beliefs. Analyzing four German SSMC, the study combines transformational leadership with the normative reference of equity, using qualitative data from guided problem-centered interviews with leaders. Two schools have established clear teaching structures, which teachers perceive as supportive, though only one has an explicit vision. At the third school, the principal struggles to promote a vision of equity due to the school culture, while the fourth shows signs of *threat rigidity*, focusing on stress reduction over improving student learning. Without an equity vision, leaders and staff lack the foundation needed to address student marginalization. The findings suggest that having an equity vision can help principals implement organizational structures that empower teachers and reduce pessimistic beliefs. The article discusses possible conclusions and identifies areas for further research.

Keywords

Educational Equity, Transformational Leadership, Instructional Improvement, Schools Serving Marginalized Communities

---

1 Shared authorship

Führung mit einer Vision der Bildungsgerechtigkeit als Motor für Unterrichtsentwicklung an Schulen an sozialräumlich benachteiligten Standorten?

Befunde aus vier deutschen Schulen

Zusammenfassung
Trotz aller Herausforderungen verfolgen einige Schulen an sozialräumlich benachteiligten Standorten eine auf Bildungsgerechtigkeit ausgerichtete Vision, doch nur wenige Studien untersuchen systematisch, wie diese Vision zur Verbesserung des Unterrichts beiträgt. In diesem Beitrag wird argumentiert, dass eine Vision von entscheidender Bedeutung ist, da die Lehrkräfte angesichts wiederholter Misserfolgserlebnisse eine klare Vision und unterstützende Strukturen benötigen, um pessimistischen Überzeugungen entgegenzuwirken. Die Studie analysiert vier deutsche Schulen und kombiniert transformationale Führung mit einem normativen Bezug zu Bildungsgerechtigkeit, wobei qualitative Daten aus leitfadengestützten, problemzentrierten Interviews mit Führungskräften verwendet werden. Zwei Schulen haben klare Unterrichtsstrukturen geschaffen, die von den Lehrer*innen als unterstützend empfunden werden, obwohl nur eine Schule eine explizite Vision hat. An der dritten Schule fällt es der Schulleitung aufgrund der Schulkultur schwer, eine Vision der Bildungsgerechtigkeit zu fördern, während die vierte Schule Anzeichen von *Thread Rigidity* zeigt und sich auf den Abbau von Belastung statt auf die Entwicklung des Schülerlernens konzentriert. Ohne eine Vision der Bildungsgerechtigkeit fehlt der Schulleitung und dem Personal die Grundlage, um in ihrem Handeln die Marginalisierung von Schüler*innen zu adressieren. Die Ergebnisse deuten darauf hin, dass eine Vision der Bildungsgerechtigkeit Schulleitenden dabei helfen kann, Organisationsstrukturen zu schaffen, die Lehrkräfte stärken und pessimistische Überzeugungen abbauen. Der Beitrag erörtert mögliche Schlussfolgerungen und zeigt Forschungsdesiderata auf.

Schlüsselbegriffe
Bildungsgerechtigkeit, transformationale Führung, Unterrichtsverbesserung, Schulen für marginalisierte Gemeinschaften

1. Introduction

School improvement initiatives targeting schools serving marginalized communities (SSMC) have been a focal point of educational research since the 1970s. Many of these schools encounter significant adversity that impedes instructional change (Zumpe, 2024), yet some manage to thrive. Research has identified that, among others, a clear vision and defined goals can help educators work towards change and improvement (Hemmings, 2012; Potter, Reynolds & Chapman, 2002). Case studies of successful SSMC often illustrate a school vision and mission centered around educational equity (for an overview: Klein, 2018). However, although leadership research underscores the relevance of goal-oriented leadership in various aspects of schooling, from teacher motivation to school improvement planning (Sun & Leithwood, 2015), research often leaves out a normative frame regarding the goals, and there are only a few studies analyzing how leading with a vision that is focused on educational equity can facilitate instructional improvement specifically at schools facing chronic adversity. The approach of transformational leadership serves as an analytical framework, where the development of a compelling vision is the core element. Teachers are empowered through individual support and intellectual stimulation to embrace this vision (e.g. Brown & Treviño, 2006). Such a vision may be relevant for systematically developing strategies that not only contribute to instructional improvement but also embed the idea of educational equity in teaching and focus on the academic learning of students (Klein, 2022).

Combining transformational leadership with the normative reference of equity, and using qualitative data from four German schools, this paper explores how a vision centered on educational equity shapes leadership strategies for instructional improvement amidst the challenges posed by chronic adversity in schools serving disadvantaged communities in Germany. To do so, we use data from guided problem-centered interviews.

2. The Role of Leading with an Equity Vision at SSMC

SSMC typically enroll more students from communities that are historically marginalized, such as economically disadvantaged or racialized groups. These students face greater challenges in navigating the education system successfully and accessing higher education, and they receive less acknowledgment at school and thus struggle to develop a positive academic self-concept (OECD, 2019). Consequently, they often experience lower life chances compared to students from more privileged communities.

2.1 Challenges of SSMC

In discussions about SSMC, the adversities facing schools are often attributed to student and community characteristics. However, research indicates that adversity arises from a poor fit between these characteristics and the educational system's requirements, as well as unfavorable school strategies (Bremm, Klein & Racherbäumer, 2016). Educators at SSMC must provide educational support that the system expects families to offer, such as the introduction to relevant cultural assets and formal language registers before school. In addition, there's a mismatch between the students' milieu-specific habitus and the educators' expectations (Kramer & Helsper, 2010), leading to perceived challenges in behavior and abilities (Bremm et al., 2016; Forell, 2020). This adversity is exacerbated by a mismatch between demands on teachers and available resources (Zumpe, 2024).

Consequently, educators at SSMC often experience their efforts to help students succeed as failures, fostering helplessness and defensiveness (Zumpe, 2024). Teachers may attribute student failure to internal deficits like lower linguistic skills or behavioral problems (e.g., Jacobson et al., 2022; van den Bergh et al., 2010), linked to socio-economic status, ethnicity, or family socialization (Valencia, 2010). This perceived lack of control affects their ability to reflect on and improve their teaching practices.

As a result, less successful SSMC often harbor pessimistic views, hindering critical reflection of their pedagogical practice (Potter et al., 2002). A key development task for SSMC is to challenge such pessimism and help educators develop a positive outlook and agency (Zumpe, 2024).

2.2 The Role of an Equity Vision

For teachers facing long-term adversity, admitting they may have negatively impacted students can be painful and threatening. Senge (2006) argues that

> "[w]ithout a pull toward some goal which people truly want to achieve, the forces in support of the status quo can be overwhelming. […] Learning can be difficult, even painful. With a shared vision, we are more likely to expose our ways of thinking, give up deeply held views, and recognize personal and organizational shortcomings" (p. 195).

Senge (2006) describes a vision as "a force in people's hearts" (p. 192). We assume that a lack of vision may emotionally burden teachers, as it is difficult to acknowledge their role in students' lack of success without threatening their self-esteem. Goals direct actions, increase persistence, and activate relevant knowledge (Locke & Latham, 2002). Sun and Leithwood (2015) highlight that goal-setting strengthens teachers' self-efficacy and commitment, aids in prioritization, and enables strategic planning.

Less successful SSMC often lack a vision and goals (Muijs et al., 2004; Potter et al., 2002), which entails ineffective structures, hindering teacher and student success (Hemmings, 2012). Case studies indicate that successful SSMC in contrast, often have an *equity vision.* Equity vision in this context means an image of a future in which their students have the same access to educational resources as other students; this image is connected to the belief that the school's mission is to empower students by providing opportunities society may deny them (for an overview: Klein, 2018). Without such an equity-centered vision that addresses the educators as advocates for their students rather than 'victims' of external circumstances, and structures built around that vision, teachers may focus on external factors rather than reflecting their practices. Thus, leading with an equity vision is crucial for SSMC to change pedagogical and instructional practices.

2.3 Transformational Leadership

One concept to theoretically underpin *leading with an equity vision* is transformational leadership (TL). At its core, the theory of action of TL is that leaders convince those they lead to pursue a common goal – or a shared vision – out of intrinsic motivation (Bass & Avolio, 1994). Based on this, Leithwood et al. (2006) describe four strategic components of effective transformational leadership in schools that have been shown to be effective in several empirical studies.

- *Setting directions*: Leadership develops a shared vision, motivates individuals with meaningful and challenging goals, and sets high expectations (e.g., identifying and articulating a vision, holding high performance expectations).
- *Developing people:* Leaders enhance educators' competencies with intellectual stimulation, individual support, and role modeling (e.g., modeling valued behaviors, beliefs, and values).
- *Restructuring the organization:* Leaders restructure schools to support educators, foster collaboration, and adapt flexibly to achieve goals (e.g., creating collaborative cultures, restructuring to foster collaboration).
- *Managing the instructional program*: Leaders guide instruction, supervise teaching, support educators, review progress, and shield teachers from distractions (e. g., planning and supervising instruction providing instructional support).

The concept illustrates that the main drivers of change are an inspiring vision, clear improvement goals, and conditions that motivate educators to take ownership and enable them to work towards the goals.

2.4 Effects of TL

TL in schools indirectly affects student learning through teacher engagement, self-efficacy, job satisfaction, wellbeing, and school culture or organizational learning (e.g., Leithwood & Sun, 2012; Witziers, Bosker & Kruger, 2003). Moreover, case studies of successful SSMC show that leaders often anchor their vision in beliefs about social justice and use strategies to reinforce this perspective (Jacobson et al., 2007; Ylimaki, Jacobson & Drysdale, 2007).

However, the impact of TL is strong in US studies, but smaller in other international contexts (e.g., Witziers et al., 2003). Research from Germany – the setting of our research – indicates that TL affects teacher motivation and well-being (e.g., Gerick, 2014), but not instructional practice (Pietsch & Tulowitzki, 2017). Comparative studies between the US and Germany moreover show that German principals lead less in instructional or professional development compared to US principals (e.g., Klein et al., 2022).

Principals at SSMC are more likely to exhibit visionary leadership than those in more privileged communities (Graw-Krausholz & Pietsch, 2020). This, however, depends on their belief in their influence, feeling of acceptance, and perceived teacher innovativeness (Klein et al., 2024; Tulowitzki et al., 2023).

3. Study Design

To date, there are no studies that systematically delineate what consequences an equity vision has for leadership, professional development and instructional improvement at SSMC. This paper aims to analyze the extent to which the four dimensions of *Setting Directions, Helping People, Restructuring the Organization,* and *Managing the Instructional Program* (Leithwood et al., 2006) can be identified in the leadership practices of principals at SSMC in Germany, and how they feed into the ability of the school to effectively address professional development and instructional improvement.

The paper uses qualitative data from the project "Leadership and School Improvement in Context", which was carried out through the University of Duisburg-Essen and funded by the German Research Foundation (Grant Number 279117534).

3.1 Data Source

We examined principals' role perceptions and leadership strategies at SSMC with varying improvement needs. The study sequentially combined quantitative and qualitative data in two sub-studies. We identified SSMC based on the state's socioeconomic index, which categorizes schools into five categories based on welfare recipients in the catchment area, and students with an immigration background at the school. Initially, quantitative data from 16 SSMC in one German state were analyzed (Klein & Bronnert-Härle, 2020). Then, in-depth studies were conducted in four schools. The schools had, on average, 887 students. This paper focuses the qualitative in-depth studies, in which we conducted problem-centered interviews with different leaders at the schools (see tab. 1).

Table 1: Overview of data.

	Teacher assessment in quantitative survey[a]			Number of interviews	
School	Transformational leadership	Team collaboration and shared values	Teacher deficit thinking	Members of school leadership team	Other teacher leaders
Rosenschule	higher	higher	lower	3	6
Tulpenschule	higher and average	higher	average	3	6
Kornblumenschule	lower	lower	average	2	6
Geranienschule	average	average	higher	2	4

Note: [a] see Klein et al., 2022, for an overview of the scales. Table indicates whether scores of each school were significantly higher or lower ($p < .05$) than the sample average.

The leadership team at each school consists of a principal, assistant principal, and curriculum director (CD). *Rosenschule*[2], established in the 2010s and located in a large city, has had the same principal from the start. *Tulpenschule* was established in the 1980s and is located in a smaller city. The principal has been at this school for 12 years. *Kornblumenschule*, established in the 1980s and located in a large city, has a principal that has been at this school for four years. *Geranienschule* was established in the 1990s and is located in a large city as well. Their principal, too, has been at this school for four years.

3.2 Methodological Approach

Guided problem-centered interviews (Witzel, 2000) were conducted with the principals, assistant principals, CDs, and various teacher leaders[3] (tab. 1). The principals were asked about their strategies based on Leithwood et al.'s (2006) dimensions of TL. Other leaders and teachers were also asked about changes and current structures and processes of professional learning.

All interviews were recorded and transcribed, then analyzed using a structuring qualitative content analysis (Mayring, 2022). The deductive coding system contained the main codes and subcategories of Leithwood et al.'s (2006) TL dimensions. The findings were first summarized for school leaders and teachers separately per school (Hartung-Beck & Muslic, 2015), and then compared across these groups. In the analysis of the data, the focus was placed on the comparison between the schools.

4. Results

4.1 Visions of the different schools

Since the focus of this paper is on analyzing the vision centered on educational equity, the results regarding the subcategory *Identifying and articulating a vision* within the dimension *Setting Directions* are presented first.

The principal of Rosenschule (RS) has an explicit vision for her school that the entire leadership team clearly identifies with. The vision is focused on educational justice that is *owed to the students*, but hindered by current societal structures:

> "Because we got children who were first left behind in elementary school, the children who are with us because of fleeing and poverty and displacement. Highly talented children, highly talented." (RS-P; 45–47)

2 All school names are pseudonyms.

3 Teachers who take an active role in the leadership and development of their schools beyond their regular teaching responsibilities (e.g., department heads).

This political perception of the schools' situation is framed as the main reason that the educators do not feel helpless:

> "And we don't sit here and say, 'we are the poor victims.' But rather, we know what is happening to us is happening for certain reasons. That this school is a political school, and every school has to be seen in the context of socio-political things." (RS-P; 833–837)

Other interviewees confirm that the vision is shared by the teachers. The principal is open to new ideas while staying focused on the vision and the planning that is connected to it. Consensus is achieved through shared decision making, intensive communication, and systematic professional development planning as well as training for the large group of 'career jumpers' that are teaching at the school.

At Tulpenschule (TS), the leadership team describes various short- and medium-term development goals that are set with the staff at the beginning of the school year. Implicitly, the school's practices are subject to a vision of equity. For example, the principal has high expectations for student achievement and does not tolerate deficit thinking: "[...] basically, my approach is that children who have a prognosis for *Hauptschule*[4] are not necessarily Hauptschule students but can develop into something higher" (TS-P; 28–31).

However, an explicit overarching vision for development goals is missing. Instead, the leaders at Tulpenschule emphasize the importance of consensus among teaching staff; development goals are discussed at length in teacher committees and teachers are encouraged to contribute their own ideas:

> "We basically do it in such a way that we first, I'd say, 'go around the villages'. [...] And then we basically pass it on to the individual committees. [...] And then we have it discussed everywhere. [...] And then, once it has been discussed, it goes to the teachers' conference. [...] And then we talk about it together. There, too, everyone has another opportunity to say something (...)." (TS-P; 306–323)

At Kornblumenschule (KS), the principal pursues two development goals, establishing team structures and abandoning student ability tracking. While there is consensus and an improvement plan for the former, the latter is controversial, and the principal is unable to convince the teachers of its merit. Even within the leadership team, there is no consensus on this. The principal is described as someone who sometimes imposes goals against the teachers' wishes: "There simply are areas that our principal doesn't want to give away and where he has very specific ideas about how things should be. And then sometimes tries to change things without getting people on board first" (KS-L23; 146–149).

The teachers feel that school improvement lacks clear planning: some teacher-developed ideas are rejected when these rely on tracking, while other project ideas unrelated to the school's development goals are approved by the principal: "Everyone's

4 In the German secondary school system, *Hauptschule* is the lowest track school, leading to a diploma after grade 9 and qualifying graduates mostly for craftman trades.

ideas, yes, they are allowed, they are permitted, they are also supported, but there is no such thing as a master plan" (KS-L32; 287–297).

In Geranienschule (GS), the interviews do not indicate a common vision or shared improvement goals. Instead, the leadership team phrases wishes reflecting their view of their students:

> "I can't work with class sizes of 27 at this school if we have three children with special needs in the classes, two more newcomers [refugee children; the authors], and the *normal* student body – I say so in quotes – arrives at our school with below-average results as well." (GS-P; 575–579)

The principal emphasizes that high workload, stress, and limited resources keep him from developing a vision:

> "But there are still a few things where I think you could actually turn the school completely upside down. [...] The way I'm acting here at the moment, I have to say quite honestly that I lack the horizon to think about it." (GS-P; 679–683)

Throughout the interviews, the interviewees profess a deficit-oriented view of students; for example, the CD notes the need to focus on discipline management and social learning, and questions whether all students *deserve* the teachers' engagement: "But we are trying more and more to just also see the nice kids who absolutely deserve that we put a lot of effort into our job because they need us" (GS-CD; 40–42).

Although there is awareness that a lack of focus on academic learning has worsened student performance, concrete approaches are not (yet) developed. The principal expresses helplessness in convincing people of ideas. External development impulses are seen as unhelpful; according to the principal, all achievements of the school have come from within.

4.2 Strategies to implement the vision

The results of the categories *Developing People, Restructuring the Organization,* and *Managing the Instructional Program* are summarized in this section. In all four schools, team structures and distribution of leadership are at the core of organizational structures; at the same time, the approach to utilizing collaboration towards instructional improvement differs.

4.2.1 Rosenschule

In Rosenschule, the vision and its attitudes are embodied by the principal, institutionalized in practices, and reflected in structures. Leadership strongly focuses on instructional development, foregrounding it in team meetings and PD. The vision that equity necessitates empowerment is the main pillar of the school's instructional concept.

The principal emphasizes that one of the main reasons for her vision to be adopted in her school is that she has clear strategies to help educators work towards that vision, which is defined as unusual for lower track schools: "And then we started with colleagues from *Hauptschule*, who were a bit surprised that [our work; the authors] here was about quality and about somehow picking up pace" (RS-P; 38–40).

The leadership team expects teachers to reflect and improve their practice, with a focus on identifying and solving issues where teachers are struggling. To help teachers teach according to the concept, leadership has implemented regular classroom observations between teachers; additional observations by the leadership team are followed by an in-depth reflection meeting. Support strategies moreover include tandem partners for struggling teachers.

Each grade level team has a champion of the instructional concept implemented throughout classrooms. Teacher collaboration is facilitated through timetables, protocols, and leadership visibility. Leadership tasks and responsibilities are distributed broadly among staff, and transparency in decision-making is emphasized. Teachers can act autonomously but receive feedback. Knowledge management moreover includes the dissemination of external PD knowledge and using observations, feedback, and surveys to monitor developments and identify needs.

This empowerment strengthens educators' positive mindset amid school challenges by modeling the appreciative attitude expected from teachers towards students:

> "And I think you have to model what you expect from your colleagues. [...] So if I expect them to be friendly and appreciative with the children, then I have to do the same with my colleagues." (RS-P; 412–415)

The instructional program thus influences teaching practices; discipline management, in contrast, plays only a minor role in the interviews.

4.2.2 Tulpenschule

The principal at Tulpenschule describes instructional development as the core of school improvement. Instruction is built around an interdisciplinary individual learning approach that allows students to work at their own pace, based on diagnostics. The concept affects teachers' instructional work to a high degree. Classroom and discipline management is ensured through rules, structures, and teacher PD, though it is not the primary focus of instructional improvement. Leadership monitors teacher and student performance, is visible in the classrooms and proactively addresses issues based on their observations, which, however, is perceived by some as intrusive. Teachers are moreover expected to align their PD with the school goals. Data is used to track specific issues (e.g., the type of diploma students get).

The instructional concept requires close teacher collaboration. The principal encourages collaboration by promoting peer observation and scheduling collaboration time. Mandatory collaboration protocols identify and address needs. Tasks are distributed broadly among staff, and teachers have a high degree of autonomy within them.

The principal values trusting relationships with teachers; teachers describe her as approachable, visible, and appreciative. She approaches teachers for leadership roles and addresses development potentials. Teachers report that their voices are heard and respected by her.

> "I experienced her as someone who always has an open ear, so if you go to her and no matter what the problem is, she takes care of it. And always makes you feel that she's on your side." (TS-L60; 425–427)

4.2.3 Kornblumenschule

In Kornblumenschule, the leadership team shares low expectations for student performance but has diverging views of what this entails with regard to instructional development. The principal has high expectations of the teachers and emphasizes academic learning, while the CD pathologizes students and prioritizes the teachers' pedagogical autonomy over developing common instructional concepts:

> "It is actually completely irrelevant to me whether we have wonderfully elaborated curricula […]. So I don't need wonderful concepts, but I need the feeling that we live together here and that we are doing well." (KS-CD; 192–195)

Emphasizing teacher autonomy, the current CD trusts teachers' professionalism, avoiding systematic evaluations and relying on their 'gut feeling'. Development ideas are suggested without 'restrictive' structures. Instructional decisions are decentralized in the subject departments, with teachers setting their own goals. Support structures focus on ad hoc classroom issues and professional development and are primarily provided upon teacher request. Classroom observations are at the teachers' discretion; leadership only observes lessons for formal evaluation procedures of early career teachers[5]. As a result, teachers express the belief that leadership does not know what happens in classrooms.

The one development goal that staff has been able to agree on is developing a systematic team structure. However, even in this, clear collaboration structures are avoided because the CD believes that teachers can develop better when they have autonomy:

> "If we write something down, we have to stick to it. We don't want that. Please don't set us any limits, give us the pedagogical freedom to work with the groups and see what they need." (KS-CD; 181–184)

5 In the German school system, there is no regular formal teacher evaluation after that.

4.2.4 Geranienschule

At Geranienschule, the leadership team prioritizes reducing teachers' workload over instructional improvement: "that is just a bit of the difficult thing in school, that we ultimately only have limited resources" (GS-CD; 505–506). Focusing on resources and stress culminates in low expectations for both teachers and students. Instructional development is mainly focused on managing discipline, with students being described to have "no social competences whatsoever" (GS-CD; 102–103). Apart from that, leadership ideas focus on reducing stress, such as double staffing classes that is not specifically aimed at improving student learning, but rather on decreasing teachers' workload, while the principal and CD acknowledge that the school lacks a clear perspective on academic learning.

Teacher support addresses ad hoc problems with direct support, such as an assigned tandem partner or collaboration with other teachers. Classroom observations among teachers are rare "due to the high workload" (GS-CD; 447–448), and the school's PD plan is not aligned with specific improvement goals.

Organizational structures are perceived as restrictive, but nevertheless important. The school emphasizes the development of team structures, such as a school improvement committee, scheduled collaboration times, communication guidelines for grade teams, and systematic internal evaluation. Leadership aims to involve the whole teaching staff, particularly grade level leaders, in decision making and problem solving. The teachers' staff meeting is seen as the central place of school improvement, where the majority decides about what improvement goals to pursue: "And then you also have to live with the fact that you haven't found a majority" (GS-CD; 389). Teachers describe the principal as appreciative and approachable but mirror his focus on high workload.

5. Discussion

Before discussing our findings, it is important to address the limitations of our data. A qualitative study with only four schools presents a limitation regarding the representativeness of the sample and cannot provide clear evidence that leading with an equity vision can help teachers overcome a pessimistic outlook. Moreover, our study is a cross-sectional analysis. As a result, we can only describe changes based on the retrospective interpretation of those who were involved in these changes. These could be biased by particularly positive or negative experiences and how these were negotiated in the schools. Such biases are probably evident in the contrast between Rosenschule and Geranienschule. Since the goal of the research was to describe leadership strategies, we chose qualitative content analysis; a different methodological approach may have also allowed us to describe the underlying cognitions and thus uncover possible biases.

Bearing these limitations in mind, our data nevertheless allow for some insights that bear relevance for the discussion of leadership at SSMC. At Rosenschule, the principal's vision is clearly communicated and integrated into the school's structures, viewed by the principal as pivotal for the school's success and community cohesion, resonating with the concept of vision as "a force in people's hearts" (Senge, 2006, p. 192) and parallels studies from the US describing similar results. At Tulpenschule, a similarly clear vision is not explicitly evident. Interviews indicate that the principal refers to personal equity beliefs and rejects deficit thinking, yet she does not articulate a unified shared vision. Nevertheless, teachers at Tulpenschule are committed to a common instructional concept based on a shared idea about learning.

Although only one school has an explicit vision, both principals have established clear structures for instruction, and despite these 'restrictions', teachers feel largely free in their decision-making, indicating that the structures support rather than restrict them. Understanding why this is exceptional in German schools requires knowledge of the 'DNA' of German schools. Traditionally, the German school system is characterized by pronounced teacher autonomy and isolation in instructional practice, with principals having limited authority to influence teachers' classroom practices (Klein et al., 2022; Klein & Bronnert-Härle, 2020). Kornblumenschule, for instance, stands out as a school where this DNA remains very active, where the principal strives towards goals, but struggles to disseminate his goals even within his leadership team. His CD's insistence on placing teacher autonomy over strategy prevents structures that could support common goals. Even in this environment, teachers sometimes feel imposed upon, making it challenging for the principal to sell his vision of equity to the staff, and the only goal that staff was able to agree on – team structures – does not touch on teaching and learning at all. One could say that while the principal actually has an equity vision, he is kept from systematically leading with it by the school's organizational culture and lacks the strategies to address this culture.

Finally, Geranienschule represents a school with thread rigidity (Staw, Sandelands & Dutton 1981), where the challenges are seen as overwhelming and beyond manageable with current resources. While the school and its staff see themselves as effective, students are viewed as having significant 'deficits' that the school is unable to address. The description of teachers' suffering legitimizes the school's focus on alleviating teacher burdens rather than prioritizing student learning. Vision-wise, the thread rigidity manifests in the principal's inability to paint a positive future for the school, and the primary focus in efforts to improve instruction is to reduce stress for the teachers rather than improve learning. The focus on stress reduction seems to prevent the school from considering improvements in teaching, creating a cycle where educators' exhaustion due to a lack of goals or strategies hinders their development of both goals and strategies.

6. Conclusion

In this paper, we argued that leading with an equity vision is essential for influencing pedagogical practices and instruction at less successful SSMC, as teachers who have faced repeated experiences of failure may need a clear and sweeping vision and supportive structures that enable them to work towards the vision to overcome pessimistic beliefs. Our findings on this issue are not clear-cut. In our sample, two schools have clear instructional concepts aimed at the academic success of students. However, only one of these schools has an explicitly formulated and shared vision focused on equity, integrated with goal-oriented work and support structures. On the other end of the continuum, there is Geranienschule, where we might argue that a lack of an equity vision keeps both leaders and educators from shifting their attention from their own 'suffering' to the marginalization of their students.

Considering the limitations of our data, the findings suggest that having an equity vision can aid principals in implementing organizational structures, which can then facilitate teachers' development of practices that help them feel self-efficacious and, in the long run, reduce their pessimistic beliefs. In those schools of our sample where the principals had a strong sense of purpose, either explicit as in Rosenschule, or implicit as in Tulpenschule, the structures that the principals created were more restrictive, but teachers did not perceive them as such because they helped them structure their work and reduce the complexity and responsibility that comes with teacher autonomy, and especially when teachers are not prepared for culturally-responsive teaching (Gay, 2021), as is often the case in Germany. The data from Kornblumenschule and Geranienschule, on the other hand, also point to the need for support structures, such as professional development programs or networks for school leaders. These can help leaders use their equity vision to systematically lead their school or help them develop such a vision amidst the experience of adversity and overwhelm in the first place.

References

Bass, B. M., & Avolio, B. J. (1994). *Improving organizational effectiveness: Through transformational leadership*. Sage.

Bremm, N., Klein, E. D., & Racherbäumer, K. (2016). Schulen in „schwieriger" Lage?! Begriffe, Forschungsbefunde und Perspektiven [Schools in a "difficult" contexts?! Concepts, research findings and perspectives]. *Die Deutsche Schule, 108*(4), 323–339.

Brown, M. E., & Treviño, L. K. (2006). Ethical leadership: A review and future directions. *The Leadership Quarterly, 17*(6), 595–616. https://doi.org/10.1016/j.leaqua.2006.10.004

Forell, M. (2020). *Öffnung und Begrenzung des Gymnasiums: Institutionsverständnisse angesichts einer sich verändernden gymnasialen Schülerschaft [Opening up and limiting the German Gymnasium: Institutional understandings in the face of a changing pupil community]*. Waxmann.

Gay, G. (2021). Culturally Responsive Teaching. Ideas, Actions, and Effects. In H. R. Milner & K. Lomotey (Eds.), *Handbook of Urban Education* (pp. 210–233). Routledge. https://doi.org/10.4324/9780429331435-16

Gerick, J. (2014). *Führung und Gesundheit in der Organisation Schule. Zur Wahrnehmung transformationaler Führung und die Bedeutung für die Lehrergesundheit als Schulqualitätsmerkmal [Leadership and health in schools as organizations. On the perception of transformational leadership and its significance for teacher health as a feature of school quality]*. Waxmann.

Graw-Krausholz, S., & Pietsch, M. (2020). Wie führen Schulleitungen? – Eine Mehrebenenbetrachtung verschiedener Führungstypen an Hamburger Schulen [How do school principals lead? A multi-level analysis of different types of leadership at schools in Hamburg]. In M. Warmt, M. Pietsch, S. Graw-Krausholz & S. Tosana (Eds.), *Schulinspektion in Hamburg. Der zweite Zyklus 2012–2020: Perspektiven aus Theorie, Empirie und Praxis* (pp. 45–67). wbv.

Hartung-Beck, V., & Muslic, B. (2015). Herausforderungen qualitativer Interviewstudien innerhalb von Organisationen. Methodologische Überlegungen zu einer empirischen Rekonstruktion schulischer Organisationen am Beispiel des Forschungsprojektes „Realisierung testbasierter Schulreform" [Challenges of qualitative interview studies within organizations. Methodological considerations on an empirical reconstruction of school organizations using the example of the research project "Realization of test-based school reform"]. *Zeitschrift für qualitative Forschung, 16*(1), 57–72. https://doi.org/10.3224/zqf.v16i1.22854

Hemmings, A. (2012). Four Rs for Urban High School Reform. Re-envisioning, Reculturation, Restructuring, and Remoralization. *Improving Schools, 15*(3), 198–210. https://doi.org/10.1177/1365480212458861

Jacobson, E., Cross Francis, D., Willey, C., & Wilkins-Yel, K. (2022). Race, Gender, and Teacher Equity Beliefs: Construct Validation of the Attributions of Mathematical Excellence Scale. *AERA Open*, 8. https://doi.org/10.1177/23328584221130999

Jacobson, S. L., Brooks, S., Giles, C., Johnson, L., & Ylimaki, R. (2007). Successful Leadership in Three High-Poverty Urban Elementary Schools. *Leadership and Policy in Schools, 6*(4), 291–317. https://doi.org/10.1080/15700760701431553

Klein, E. D. (2018). *Erfolgreiches Schulleitungshandeln an Schulen in sozial deprivierter Lage. Eine Zusammenschau zentraler Grundlagen und Befunde aus der nationalen und internationalen Bildungsforschung. Expertise im Auftrag der Wübben Stiftung [Successful school leadership at schools serving disadvantaged communities. A summary of central principles and findings from national and international educational research. Expertise on behalf of the Wübben Foundation]*. SHIP Working Paper Serie, No. 02.

Klein, E. D. (2022). Schulisches Handeln als Faktor von Bildungsgerechtigkeit. Eine Annäherung am Beispiel schulischer Strategien im Kontext von COVID-19 [School practice as a factor of educational equity. An approach using the example of school strategies in the context of COVID-19]. In W. Böttcher, L. Brockmann, C. Hack & C. Luig (Eds.), *Chancenungleichheit: geplant, organisiert, rechtlich kodifiziert. Tagungsband der Kommission Bildungsorganisation, Bildungsplanung und Bildungsrecht* (pp. 75–82). Waxmann.

Klein, E. D., & Bronnert-Härle, H. (2020). Mature School Cultures and New Leadership Practices – An Analysis of Leadership for Learning in German Comprehensive Schools. *Zeitschrift für Erziehungswissenschaft, 23*, 955–977. https://doi.org/10.1007/s11618-020-00968-4

Klein, E. D., Bronnert-Härle, H., Boone, W. J., & Muslic, B. (2022). Constructs of Leadership and Diverging Institutional Environments. An Exploratory Comparative Study in the United States and Germany. *School Effectiveness and School Improvement, 33*(4), 564–587. https://doi.org/10.1080/09243453.2022.2069129

Klein, E. D., Czaja, S. J., Proskawetz, F. S., van Ackeren-Mindl, I., & Becks, C. (2024). Alles eine Frage der Perspektive?! Wie Schulleitende ihren Einfluss wahrnehmen und wie dies mit ihrem Führungshandeln zusammenhängt [It's all a question of perspective?! How school principals perceive their influence and how this relates to their leadership practice]. In K. Maaz, A. Marx & K. Kronsfoth (Eds.), *SchuMaS – Schule macht stark. Sozialraumorientierte Schul- und Unterrichtsentwicklung an Schulen in schwierigen Lagen. Aufbau und erste Arbeitsergebnisse des Forschungsverbunds* (pp. 327–341). Waxmann.

Kramer, R.-T., & Helsper, W. (2010). Kulturelle Passung und Bildungsungleichheit – Potenziale einer an Bourdieu orientierten Analyse der Bildungsungleichheit [Cultural fit and educational inequality – potentials of a Bourdieu-oriented analysis of educational inequality]. In H.-H. Krüger, U. Rabe-Kleberg, R.-T. Kramer & J. Budde (Eds.), *Bildungsungleichheit revisited: Bildung und soziale Ungleichheit vom Kindergarten bis zur Hochschule* (pp. 103–125). Springer VS. https://doi.org/10.1007/978-3-531-92201-0_6

Leithwood, K., Aitken, R., & Jantzi, D. (2006). *Making Schools Smarter. Leading With Evidence* (3rd ed.). Corwin Press.

Leithwood, K., & Sun, J. (2012). The Nature and Effects of Transformational School Leadership. *Educational Administration Quarterly, 48*(3), 387–423. https://doi.org/10.1177/0013161X11436268

Locke, E. A., & Latham, G. P. (2002). Building a Practically Useful Theory of Goal Setting and Task Motivation. A 35-Year Odyssey. *American Psychologist, 57*(9), 705–717. https://doi.org/10.1037//0003-066X.57.9.705

Mayring, P. (2022). *Qualitative Inhaltsanalyse. Grundlagen und Techniken [Qualitative content analysis. Basics and techniques]* (13th ed.). Beltz. https://doi.org/10.1007/978-3-658-37985-8_43

Muijs, D., Harris, A., Chapman, C., Stoll, L., & Russ, J. (2004). Improving Schools in Socioeconomically Disadvantaged Areas. A Review of Research Evidence. *School Effectiveness and School Improvement, 15*(2), 149–175. https://doi.org/10.1076/sesi.15.2.149.30433

OECD. (2019). *PISA 2018 Results (Volume II). Where All Students Can Succeed.* PISA, OECD. https://doi.org/10.1787/b5fd1b8f-en

Pietsch, M., & Tulowitzki, P. (2017). Disentangling school leadership and its ties to instructional practices – an empirical comparison of various leadership styles. *School Effectiveness and School Improvement, 28*(4), 629–649. https://doi.org/10.1080/09243453.2017.1363787

Potter, D., Reynolds, D., & Chapman, C. (2002). School Improvement for Schools Facing Challenging Circumstances: A review of research and practice. *School Leadership & Management, 22*(3), 243–256. https://doi.org/10.1080/1363243022000020381

Senge, P. (2006). *The Fifth Discipline. The Art and Practice of the Learning Organization.* Currency.

Staw, B. M., Sandelands, L. E., & Dutton, J. E. (1981). Threat-rigidity effects in organizational behavior: A multilevel analysis. *Administrative Science Quarterly, 26*(4), 501–524. https://doi.org/10.2307/2392337

Sun, J., & Leithwood, K. (2015). Direction-setting school leadership practices: a meta-analytical review of evidence about their influence. *School Effectiveness and School Improvement, 26*(4), 499–523. https://doi.org/10.1080/09243453.2015.1005106

Tulowitzki, P., Ruf, L., Sposato, G., Witthöft, J., & Pietsch, M. (2023). *Schulleitungsmonitor Deutschland 2022 – Schulen in sozial benachteiligter und nicht benachteiligter Lage [School principals Monitor Germany 2022 – Schools in socially disadvantaged and non-disadvantaged locations].* https://doi.org/10.26041/fhnw-5748

Valencia, R. R. (2010). *Dismantling Contemporary Deficit Thinking: Educational Thought and Practice.* Routledge. https://doi.org/10.4324/9780203853214

van den Bergh, L., Denessen, E., Hornstra, L., Voeten, M., & Holland, R. W. (2010). The Implicit Prejudiced Attitudes of Teachers: Relations to Teacher Expectations and the Ethnic Achievement Gap. *American Educational Research Journal, 47*(2), 497–527. https://doi.org/10.3102/0002831209353594

Witzel, A. (2000). Das problemzentrierte Interview [The problem-centered interview]. *Forum Qualitative Sozialforschung, 1*(1), 1–9. https://doi.org/10.1007/978-3-8349-9441-7_29

Witziers, B., Bosker, R. J., & Kruger, M. L. (2003). Educational Leadership and Student Achievement: the Elusive Serach for an Association. *Educational Administration Quarterly, 39*(3), 398–425. https://doi.org/10.1177/0013161X03253411

Ylimaki, R. M., Jacobson, S. L., & Drysdale, L. (2007). Making a Difference in Challenging, High-Poverty Schools: Successful principals in the USA, England, and Australia. *School Effectiveness and School Improvement, 18*(4), 361–381. https://doi.org/10.1080/09243450701712486

Zumpe, E. (2024). School improvement at the next level of work: the struggle for collective agency in a school facing adversity. *Journal of Educational Change, 25*, 485–529. https://doi.org/10.1007/s10833-023-09500-x

Further Contributions in the Volume

Another article that focuses on schools as change agents is authored by *Mirjam Maier-Röseler, Enkeleta Shtërbani,* and *Gabriele Weigand.* They explore the implications of Art. 29 Para. 1 of the UN CRC concerning children's rights to develop their talents (pp. 103–114).

For a deeper engagement with practical implications of children's rights, we recommend reading the focus article by *Thea Jenner* on the German "Ganztagsförderungsgesetz" (pp. 139–145).

Julia Hugo, Charlotte Assmann, Andreas Schmidt (Eds.)
Educational Leadership and Children's Rights?/
Kinderrechte als Führungsaufgabe?
 https://doi.org/10.31244/9783830998259_3

Andreas Schmidt, Ruth Luzmore & Colin Cramer

Teachers as Educational Change Agents for Children's Rights

Implications and Challenges for Meta-Reflexive Teacher Education

Abstract
The UN Convention on the Rights of the Child (UN CRC) highlights children's educational rights in Articles 28 and 29. Article 28 mandates universal access, while Article 29 emphasises education's role in fostering respect for human rights, culture, and the environment. However, many states' educational policies do not fully reflect these principles. Teacher agency is vital, as educators act as state agents, shaping student outcomes and embodying the UN CRC's objectives. To implement these rights, teachers must balance competing educational goals and fully understand their roles. The concept of *meta-reflexivity* in teacher education is proposed to enhance teachers' ability to adapt and reflect on complex situations, enabling them to uphold children's rights. First, the meta-reflexive principles of teacher education are presented. The systematic professionalisation of teachers is a general concern in teacher education, and we use this as a framework to explore how Article 29 can be applied as an exemplary case for meta-reflexivity. The role of teachers in relation to the educational objectives mentioned in Article 29 is then reflected upon with the help of relevant research literature on children's rights. The analysis results in a theoretical typology of teachers. The conclusion stresses the importance of preparing teachers to embody these roles and fulfil the UN CRC's vision, underscoring that achieving these goals requires a collective effort, as no single teacher can achieve them in isolation.

Keywords
Children's rights, Meta-reflexivity, Teacher education, UN Convention on the Rights of the Child

Lehrer*innen als Change Agents für Kinderrechte

Implikationen und Herausforderungen für eine meta-reflexive Lehrer*innenbildung

Zusammenfassung

Die UN-Konvention über die Rechte des Kindes (UN-KRK) hebt in den Artikeln 28 und 29 die Rechte der Kinder auf Bildung hervor. Artikel 28 adressiert den allgemeinen Zugang zu Bildung, während Artikel 29 die Rolle der Bildung bei der Förderung der Achtung der Menschenrechte, der Kultur und der Umwelt betont. Die Bildungspolitik vieler Staaten berücksichtigt diese Grundsätze jedoch nicht vollständig. Die Handlungsfähigkeit der Lehrkräfte ist von entscheidender Bedeutung, da sie als staatliche Akteure die Bildung der Schüler*innen beeinflussen und die Ziele der UN-KRK verkörpern. Um diese Rechte umzusetzen, müssen Lehrer*innen konkurrierende Bildungsziele ausbalancieren und ihre Rolle vollständig verstehen. Dieser Beitrag argumentiert, dass das Konzept der Meta-Reflexivität in der Lehrer*innenausbildung geeignet ist, um die Fähigkeit der Lehrer*innen zu verbessern, sich anzupassen und über komplexe Situationen zu reflektieren, damit sie so die Rechte der Kinder wahren können. Zunächst werden die meta-reflexiven Grundsätze der Lehrer*innenbildung vorgestellt. Die systematische Professionalisierung von Lehrer*innen ist ein allgemeines Anliegen in der Lehrer*innenausbildung und wir verwenden dies als Rahmen, um zu untersuchen, wie Artikel 29 als Beispiel für Meta-Reflexivität angewendet werden kann. Die Rolle der Lehrer*innen in Bezug auf die in Artikel 29 genannten Bildungsziele wird dann mit Hilfe der einschlägigen Forschungsliteratur über Kinderrechte reflektiert. Die Analyse führt zu einer theoretischen Typologie von Lehrer*innen. In der Schlussfolgerung wird betont, wie wichtig es ist, Lehrer*innen darauf vorzubereiten, diese Rollen zu verkörpern und die Vision der UN-KRK zu erfüllen, und es wird hervorgehoben, dass das Erreichen dieser Ziele eine kollektive Anstrengung erfordert, da keine einzelne Lehrkraft sie allein erreichen kann.

Schlüsselbegriffe

Kinderrechte, Meta-Reflexivität, Lehrer*innenbildung, UN-Konvention über die Rechte des Kindes

1. Introduction

The United Nations Convention on the Rights of the Child (UN CRC), through its 54 articles, advocates for a distinct set of rights specifically for children, extending beyond existing international or local human rights legislation. It addresses the rights that should be guaranteed throughout childhood and how these rights prepare children for adulthood and responsible citizenship. Articles 28 and 29 of the UN CRC focus mainly on the children's right to education, though other articles indirectly relate to a child's development. Article 28 calls for the universal provision of education for all children, though debates may arise regarding the boundaries of compulsory education. In contrast, Article 29 outlines a broader vision for the aims and quality of education, stressing the holistic development of children. It requires that education not only focuses on academic achievement but also foster the development of a child's personality, talents, and respect for human rights, cultural diversity, and the environment. In essence, states must ensure children receive an education that supports their overall development, preparing them for a responsible life in a free society (United Nations, 1989). However, it would be challenging to claim that these rights, described as ambitious and idealistic (Lundy & Sainz, 2018), are universally experienced by children in all countries that have ratified the convention. In 2001, the UN Committee drew particular attention to Article 29 as the wide-ranging values embodied within it "led many State parties to assume it is unnecessary, or even inappropriate, to ensure that the relevant principles are reflected in legislation or administrative directives" (United Nations, 2001, § 17). The Committee argued that fulfilling Article 29's aims means states must consider other related articles when designing, monitoring, and reviewing the curriculum, the learning environment, and the pedagogical methods in schools (United Nations, 2001, § 8). In other words, the goals of Article 29 can only be fully realised when states implement its principles across all aspects of education – a complex but vital task. The role of Article 29 as a foundation for implementing other rights within the UN CRC may explain why it has received relatively little attention in the literature (Gillett-Swann, Thelander & Hanna, 2021), making it particularly relevant to this paper.

While education can occur in various contexts, many children first encounter the state through formal education, where teachers serve as *state agents*, fulfilling the obligations of Article 28 (Gillett-Swann et al., 2021). Despite their role as state actors carrying out national and local policies (Ball et al., 2011), the concept of *teacher agency* – referring to teachers' actions within schools – has received limited attention in research (Vongalis-Macrow, 2007). Biesta and colleagues (2015) argue that agency is not a fixed trait of individuals but rather something teachers actively perform in response to their contexts. Teacher agency reflects how teachers engage with the specific demands of their work rather than being an inherent quality. Even though teachers are expected to follow national policies, they still have considerable influence over student outcomes depending on how they enact their roles in the classroom. Despite ongoing debates about how much agency teachers should have (Biesta et al., 2015), we argue that teachers are *change agents* because of their direct impact on students. Teachers influence their students' outcomes and have varying degrees of autonomy in implementing education. To meet the UN CRC's aims regarding education, teachers must balance complex and often competing objectives. Their ability to act as change agents within classrooms directly affects student outcomes and aligns with broader frameworks like the UN CRC.

The relationship between teacher agency and implementing children's rights under Article 29 highlights the importance of empowering teachers to navigate their roles effectively. Therefore, teacher education must go beyond basic pedagogical skills to include a deeper understanding of reconciling competing educational policy and practice objectives. This is essential to enable teachers to enact Article 29 in the classroom, leading us to ask: What form of teacher education could support the professional implementation of Article 29? A key concept here is meta-reflexivity. It enables teachers to recognise and navigate the tensions between educational goals, such as academic achievement and the holistic development required by Article 29. A meta-reflexive teacher can weigh different options for action, balancing tensions and acting appropriately in complex situations (Cramer, Brown & Aldridge, 2023). A teacher who is aware of the complex dynamics of their role in the classroom and school and thus can relate to the aims of the UN CRC professionally can be described as meta-reflexive.

First, the meta-reflexive principles of teacher education are presented. The systematic professionalisation of teachers is a general concern in teacher education, and we use this as a framework to explore how Article 29 can be applied as an exemplary case for meta-reflexivity. The role of teachers in relation to the educational objectives mentioned in Article 29 is then reflected upon with the help of relevant research literature on children's rights. The analysis results in a theoretical typology of teachers. In conclusion, further implications for teacher education are discussed.

2. Meta-reflexive Principles in Teacher Education

We begin by assuming that teachers are committed to a professional approach – one that is autonomous, competent, and dedicated to implementing Article 29. This raises an important question: What requirements should be placed on teacher professionalism, and what are the implications for teacher education? To explore this, we draw on the recently introduced professional theory of *meta-reflexivity.* This approach goes back to basic theoretical considerations in relation to western history of ideas as a precondition, reflection, the discourse on personal epistemology, complexity theory and the long-lasting academic debate on teacher professionalism (Cramer et al., 2023). Teacher professionalism suggests that teachers must confidently navigate uncertainty and complexity. This involves reflecting on specific professional situations and critically examining the assumptions and positions that shape these reflections.

When applied to the aims of Article 29, this approach reveals the embedded claims and values, shows why the maxim formulated with it is often undermined in educational contexts, and highlights the challenges of implementing it in practice. However, it also helps identify viable strategies for promoting and enforcing children's rights within classrooms. Meta-reflexive teachers can develop a range of exemplary interpretations (as introduced in teacher education) and apply these to real-world classroom situations. These teachers can adapt their actions by weighing options and making informed decisions based on critically engaging with these interpretations. While appropriate situational responses can occur intuitively (Evans, 2008), meta-reflexivity is distinct because it allows teachers to consciously and critically engage with their decisions. As Cramer et al. (2023) point out, "Meta-reflexivity manifests itself in the secure handling of uncertainty" (p. 474). Ten principles of meta-reflexivity are postulated (Cramer, 2020; Cramer et al., 2023) that can help teachers adopt a more nuanced understanding of the complexities involved in upholding children's rights in diverse educational contexts:

1) A *multi-perspective* approach to situation-specific challenges helps teachers understand the barriers to implementing children's rights and identify possible solu-

tions. By considering different perspectives, teachers can find more effective ways to uphold these rights in various contexts.

2) The principle of *distancing* means gaining distance from initial and overly simple interpretations of complex action situations and recognising the added value of critical-constructive, i.e., distanced (temporally relieved) considerations of a complex situation. For example, a teacher who realises that lessons focused too much on memorisation and testing may not fully reflect Article 29's emphasis on creativity and cultural understanding might introduce projects exploring students' cultural backgrounds or global issues, promoting academic skills and respect for diversity.
3) *Historicization* signifies a sensitivity to the historical circumstances of the emergence of a specific way and why children's rights are neglected, challenged, or promoted. This sensitivity helps teachers appreciate how different cultural, legal, and educational systems have shaped perceptions of children's roles in society and education.
4) As one result of this awareness, the *contextuality* of academic cognition in theory and empiricism is to be disclosed. Global declarations like the UN CRC do not guarantee uniform implementation, and the chances of their implementation vary in specific political and social contexts and different situations. A teacher who understands this might ask students to reflect on how children's rights are upheld in their community, encouraging them to advocate for their rights in practical ways, such as forming a student council.
5) Regularly emphasising all knowledge's *alternativity* or provisional nature can highlight that no theory, empirical approach, or normative principle, including Article 29, can fully explain school practices. Despite the legal authority of children's rights, some teachers may still undermine or fail to enforce them in specific situations.
6) The *independence* of specific ways of looking at things points to different settings (concepts, theorems, paradigms, etc.) that place theories in a non-hierarchical relationship to each other. In consideration of Article 29, this meta-reflexive principle illustrates that, on the one hand, it asserts absolute validity irrespective of the specific requirements for action and personal attitudes that may be present in any given situation. On the other hand, it is also important to note that numerous other maxims for society similarly claim unconditional validity and must be considered. Consequently, conflicts may arise between several normative orientations that are indisputable in themselves, particularly given that the implementation of all maxims is never explicitly addressed in school or teaching.
7) Awareness of each axiomatic points to the relevance of *transparency in* teacher education by disclosing the meta-reflexive principles to student teachers and discussing them together. This claim is linked to the need to understand this joint reflection on a specific content. While academic theories and empirical research results have been the focus, it becomes clear here that human rights and fundamental social maxims can also become the subject of meta-reflexive considerations.

8) Therefore, *meta-communication* is necessary regarding how different theories, empirical findings, and normative demands on schools and education are considered in a meta-reflexive perspective in teacher education programs. For instance, by encouraging students to reflect on the balance between academic achievement and creativity or cultural respect, a teacher can adjust their methods to better align with the holistic goals of Article 29. In contrast, a teacher who does not use meta-communication may follow the curriculum without questioning how well it aligns with children's rights.
9) Teacher educators must *justify* the selection of theories and findings presented to student teachers. In the present case, it becomes evident that teacher education cannot be based solely on scientifically acquired theories and empirical findings. It must also explicitly address fundamental normative and widely shared maxims, such as children's rights, and allow teacher action to be guided by these. This implies that the guiding principle of evidence-based teacher education is joined by one of values-driven teacher education.
10) The principle of *dynamics* as a gradual increase of complexity in their courses and lectures appears necessary to avoid overtaxing students. The challenge of balancing the need for evidence-based action with value-based action is a remarkably complex one. In the context of teacher education, this raises the question of how different maxims of action can be integrated and how professionalism can be gradually developed in a way that does not overwhelm prospective teachers.

3. The Role of the Teacher

3.1 Perspectives on Children's Rights Education

Existing research on children's educational rights can heuristically be categorised in three ways: 1) *rights to education*, focusing on the state's provision of education; 2) *rights in education*, focusing on how educational institutions fulfil children's rights, mainly how children's voices are heard; and 3) *rights through education*, where education serves as a means for children to learn about citizenship and human rights (Quennerstedt & Moody, 2020). The existing literature often explores the role of teachers in designing and delivering citizenship and human rights education (Jerome, 2018; Jerome & Starkey, 2022; Brantefors & Thelander, 2017; Burridge & Chodkiewicz, 2017), as well as their knowledge of and attitudes towards children's rights (Leung, Yuen & Chong, 2011; Isenström, 2022; Banko-Bal & Guler-Yildiz, 2021).

While some argue that the challenge lies not in understanding educational rights but in how they are enacted (Lundy & Sainz, 2018), we propose that a teacher's meta-reflexive understanding of these rights is crucial to their actions in the classroom. Jerome's (2016) work on Children's Rights Education (CRE) provides a helpful framework by theorising three different perspectives on CRE:

1) In the *legalistic worldview*, implementing CRE is a straightforward process. Toolkits, checklists, and documentation provided by agencies like the UN offer a

framework for aligning policies with school practices. Such a view ignores the possible challenges when implementing a legal requirement in actual educational practice.

2) The *reformist worldview* adopts a more critical stance towards CRE, focusing on ideological issues. Jerome (2016) draws upon comments from the Committee on the Rights of the Child, which criticises education for lacking child participation and "prioritises competition and a narrow focus on knowledge acquisition" (p. 147). These comments have been seen as problematic when considering the prevalence of schooling systems where standardised testing drives competition and arguments around 'powerful knowledge' (Young & Muller, 2013) rather than a curriculum driven by relevance to a child's life is seen as the best vehicle to narrow inequalities. Such tension indicates the need to place these different rationalities in a relationship.
3) The *radical worldview* sees CRE as the 'contested terrain' (Jerome, 2016, p. 148) with two different outlooks. The first group supports a utopian vision of critical pedagogy, recognising children as rights-holders and agents for promoting rights. The second group critiques this view, arguing that rights can be overly individualistic and rooted in Western thinking. Teachers must navigate these conflicting perspectives and position themselves accordingly.

Jerome's (2016) differentiation of these worldviews helps identify three corresponding types of teachers. This leads us to the next step in our argument: applying Article 29 to outline the qualities of an ideal teacher. Article 29 focuses on the child's holistic development, including fostering respect for human rights, cultural diversity, and the environment. With the meta-reflexive principles in mind, teachers must navigate the tension between these three perspectives and critically reflect on the typology. A *meta-reflexive teacher education*, discussed in the conclusion section, encourages future educators to critically engage with these perspectives and their role in implementing children's rights.

3.2 A Teacher Typology

Delivering the overall aims of Article 29 is ambitious and holistic in its outcomes for children to prepare them to live a "responsible life in a free society". This goes beyond delivering a curriculum that instructs children on the legalistic contents of rights legislation and prepares them by addressing the development of attitudes and behaviours in children (Osler & Solhaug, 2018) to prepare them for adulthood. The UN CRC establishes that children are holders of rights and should be acknowledged as potential and often actual human rights defenders rather than "recipients of concern, goodwill or charity" (UN Committee on the Rights of the Child, 2018). In other words, children's rights should be taken seriously. However, teachers' views on this understanding of children's rights can vary significantly. Some teachers may see children's rights as a threat to adult authority (Leung et al., 2011) or feel these rights conflict with their legal responsibility to act in *loco parentis* in the classroom. For example, the most recent comments from the UN Observation on Children's Rights for the UK urged policymakers to ensure that children have the right to "appeal their exclusion and provide them with legal advice and recommendations, where appropriate" (United Nations, 2023, p. 17). Given the increasing number of school exclusions in the country (Department for Education, 2024), one can imagine that school leaders and teachers making these decisions – legal only in severe disruption or violence – would unlikely support this right. Therefore, individual teachers will likely have a range of rights-teaching mentalities (Isenström, 2020, 2022; Robinson, Phillips & Quennerstedt, 2018), which they will bring into the classroom and influence their decisions and actions. Building on Jerome's (2016) earlier work on Children's Rights Education (CRE), he identifies three types of teachers:

1) *Implementors:* These teachers need to gain more knowledge about children's rights and passively deliver education in line with the legalistic worldview, which tends to overlook the practical challenges of implementation.
2) *Gatekeepers:* These teachers understand CRE but may show caution or scepticism about how much children's rights should be embedded in the classroom. This aligns with the reformist worldview. Isenström's (2022) research in Swedish primary schools offers insight into this view, where teachers argue that "competence and maturity determine access to rights" (p. 285), meaning that children's voices are present but restricted to specific topics. This approach tends to avoid addressing more challenging issues.
3) *Change agents*: These teachers embrace CRE fully, shifting their role from agents of the state to advocates of children's rights (Jerome & Starkey, 2022). Aligned with the radical worldview, they actively draw on ideas from CRE to integrate them into their daily teaching practices. These teachers know the tensions that arise and work to balance the various external and internal demands placed on them.

However, teachers do not operate exclusively within one of these roles; they must often move between them depending on the situation (Devine & McGillicuddy, 2016). For example, teachers must act within the boundaries of the state's legislation. As they work with minors in their care, teachers must act as gatekeepers and judge what is and is not appropriate for their students. Finally, regardless of the system they work in, there is always some agency in how a teacher implements curriculum requirements, makes pedagogical choices, responds to children's behaviour, presents themselves, etc. A teacher's worldview – whether aligned with Jerome's categories or others – and beliefs about their role (Biesta et al., 2015) will influence their actions and, by extension, how well they achieve the core outcomes of Article 29. We argue that being a teacher inherently means being an educational change agent, which makes every teacher an educational leader within their specific role. Article 29 provides the normative goals that guide this educational agency. Therefore, teacher education must equip future teachers with strategies to improve student outcomes and become change agents for children's rights. In the next section, we will explore how adopting a meta-reflexive perspective can help future teachers engage with different worldviews and better understand their roles in promoting children's rights.

4. Conclusion

The preparation of teachers to be educational change agents in a meta-reflexive manner can be effectively demonstrated by focusing on children's rights. While the UN CRC provisions on children's rights represent a high legal and social standard – whether seen from a legalistic, reformist, or radical perspective – other critical social values could also be addressed in teacher education. In practice, few teachers are likely to know the exact wording of these provisions, and they should not necessarily be the focus of teacher education. If we required teachers to learn all details, the curriculum would become even more overloaded. For instance, we could argue that students should also be educated on the contents of the Convention on Human Rights, the Convention on the Rights of Persons with Disabilities, and so on. Therefore, it is more realistic to prepare teachers to develop a general awareness and sensitivity to these complex social and educational demands. Meta-reflexivity becomes critical here – a core feature of professional teaching that can help safeguard, promote, and observe children's rights. Teachers need to switch between different roles depending on the situation, and this flexibility requires a professional attitude shaped by a multi-perspective approach to their work.

The typology of teacher roles discussed earlier should be critically examined through a meta-reflexive lens in teacher education and possibly even questioned. Based on Article 29 of the UN CRC, one could argue that teachers have a moral, or even legal, obligation to adopt the role of a change agent. In this text, we argue that teachers are already educational change agents in their professional roles. Therefore, teacher education must make teachers aware of this responsibility. Meta-reflexivity provides a valuable framework for shaping this kind of teacher education. Ultimately, it is about future teachers seeing themselves consciously as educational change agents and being able to act professionally in the complex and often challenging environment of schools, where many expectations are placed on them. In Article 29, we have developed an exemplary case to illustrate how meta-reflexive teacher education could be structured. While a single teacher cannot meet all the goals of Article 29 – especially since it cannot be fully realised in isolation from the rest of the UN CRC – meta-reflexivity helps teachers gain the critical distance needed to act professionally. With this paper, we want to stimulate research to explore this gap in the literature and address this research desideratum.

References

Ball, S. J., Maguire, M., Braun, A., & Hoskins, K. (2011). Policy actors: Doing policy work in schools. *Discourse Studies in the Cultural Politics of Education, 32*(4), 625–639.

Banko-Bal, C., & Guler-Yildiz, T. (2021). An investigation of early childhood education teachers' attitudes, behaviours, and views regarding the rights of the child. *International Journal of Child Care and Education Policy, 15*(5), 1–26.

Biesta, G., Priestley, M., & Robinson, S. (2015). The role of beliefs in teacher agency. *Teachers and Teaching, 21*(6), 624–640.

Brantefors, L., & Thelander, N. (2017). Teaching and learning traditions in children's human rights: Curriculum emphases in theory and practice. *The International Journal of Children's Rights, 25*(2), 456–471.

Burridge, N., & Chodkiewicz, A. (2017). Educating teachers about human rights: building a rights based culture in Australian schools. *Asia-Pacific Journal of Teacher Education, 45*(5), 455–468.

Cramer, C. (2020). Meta-Reflexivität in der Lehrerinnen- und Lehrerbildung [Meta-reflexivity in teacher education]. In C. Cramer, J. König, M. Rothland & S. Blömecke (Eds.), *Handbuch Lehrerinnen- und Lehrerbildung* (pp. 204–214). Klinkhardt/utb.

Cramer, C., Brown, C., & Aldridge, D. (2023). Meta-Reflexivity and Teacher Professionalism: Facilitating Multiparadigmatic Teacher Education to Achieve a Future-Proof Profession. *Journal of Teacher Education, 74*(5), 467–480.

Department for Education. (2024). Suspensions and permanent exclusions in England, Spring term 2022/23. *Explore education statistics.* GOV.UK. https://explore-education-statistics.service.gov.uk.

Devine, D., & McGillicuddy, D. (2016). Positioning pedagogy – a matter of children's rights. *Oxford Review of Education, 42*(4), 424–443.

Evans L. (2008). Professionalism, professionality and the development of education professionals. *British Journal of Educational Studies, 56*(1), 20–38.

Gillett-Swan, J., Thelander, N., & Hanna, A. (2021). Setting the Scene for Children's Rights and Education: Understanding the Aims of Education. In J. Gillett-Swan & N. Thelander (Eds.), *Children's Rights from International Educational Perspectives: Wicked Problems for Children's Education Rights* (pp. 1–11). Springer.

Isenström, L. (2020). Children as Growing Rights Subjects – The Significance of Teachers' Actions. *The International Journal of Children's Rights, 28*(2), 258–287.

Isenström, L. (2022). Teachers' rights-teaching mentalities – what teachers do and why. *Scandinavian Journal of Educational Research, 66*(2), 275–289.

Jerome, L. (2016). Interpreting children's rights education: Three perspectives and three roles for teachers. *Citizenship, Social and Economics Education, 15*(2), 143–156.

Jerome, L. (2018). Hypocrites or heroes? Thinking about the role of the teacher in human rights education. *Human Rights Education Review, 1*(2), 46–64.

Jerome, L., & Starkey, H. (2022). Developing children's agency within a children's rights education framework: 10 propositions. *Education 3-13. International Journal of Primary, Elementary and Early Years Education, 50*(4), 439–451.

Leung, Y. W., Yuen, T. W. W., & Chong, Y. K. (2011). School-based human rights education: Case studies in Hong Kong secondary schools. *Intercultural Education, 22*(2), 145–162.

Lundy, L., & Sainz, G. M. (2018). The role of law and legal knowledge for a transformative human rights education: Addressing violations of children's rights in formal education. *Human Rights Education Review, 1*(2), 4–24.

Osler, A., & Solhaug, T. (2018). Children's human rights and diversity in schools: Framing and measuring. *Research in Comparative and International Education, 13*(2), 276–298.

Quennerstedt, A., & Moody, Z. (2020). Educational children's rights research 1989–2019: Achievements, gaps and future prospects. *The International Journal of Children's Rights, 28*(1), 183–208.

Robinson, C., Phillips, L., & Quennerstedt, A. (2018). Human rights education: developing a theoretical understanding of teachers' responsibilities. *Educational Review, 72*(2), 220–241.

UN Committee on the Rights of the Child. (2018). *Day of General Discussion 2018 Outcome Report: Protecting and Empowering Children as Human Rights Defenders*. https://www.ohchr.org/sites/default/files/Documents/HRBodies/CRC/Discussions/2018/crc_dgd_2018_outcomereport_en.pdf.

United Nations. (UN). (1989). *UN Convention on the Rights of the Child*. United Nations.

United Nations. (UN). (2001). *UN Committee on the Rights of the Child, General Comment No. 1 Article 29: The aims of education. CRC/GC/2001/1*. United Nations.

United Nations. (UN). (2023). *Concluding observations on the combined sixth and seventh periodic reports of the United Kingdom of Great Britain and Northern Ireland. CRC/C/GBR/CO/6-7*. United Nations.

Vongalis-Macrow, A. (2007). I, Teacher: Re-territorialization of teachers' multi-faceted agency in globalized education. *British Journal of Sociology of Education, 28*, 425–439.

Young, M., & Muller, J. (2013). On the powers of powerful knowledge. *Review of Education, 1*(3), 229–250.

Further Contributions in the Volume

For a complimentary international perspective on the professionalization needs of principals regarding children's rights, we recommend the article by *Carolina Dahle* and *Tine Sophie Prøitz* on the Norwegian zero-tolerance-policy against bullying in schools (pp. 89–101).

A focus on a specific type of leadership is provided by *Hanna Luise Bronnert-Härle* and *Esther Dominique Klein*, who empirically explore transformational leadership as an answer to issues of schools in marginalized communities (pp. 23–39).

Julia Hugo, Charlotte Assmann, Andreas Schmidt (Eds.)
Educational Leadership and Children's Rights?/
Kinderrechte als Führungsaufgabe?
 https://doi.org/10.31244/9783830998259_4

Robert Pham Xuan & Dong Nguyen

Academic Tracking in Germany as a Challenge to Children's Rights

Implications for School Leadership

Abstract
Academic tracking in education is the process of assigning students to different classes or schools based on an assessment of their abilities or interests. The aim of tracking policies is to improve the efficiency of the education system by grouping students. This article provides an overview of the tracking system in Germany and focuses on some of the challenges associated with academic tracking in relation to children's right to education. These include access to academically oriented secondary schools for children from disadvantaged backgrounds, unequal learning conditions between hierarchically structured tracks, and limited educational opportunities. There is also a lack of clear evidence on the direct effects of tracking itself on enhanced student learning, and on whether and how the mobility between tracks in German secondary schools could address these challenges. These phenomena are discussed using Tomaševski's 4A framework to consider how these challenges relate to the availability, accessibility, acceptability, and adaptability of formal educational settings. Finally, the article discusses some implications for school leadership in ensuring robust and equitable tracking recommendations, raising parental awareness, and advocating for innovative and inclusive policy changes.

Keywords
Academic Tracking, Children's Rights, School Leadership, Educational Inequality

Schulische Selektion in Deutschland als Herausforderung für die Rechte der Kinder

Implikationen für schulisches Leadership

Zusammenfassung
Im Bildungswesen wird unter „Tracking" die Selektion von Schüler*innen zu verschiedenen Klassen oder Schulen auf der Grundlage einer Bewertung ihrer Fähigkeiten oder Interessen verstanden. Das Ziel des Tracking ist es, die Effizienz des Bildungssystems durch die Gruppierung von Schüler*innen zu verbessern. Dieser Artikel gibt einen Überblick über das Tracking-System in Deutschland und konzentriert sich auf einige der Her-

ausforderungen, die mit der Selektion im Zusammenhang mit dem Recht des Kindes auf Bildung verbunden sind. Dazu gehören der Zugang zu akademisch orientierten Sekundarschulen für Kinder aus benachteiligten Verhältnissen, ungleiche Lernbedingungen zwischen hierarchisch strukturierten Bildungsgängen und eingeschränkte Bildungschancen. Darüber hinaus gibt es keine eindeutige Evidenz dafür, dass die Trennung der Schularten einen direkten Einfluss auf den Lernfortschritt der Schüler*innen hat und ob und wie die Möglichkeit der Mobilität zwischen den Schularten in deutschen Sekundarschulen diesen Herausforderungen begegnen könnte. Diese Phänomene werden anhand des 4A-Rahmens von Tomaševski diskutiert, um zu zeigen, wie diese Herausforderungen mit der Verfügbarkeit, Zugänglichkeit, Akzeptanz und Anpassungsfähigkeit formaler Bildungseinrichtungen zusammenhängen. Abschließend werden einige Implikationen für schulisches Leadership erörtert, um solide und faire Schullaufbahnempfehlungen zu gewährleisten, Eltern zu sensibilisieren und innovative und inklusive Policies zu fördern.

Schlüsselbegriffe
„Tracking“, Kinderrechte, schulisches Führungshandeln, Bildungsungleichheit

1. Introduction

Academic tracking in education involves sorting students into different classrooms or schools based on an assessment of their abilities and/or interests. Originating in Western and European schools in the 19th century, tracking gained traction with the rise of compulsory education and social stratification (Oakes, 2005; Blossfeld et al., 2016). In the early 20th century, psychometric testing began to classify students by cognitive ability (Oakes, 2005). Economic growth after the Second World War increased the demand for skilled workers, leading to more formalised tracking systems (Hallinan, 1994). Tracking school systems have therefore been developed to meet the need for a qualified labour force. Since then, academic tracking has been formalised in national education policies and implemented in many countries, including OECD countries (OECD, 2013).

Academic tracking policies are formulated with the intention of optimising the efficiency and effectiveness of the education system. A primary aim is to simplify the organisation and delivery of education by grouping students according to their academic ability (Hallinan, 1994; Esser, 2021). Educational policymakers tend to argue that by grouping students into different tracks, more focused and specialised teaching can be provided to better prepare students for their future educational and career pathways (Anderson & Oakes, 2014). For example, academic tracks are designed to prepare students for post-secondary education, while vocational tracks are designed to equip students with specific skills required in the labour market. Tracking has also been justified as an instrument to more effectively manage diverse classroom environments (Loveless, 2021).

While these good intentions appear clear, it is important to discuss the impact of academic tracking policies, informed by evidence, on issues such as educational equity and excellence, in specific contexts. This article centres on one critical aspect of these broad issues – academic tracking in relation to children's rights to non-discriminatory access to and benefit from quality education, with particular reference to Articles 2, 12 and 28 of the United Nations Convention on the Rights of the Child (UN CRC, 2024 [1989]) and the 4A framework of Tomaševski (2001). It considers Germany as a case for discussion because the country has a multi-track structure for children at an early age through a predominant form of between-school tracking. Early tracking systems between schools raise concerns about increasing inequalities in children's educational opportunities (Wößmann et al., 2023) that need to be critically discussed and addressed.

The discussion in this article is guided by the following two questions (Q).

Q1. What are the major issues of academic tracking in relation to children's rights in Germany?

Q2. What are the key implications and recommendations for school leadership to address these issues?

The article continues with an overview of academic tracking policy in Germany for background information, followed by a discussion of major issues on academic tracking in Germany (to respond to Q1) and some implications and recommendations for school leadership (to address Q2).

2. An Overview of Academic Tracking Policy in Germany

The German school system is basically divided into three levels: Primary school (Grundschule), lower secondary (Sekundarstufe I), and upper secondary (Sekundarstufe II; KMK, 2020 a, b). Full-time schooling is compulsory from the age of six for nine or ten years, depending on the regulations of each of the 16 federal states. At the primary level, pupils mainly attend comprehensive schools. Tracking starts typically after grade four, when students move from primary to secondary education (Lauterbach, 2021). After this period, students are usually placed in further vocational schools or start an apprenticeship for at least three years if they do not continue with general higher education (Henninges, Traini & Kleinert, 2019).

Germany's federal states have the autonomy to shape their education policies within national guidelines (Lauterbach, 2021). As a result, the implementation of tracking varies from state to state, although certain core principles are consistent across the country (Döbert et al., 2017). Germany has a multi-track secondary school structure. The federal states use either a two-track or a three-track system, with an academic track and one or two non-academic tracks (Lauterbach, 2021). In many German federal states, there has been a gradual shift from a three-track to a two-track secondary school structure. The multi-track system is hierarchical across all 16 federal states, with the highest track (Gymnasium) receiving the most recognition. The next section discusses some issues of academic tracking in Germany.

3. Issues of Academic Tracking in Germany

The tracking process is primarily based on students' previous academic performance, including grades, teacher recommendations and parental choice (Döbert et al., 2017). In nine of the 16 federal states, parents can choose where their children attend secondary school (Lauterbach, 2021). A close look at the academic tracking system in Germany reveals some challenges that are likely to underline children's rights to equal access to quality education.

The *first issue* is that the tracking process risks exacerbating educational inequalities, as the process might be influenced by so-called origin effects (Boudon, 1974; Esser, 2021). As school performance is linked to family background, the primary effects of origin influence school transfer options (ibid.). Parental choice also risks intensifying educational inequalities (secondary effects of origin), as families with higher socio-economic status may have more resources and knowledge to navigate the system to their advantage (Boudon, 1974; Henderson, 2020). However, the primary effects of origin tend to be stronger than the secondary effects of origin (Scharf et al., 2020). Teacher recommendations often carry considerable weight and are based on assessments of a student's academic ability, work habits and perceived potential (Helbig & Morar, 2017). Parental choice is largely influenced by teacher recommendations and academic assessments, as well as family attitudes towards education (Pham Xuan, 2023). These recommendations are not immune to bias, and socio-economic factors can influence the outcomes of teacher recommendations, which can lead to inequalities in course placement (tertiary effects of origin; Esser, 2021; Helbig & Morar, 2017).

The *second issue* relates to inequitable learning conditions between school types. While the desirable effects of academic tracking are to support personalised learning for groups of students, there is no clear evidence on the direct effects of academic tracking on student learning (Hattie, 2002; Fauth et al., 2021). However, these effects could be indirect through the learning conditions in schools. The disparities in learning conditions between school tracks may be due to differences in the quality of curricula, teacher training and teaching (Angelone, 2019). Evidence (e.g. Weber, 2020; Stanat et al., 2023) suggests that learning conditions in academic tracks tend to be more favourable than those in non-academic tracks.

Thirdly, the opportunities for children from lower socio-economic backgrounds to attend academic track secondary schools, particularly Gymnasiums, are limited. The report by the Autoren:innengruppe Bildungsberichterstattung (2024) highlights this pattern. Children from lower socio-economic backgrounds (17 %) are more than twice as likely as those from privileged backgrounds (7 %) not to receive a recommendation for the academic track. Children aged 12–17 from socio-economically disadvantaged families are 18 percent less likely to attend upper secondary school (Gymnasium) than the average for this age group. These children are most likely (43 %) to go to multi-track schools that do not offer the highest level of education (Abitur). Conversely, children from socio-economically privileged backgrounds are the most likely to attend a Gymnasium nationally (68 %) and are over-represented in this type of school.

The report by the Autoren:innengruppe Bildungsberichterstattung (2024) shows that 78 percent of children from higher socio-economic backgrounds receive recommendations for academically oriented upper secondary education, as compared with only about a third from disadvantaged backgrounds. Even when school performance is taken into account, 59 percent of privileged children are recommended for upper secondary education, as compared with 51 percent from lower socio-economic backgrounds. However, this does not guarantee higher qualifications for students from disadvantaged households but suggests that their access is limited. Transition rates are also higher for children from more affluent backgrounds (58 %) than for those from less privileged backgrounds (44 %).

Fourthly, there is no clear evidence on how mobility between tracks in Germany could minimise or mitigate the possible consequences of early tracking as noted above. The current German tracking policy allows for movement between types of secondary schools (Lauterbach, 2021). Mobility between tracks in Germany is often linked to the social background of pupils, and follows a social gradient (Hillmert & Jacob, 2010). Children from socio-economically disadvantaged backgrounds appear to be more exposed to downward mobility than those from more privileged backgrounds (Buchholz et al., 2016; Autoren:innengruppe Bildungsberichterstattung, 2024). Furthermore, while the system theoretically allows for movement between tracks, this permeability tends to be limited in practice. Transitions from lower to higher tracks are less frequent and more difficult than downward movements (Bellenberg & Forell, 2012; Meißner, 2024), reflecting broader socio-economic trends and reinforcing existing inequalities. Overall, mobility and permeability in the German school system have increased slightly in the long term (Kühne et al., 2021).

The four issues mentioned above in the German school system challenge protection of children's right to education, as highlighted in the non-governmental organisation (NGO) report of the National Coalition Germany (2020). More specifically, they are real barriers to promoting non-discriminatory access to education (as noted in Article 2, United Nations, Convention of the childrens rights, UN CRC, 2024 [1989]); equal distribution of educational opportunities (Article 12 UN CRC); and, more broadly, children's right to education (Article 28 UN CRC). From an inclusion perspective, these issues of early tracking policies may increase segregation by separating pupils from the mainstream education system on the basis of social characteristics such as social class, ethnicity or special educational needs. Contextualising these four issues within the 4A *(Availability, Accessibility, Acceptability, and Adaptability)* framework (Tomaševski, 2001), the current tracking system in Germany is exposed to the following worrying issues:

- Availability: Although there seems to be no clear evidence on significant problems with the availability of formal education in Germany, the uneven educational quality between school tracks is concerning. This difference is mainly due to institutional effects such as differed teaching quality and curricular requirements, which in turn can differentiate student learning and development environments (Kunter et al., 2011; Bos & Scharenberg, 2010; Neumann et al., 2007; Angelone, 2019). Unfortuantely, this difference disadvantages children from less privileged backgrounds.

- Accessibility: As discussed in the third issue above, tracking can create barriers for disadvantaged students, and therefore initial placement in lower tracks may limit their opportunities for higher education (Autoren:innengruppe Bildungsberichterstattung, 2024).
- Acceptability: Stigmatisation effects disadvantage children placed in less prestigious school tracks (Helsper & Wiezorek, 2006). There is also a concern that curricula in non-academic school track might not effectively prepare students for a possible academic career (Bos et al., 2010).
- Adaptability: As discussed in the fourth issue above, the inequitable movement between tracks in Germany, with the evidence on the high odds of downward movement for disadvantaged children, is a constraint on adaptability (Buchholz et al., 2016; Meißner, 2024). The disproportionate distribution of disadvantaged pupils in non-academic tracks can also raise the risk that pupils in these schools do not receive the best possible support, as teachers may be overburdened (OECD, 2012; Kunter et al., 2011).

4. Implications and Recommendations for School Leadership

The previous section has presented four major concerns on the current tracking system in Germany. These issues highlight the importance of well-coordinated efforts to address and minimise the negative effects of academic tracking on educational equity for all children. These efforts require the collective responsibility and active involvement of policy makers, educational leaders, educators and the wider community. The following implications and recommendations aim, within the scope and space of this article, to offer some important, albeit probably incomplete, perspectives in response to the complex issues of academic tracking in the current German school system. Discussion on whether to completely de-track school systems goes beyond the scope of this article.

The literature highlights the importance of school leadership in supporting educational equity and children's rights (Leithwood, 2021; Poekert et al., 2020). In the context of academic tracking, school leaders are critical in promoting children's educational rights and potential. These important roles include ensuring robust and equitable teacher referrals, raising parental awareness, and advocating for innovative and inclusive changes to current policies around tracking.

As noted above, teacher recommendation is an important element in sorting students into tracks. It is important to ensure that this recommendation is robust, fair and bias-minimised. The international review by Batruch et al. (2023) found biases against students from disadvantaged socio-economic backgrounds in teachers' track recommendations. School-level contexts could mitigate teachers' stereotypes and prejudices in making track recommendations (Batruch et al., 2019). School leaders could allocate resources for ongoing professional development for teachers in assessing student learning and making track recommendations. Professional development activities should raise teachers' awareness of possible bias and increase their competence in student learning assessment. These activities could be organised within the teacher workload structure and in different forms such as structured courses, workshops, professional learning communities and peer mentoring.

Equally important, school leaders across schools should work together to develop school-wide policies and processes to support robust track recommendations. These policies and processes must take into account the voices of all school stakeholders and the potential of children from all backgrounds. They should recognise the responsibility and accountability of teachers and school leaders for track recommendations. In secondary schools, the development and implementation of rigorous processes to enable timely and appropriate movement between tracks is paramount to maximising children's potential and promoting their educational rights. The development and implementation of these processes requires strong school-family partnerships.

Effective communication between schools and families could help to better inform parental choices about pathways to optimise children's potential. Evidence suggests that school leaders could influence learning and teaching through a professional relationship with families (Leithwood, Harris & Hopkins, 2020). Parents' decisions about their children's educational pathways are a long-term process, based on their attitudes and knowledge about education, rather than a single moment of rational judgement (Bourdieu, 1987/2014). It is concerning if parents' choices fail to place a child's potential as a key factor as it should be. Therefore, the role of school leaders and teachers in sensitising parents to child-centred decision-making through contextualised, diversity-sensitive and sustainable activities is crucial.

Sorting children into different tracks is likely to affect their perceived self-efficacy for learning, as their perceptions may vary according to the environment, including interactions and comparisons with their peers (Grünthal, Kretschmann & Brunner, 2024). Children in academically oriented tracks may feel less competent despite equal performance, whereas educational self-concept may be higher in less academically oriented tracks. This may lead to lower motivation and achievement in the long term. Especially for pupils from less privileged backgrounds, this effect could lead to a faster transition from the higher to the lower track. School leaders should promote a positive learning environment to enhance children's self-efficacy and educational experiences (Thapa et al., 2013). They are central in fostering a climate where teachers can develop and demonstrate high-quality adaptive teaching skills (Fischer et al., 2014), ensuring an equitable, inclusive, and compensatory learning environment for all. This includes organising teaching in such a way that skill gaps, e.g. in reading, are closed before the regular assessments that influence students' academic careers (as a way of compensating for the primary effects of origin). This approach challenges the meritocratic myth by acknowledging that not all students start from the same level (Pham Xuan, 2023).

The issues and recommendations clearly underscore the urgent need for more inclusive and innovative policies to promote both student learning effectiveness and equity. The policy-making process on (de)tracking must also include meaningful consultation on the perspectives of school leaders and other stakeholders, as well as frameworks on children's rights (e.g. the 4A framework). Rigid tracking policy is a negation of the guiding principles of the 4A framework. As a key school-based stakeholder, arguably the most influential in the policy-making process, school leaders should use their expertise and voices to influence federal and national policy changes to promote children's educational rights.

References

Anderson, L., & Oakes, J. (2014). The truth about tracking. In P. C. Lugg & J. C. Weaver (Eds.), *The Big Lies of School Reform* (pp. 109–127). Routledge. https://doi.org/10.4324/9781315886367

Angelone, D. (2019). Schereneffekte auf der Sekundarstufe I? Zum Einfluss des Schultyps auf den Leistungszuwachs in Deutsch und Mathematik [Scissor effects at lower secondary level? On the influence of school type on performance growth in German and maths]. *Schweizerische Zeitschrift für Bildungswissenschaften, 41*(2), 446–466. https://doi.org/10.25656/01:20350

Autor:innengruppe Bildungsberichterstattung. (2024). *Bildung in Deutschland 2024 [Education report 2024]*. wbv. https://doi.org/10.3278/6001820iw

Batruch, A., Autin, F., Bataillard, F., & Butera, F. (2019). School selection and the social class divide: How tracking contributes to the reproduction of inequalities. *Personality and Social Psychology Bulletin, 45*(3), 477–490. https://doi.org/10.1177/0146167218791804

Batruch, A., Geven, S., Kessenich, E., & van de Werfhorst, H. G. (2023). Are tracking recommendations biased? A review of teachers' role in the creation of inequalities in tracking decisions. *Teaching and Teacher Education, 123*(10385), 1–18. https://doi.org/10.1016/j.tate.2022.103985

Bellenberg, G., & Forell, M. (2012). *Schulformwechsel in Deutschland. Durchlässigkeit und Selektion in den 16 Schulsystemen der Bundesländer in der Sekundarstufe I [Changing school type in Germany. Permeability and selection in the 16 school systems of the federal states at lower secondary level]*. Bertelsmann Stiftung.

Blossfeld, H. P., Buchholz, S., Skopek, J., & Triventi, M. (Eds.). (2016). *Models of secondary education and social inequality: An international comparison*. Edward Elgar. https://doi.org/10.4337/9781785367267

Boudon, R. (1974). *Education, opportunity, and social inequality: changing prospects in western society*. John Wiley & Sons.

Bourdieu, P. (1987/2014). *Die feinen Unterschiede: Kritik der gesellschaftlichen Urteilskraft [The subtle differences: Critique of social judgement]*. Suhrkamp.

Bos, W., Müller, S., & Stubbe, T. C. (2010). Abgehängte Bildungsinstitutionen: Hauptschulen und Förderschulen [Educational institutions left behind: Secondary schools and special schools]. In G. Quenzel & K. Hurrelmann (Eds.), *Bildungsverlierer: Neue soziale Ungleichheiten in der Wissensgesellschaft* (pp. 375–397). Springer VS.

Bos, W., & Scharenberg, K. (2010). Lernentwicklung in leistungshomogenen und -heterogenen Schulklassen [Learning development in homogeneous and heterogeneous school classes]. In W. Bos, E. Klieme & O. Köller (Eds.), *Schulische Lerngelegenheiten und Kompetenzentwicklung. Festschrift für Jürgen Baumert* (pp. 173–194). Waxmann.

Buchholz, S., Skopek, J., Zielonka, M., Ditton, H., Wohlkinger, F., & Schier, A. (2016). Secondary school differentiation and inequality of educational opportunity in Germany. In H. P. Blossfeld, S. Buchholz, J. Skopek & M. Triventi (Eds.), *Models of secondary education and social inequality* (pp. 79–92). Edward Elgar. https://doi.org/10.4337/9781785367267.00014

Döbert, H., Hörner, W., Kopp, B. von, & Reuter, L. R. (Eds.). (2017). *Die Bildungssysteme Europas: Albanien, Andorra, Armenien, Aserbeidschan, Belarus, Belgien, Bosnien-Herzegowina, Bulgarien, Dänemark, Deutschland, Estland, Färöer-Inseln, Finnland, Frankreich, Georgien, Griechenland, Irland, Island, Italien, Kosovo, Kroatien, Lettland, Liechtenstein, Litauen, Luxemburg, Malta, Makedonien, Moldawien, Monaco, Montenegro, Niederlande, Norwegen, Österreich, Polen, Portugal, Rumänien, Russische Föderation, San Marino, Schweden, Schweiz, Serbien, Slowakische Republik, Slowenien, Spanien, Tschechische Republik, Türkei, Ukraine, Ungarn, Vereinigtes Königsreich, Zypern [The education systems of Europe: Albania, Andorra, Armenia, Azerbaijan, Belarus, Austria, Belgium, Bosnia-Herzegovina, Bulgaria, Croatia, Denmark, Estonia, Faroe Islands, Finland, France, Georgia, Germany, Greece, Iceland, Ireland, Italy, Kosovo, Latvia, Liechtenstein, Lithuania, Luxembourg, Malta, Macedonia, Moldova, Monaco, Montenegro, Netherlands, Norway, Austria, Poland, Portugal, Romania, Russian Federation, San Marino, Sweden, Switzerland, Serbia, Slovak Republic, Slovenia, Spain, Czech Republic, Turkey, Ukraine, Hungary, United Kingdom, Cyprus]* (4th fully rev. and exp. ed.). Baltmannsweiler.

Esser, H. (2021). *Wie kaum in einem anderen Land? Die Differenzierung der Bildungswege nach Fähigkeiten und Leistungen und ihre Wirkung auf Bildungserfolg, -ungleichheit und -gerechtigkeit (Band 1, Theoretische Grundlagen) [Like hardly any other country? The differentiation of educational pathways by ability and achievement and its effect on educational success, inequality and equity (Volume 1: Theoretical basis)].* Campus.

Fauth, B., Atlay, C., Dumont, H., & Decristan, J. (2021). Does what you get depend on who you are with? Effects of student composition on teaching quality. *Learning and Instruction, 71*. https://doi.org/10.1016/j.learninstruc.2020.101355

Fischer, C., Kopmann, H., Rott, D., Veber, M., & Zeinz, H. (2014). Adaptive Lehrkompetenz und pädagogische Haltung [Adaptive teaching skills and pedagogical attitude]. *Jahrbuch für allgemeine Didaktik, 4*, 16–33.

Grünthal, S., Kretschmann, J., & Brunner, M. (2024). Wo soll's hingehen, kleiner Fisch? Eine konzeptuelle Replikation von Dumont et al. (2017) zu Schulformeffekten auf akademisches Selbstkonzept, schulische Motivation und die Einschätzung eigener Ausbildungschancen am Ende der Sekundarstufe I [Where to, little fish? A conceptual replication of Dumont et al. (2017) on school form effects on academic self-concept, school motivation and the assessment of own educational opportunities at the end of lower secondary level]. *Zeitschrift für Erziehungswissenschaft, 27*, 1087–1116. https://doi.org/10.1007/s11618-024-01243-6

Hallinan, M. T. (1994). Tracking: From theory to practice. *Sociology of Education, 67*(2), 79–84. https://doi.org/10.2307/2112697

Hattie, J. A. C. (2002). Classroom composition and peer effects. *International Journal of Educational Research, 37*, 449–481. https://doi.org/10.1016/S0883-0355(03)00015-6

Helbig, M., & Morar, T. (2017). Warum Lehrkräfte sozial ungleich bewerten: Ein Plädoyer für die Etablierung tertiärer Herkunftseffekte im werterwartungstheoretischen Standardmodell der Bildungsforschung [Why teachers evaluate socially unequal: A plea for the establishment of tertiary origin effects in the standard model of educational research based on value expectations theory]. In R. Becker (Ed.), *Integration durch Bildung* (pp. 145–163). Springer. https://hdl.handle.net/10419/173280.

Helsper, W., & Wiezorek, C. (2006). Zwischen Leistungsforderung und Fürsorge. Perspektiven der Hauptschule im Dilemma von Fachunterricht und Unterstützung [Between performance demands and care. Perspectives of the Hauptschule in the dilemma of specialised teaching and support]. *Die Deutsche Schule, 98*(4), 436–555. https://doi.org/10.25656/01:27349

Henderson, L. (2020). Children's education rights at the transition to secondary education: School choice in Northern Ireland. *British Educational Research Journal, 46*(5), 1131–1151. https://doi.org/10.1002/berj.3620

Henninges, M., Traini, C., & Kleinert, C. (2019). *Tracking and sorting in the German educational system.* Leibniz Institute for Educational Trajectories (LIfBi) Working Paper No. 83.

Hillmert, S., & Jacob, M. (2010). Selections and social selectivity on the academic track: A life-course analysis of educational attainment in Germany. *Research in Social Stratification and Mobility, 28*(1), 59–76. https://doi.org/10.1016/j.rssm.2009.12.006

Kühne, S., Maaz, K., Mank, S., Ordemann, J., & Schulz, S. M. (2021). Höhere Durchlässigkeit bei steigenden Bildungsbedarfen: Aktuelle Trends und Herausforderungen im deutschen Bildungswesen [Greater permeability with increasing educational needs: Current trends and challenges in the German education system]. *Recht der Jugend und des Bildungswesens (RdJB), 68*(3), 272–278. https://doi.org/10.5771/0034-1312-2020-3-272

Kunter, M., Baumert, J., Blum, W., Klusmann, U., Krauss, S., & Neubrand, M. (2011). *Professionelle Kompetenz von Lehrkräften. Ergebnisse des Forschungsprogramms COACTIV [Professional competence of teachers. Results of the research programme COACTIV].* Waxmann.

Lauterbach, W. (2021). Sekundäre Bildung in Deutschland [Secondary education in Germany]. In H. H. Krüger, H. Heinz-Hermann & A. S. Bosse (Eds.), *Handbuch Bildungs- und Erziehungssoziologie* (pp. 1–26). Springer. https://doi.org/10.1007/978-3-658-31395-1_45-1

Leithwood, K. (2021). A review of evidence about equitable school leadership. *Education Sciences, 11*(8), 377. https://doi.org/10.3390/educsci11080377

Leithwood, K., Harris, A., & Hopkins, D. (2020). Seven strong claims about successful school leadership revisited. *School leadership & management, 40*(1), 5–22. https://doi.org/10.1080/13632434.2019.1596077

Loveless, T. (2021). *Does detracking promote educational equity?* Brookings. Brown Center of Educational Policy. https://www.brookings.edu/articles/does-detracking-promote-educational-equity/

Meißner, C. (2024). *Bildungserträge atypischer Bildungsverläufe in Deutschland [Educational outcomes of atypical educational pathways in Germany].* Springer VS. https://doi.org/10.1007/978-3-658-44830-1

National Coalition Germany. (2020). *Die Umsetzung der UN-Kinderrechtskonvention in Deutschland. 5./6. Ergänzender Bericht an die Vereinten Nationen [The implementation of the UN Convention on the Rights of the Child in Germany. 5/6 supplementary report to the United Nations].* https://umsetzung-der-kinderrechtskonvention.de/wp-content/uploads/2019/10/NC_ErgaenzenderBericht_DEU_Web.pdf.

Neumann, M., Schnyder, I., Trautwein, U., Niggli, A., Lüdtke, O., & Cathomas, R. (2007). Schulformen als differenzielle Lernmilieus: Institutionelle und kompositionelle Effekte auf die Leistungsentwicklung im Fach Französisch [School types as differential learning environments: institutional and compositional effects on performance development in French]. *Zeitschrift für Erziehungswissenschaft, 10*(3), 499–420. https://doi.org/10.1007/s11618-007-0043-6

Oakes, J. (2005). *Keeping track: How schools structure inequality.* Yale University Press.

Organisation for Economic Cooperation and Development. (OECD). (2012). *Equity and quality in education: Supporting disadvantaged students and schools.* OECD. https://doi.org/10.1787/9789264130852-en

Organisation for Economic Cooperation and Development. (OECD). (2013). *PISA 2012 results: What makes schools successful? Resources, policies and practices (vol. IV).* OECD. https://doi.org/10.1787/9789264201156-en

Pham Xuan, R. (2023). *Die feinen Unterschiede in der Schullaufbahn. Rekonstruktionen zum Schüler*innenhabitus beim Übertritt von der Mittelschule in ein Gymnasium [The subtle differences in the school career. Reconstructions of pupils' habitus when transferring from secondary school to grammar school].* Barbara Budrich. https://doi.org/10.25656/01:26651

Poekert, P. E., Swaffield, S., Demir, E. K., & Wright, S. A. (2020). Leadership for professional learning towards educational equity: A systematic literature review. *Professional Development in Education, 46*(4), 541–562. https://doi.org/10.1080/19415257.2020.1787209

Scharf, J., Becker, M., Stallasch, S. E., Neumann, M., & Maaz, K. (2020). Primäre und sekundäre Herkunftseffekte über den Verlauf der Sekundarstufe. Eine Dekomposition an drei Bildungsübergängen [Primary and secondary effects of origin over the course of secondary education. A decomposition at three educational transitions]. *Zeitschrift für Erziehungswissenschaft, 23*(6), pp. 1251–1282. https://doi.org/10.25656/01:23308

Sekretariat der Ständigen Konferenz der Kultusminister. (KMK). (2020a). *The Education System in the Federal Republic of Germany 2019/2020.* https://www.kmk.org/fileadmin/Dateien/pdf/Eurydice/Bildungswesen-engl-pdfs/primary.pdf.

Sekretariat der Ständigen Konferenz der Kultusminister. (KMK). (2020b). *The Education System in the Federal Republic of Germany 2019/2020.* https://www.kmk.org/fileadmin/Dateien/pdf/Eurydice/Bildungswesen-engl-pdfs/secondary.pdf.

Stanat, P., Schipolowski, S., Schneider, R., Weirich, S., Henschel, S., & Sachse, K. A. (2023). *IQB-Bildungstrend 2022. Sprachliche Kompetenzen am Ende der 9. Klasse [IQB Education Trend 2022: Language skills at the end of year 9].* Bertelsmann Stiftung.

Thapa, A., Cohen, J., Guffey, S., & Higgins-D'Alessandro, A. (2013). A Review of School Climate Research. *Review of Educational Research, 83*(3), 357–385. https://doi.org/10.3102/0034654313483907

Tomaševski, K. (2001). Human rights obligations*: making education available, accessible, acceptable and adaptable. Right-to-education.* https://www.right-to-education.org/sites/right-to-education.org/files/resource-attachments/Tomasevski_Primer%203.pdf.

United Nations. (UN). (1989/2024). *Convention of the children's rights, UN CRC.* https://www.unicef.org/media/52626/file.

Weber, C. (2020). Herkunftsbedingte Bildungsungleichheiten – Die Rolle von Bildungsübergängen [Educational inequalities due to origin – The role of educational transitions]. *Erziehung & Unterricht, 3*(4), 299–308.

Wößmann, L., Schoner, F., Freundl, V., & Pfaehler, F. (2023). Der ifo-„Ein Herz für Kinder"-Chancenmonitor: Wie (un-)gerecht sind die Bildungschancen von Kindern aus verschiedenen Familien in Deutschland verteilt? [The ifo "A Heart for Children" opportunity monitor: How (un)fairly are the educational opportunities of children from different families in Germany distributed?]. *ifo Schnelldienst, 76*(4), pp. 29–47. https://www.ifo.de/publikationen/2023/aufsatz-zeitschrift/der-ifo-ein-herz-fuer-kinder-chancenmonitor.

Further Contributions in the Volume

Another article focusing on leadership at the system level is authored by *Philipp Schubert, Melanie Hochmuth, Julia Hufnagl,* and *Silvia Annen* on recognition procedures in Germany as a leadership task (pp. 65–78).

For insights into the teachers' needs for professionalization, the contribution of *Andreas Schmidt, Ruth Luzmore,* and *Colin Cramer* explores the concept of meta-reflexivity in teacher education (pp. 41–51).

Julia Hugo, Charlotte Assmann, Andreas Schmidt (Eds.)
Educational Leadership and Children's Rights?/
Kinderrechte als Führungsaufgabe?
 https://doi.org/10.31244/9783830998259_5

Philipp Schubert, Melanie Hochmuth, Julia Hufnagl & Silvia Annen

Recognition Authorities as Gatekeepers?

Immigrants' Legal Opportunities to Utilize their Qualifications Acquired Abroad

Abstract
Ensuring the social participation and integration of immigrants and their children into the German education and employment system is crucial. This can be achieved through proper recognition of their qualifications acquired abroad, which promotes social inclusion and self-realisation (Englmann, 2010). However, only a moderate proportion of immigrants take advantage of the recognition opportunities available, with the success of these processes varying by group of origin. Additionally, there is a lack of transparency and political influence. Furthermore, this contributes to the educational disadvantages faced by children from migrant families. To address information asymmetries regarding recognition procedures and reduce inequalities and barriers in the labour market, structured and situational management from a meta-perspective is needed. We argue that strategic leadership among stakeholders in the recognition process is essential to enhance transparency, making these processes more intersubjective and improving the professional integration of immigrants.

Keywords
Recognition Procedures, Immigrants' Recognition Rights, Leadership, Foreign Vocational Qualifications

Anerkennungsbehörden als Gatekeeper?

Rechtliche Möglichkeiten von Zugewanderten, ihre im Ausland erworbenen Berufsabschlüsse nutzbar zu machen

Zusammenfassung
Die soziale Teilhabe und Integration von Zugewanderten und ihren Kindern in das deutsche Bildungs- und Beschäftigungssystem ist von entscheidender Bedeutung für die Gesamtgesellschaft. Die angemessene Anerkennung von im Ausland erworbenen Qualifikationen kann einen wesentlichen Beitrag zur sozialen Integration und Selbstverwirklichung leisten (Englmann, 2010). Allerdings nimmt nur ein geringer Anteil der Zugewanderten die vorhandenen Anerkennungsmöglichkeiten wahr, der Erfolg dieser Verfahren ist je nach Herkunftsgruppe unterschiedlich und es mangelt an Transparenz und

politischer Einflussnahme. Dies kann auch zur Bildungsbenachteiligung von Kindern aus Familien mit Migrationshintergrund beitragen. Um Informationsasymmetrien in Bezug auf Anerkennungsverfahren zu reduzieren und Ungleichheiten sowie Barrieren auf dem Arbeitsmarkt abzubauen, ist ein strukturiertes und situatives Management aus einer Meta-Perspektive erforderlich. Der Artikel zeigt, dass eine strategische Führung der am Anerkennungsprozess beteiligten Akteurinnen und Akteure unerlässlich ist, um diese Prozesse intersubjektiver zu gestalten, ihre Transparenz zu erhöhen und die berufliche Integration von Zugewanderten zu verbessern.

Schlüsselbegriffe
Anerkennungsverfahren, Anerkennungsrechte von Zugewanderten, Führung, ausländische Berufsabschlüsse

1. Recognition of Qualifications Acquired Abroad as a Foundation for Vocational Integration

Empirical educational research shows repeatedly that children from migrant families experience educational disadvantages (e.g. Gries, Redlin & Zehra, 2022; Sudheimer & Buchholz, 2021). In the context of education and migration, the concept of educational leadership proves to be particularly relevant with regard to children's and youth's rights. The recognition of qualifications acquired abroad is a key foundation for the professional integration of immigrants. Given current political developments, particularly the ongoing crisis in Ukraine, this issue is becoming increasingly relevant as, in particular, women and families with children have immigrated, and their right to education has to be secured in the long term. Since 2022, around 1.4 million people have come to Germany from Ukraine due to the political conflict, while a total of 834,000 people from Syria, Afghanistan, and Iraq migrated to Germany between 2014 and 2016 (Destatis, 2023). Recognition is not only a legal and administrative process but also an integral part of the social participation and self-realisation of immigrants (Englmann, 2010). This is particularly evident in the context of immigration rights, as it has a direct impact on their ability to access the labour market, secure stable employment, and fully integrate into society. These factors frequently serve as pivotal criteria in the mechanisms and processes for obtaining or retaining residence status and citizenship.

The recognition decision in Germany is the result from a complex collaboration between various stakeholders involving several regulations to ensure German standards and enable adequate professional integration. Successful recognition of qualifications is associated with an approximate 50 % increase in the probability of employment (Brücker et al., 2014; Brücker et al., 2021), and thus provides a foundation for developing a long-term economic stability, self-sufficiency, social integration, and well-being. For children from families with a refugee background, lower vocational qualifications have been identified as a significant barrier to integration into the labour and housing market, increasing the risk of child poverty (Butterwegge, 2010).

The parents' professional qualifications and their integration process also have an impact on the asylum procedure.

Nevertheless, the recognition of qualifications is not a consistently established practice. To date, approximately one-third of immigrants have submitted applications for recognition (Brücker et al., 2021). Furthermore, despite the introduction of the Recognition Act, the rate of applications has only increased marginally in the first years (Anger, Bassetto & Sandner, 2018). However, an upward trend can be observed over time. In 2022, about 5 years after the Recognition Act, 49,500 applications were submitted, a new maximum (BMBF, 2024). According to the Federal Statistical Office, out of 65,900 processed applications from 170 countries in 2022, 52,300 applicants received a full recognition of their respective qualifications acquired abroad. Most of the recognised qualifications come from Europe and are in the field of medical healthcare occupations (Böse et al., 2023). These findings indicate that structures and processes in the recognition procedure differ considerably between different professional fields and involve various organisations with several decision-making options. To ensure professional integration of immigrants and their children, a strategic orientation of leadership is therefore essential among actors involved in the recognition process in order to make these processes intersubjective comprehensible and transparent. In addition to promoting integration processes in society as a whole, this can also ensure the right of immigrants to high-quality recognition of their qualifications. From these considerations, the question can be derived which legal framework conditions immigrants with qualifications acquired abroad are confronted with and which role the stakeholders of the recognising authorities play in this regard.

2. Recognition Procedures in Germany: Status quo and Current State of Research

2.1 Existing Problems Regarding Application

Formal qualifications have an important signalling effect on the labour market and play a major role in the recruitment process of immigrants in Germany (Annen, 2021). Despite the favourable ratio of skills shortages and immigration in Germany, which statistically boosts allocation on the labour market, only around a third of refugees are employed and the jobs they do are limited to a few occupations in the rather low-skilled sector (Worbs & Bund, 2016). This is also confirmed by other studies, especially when informal search strategies are used in one's own social environment (Kracke & Klug, 2021; Leschke & Weiss, 2020).

Overall, most refugees have extensive work experience, but not always vocational qualifications and diplomas (Liebau & Salikutluk, 2016). This also has an impact on the future (further) education processes of those affected and leads to challenges, particularly in sectors with an increased need for skilled workers such as the care sector (Geiger et al., 2019).

2.2 Inequalities in the Residence Status and Labour Market Access

There is also a trend towards overqualification among employees with qualifications acquired abroad (Rohrbach-Schmidt & Tiemann, 2016), which can be interpreted as an indication of possible reservations or access barriers to recognition procedures. In terms of the long-term impact of low-skilled jobs, such as barriers to the labour and housing markets, there is the potential for inequalities to emerge, affecting both young people who themselves have recognised qualifications and the children of families with recognised qualifications. In a study based on the Program for the International Assessment of Adult Competencies (PIAAC) data, employees with a qualification obtained in a non-western country earn significantly lower wages, even when other factors such as cognitive skills are controlled for (Lancee & Bol, 2017). Despite the recognition of qualifications, disparities and discrepancies in origin are evident, which may also affect the recognition process and illustrate its intricacy and its long-term consequences. Another study on the integration of refugees of Arab origin between 2015 and 2020 shows differences between the arrival phases and the prevailing labour market strategies at the time, which resulted in barriers to the recognition if they were perceived as genuine or illegitimate refugees (Menke, 2024). Factors such as social skills and ideological perceptions play a central role here (Etzel, 2022) and result in hierarchies between refugees in Germany that significantly affect their educational and employment biographies (Will, 2018).

2.3 Chances and Challenges in Accessing the Labour Market with Recognition of Foreign Qualifications

The recognition procedure itself is highly complex, with numerous regulations that vary depending on the occupational field and the type of qualification. These aspects ultimately determine whether qualifications are formally recognised as valid. This has a significant impact on the effects of recognition on access to the labour market, as well as on actual access to the labour market and subsequent labour market integration. Recognition procedures for vocational qualifications are strictly regulated at national level but differ greatly in the international context and are also shaped largely by political processes (Annen & Eberhardt, 2015).

However, studies show that other factors also play a role in the chances of success in recognition procedures. A representative analysis of the survey of refugees from the German Institute for Employment Research based on the Socio-Economic Panel Study (IAB-BAMF-SOEP) shows that both a secure residence permit, completed language and integration course increase the chance for recognition (Brücker et al., 2018). This reflects the high decision-making power of the stakeholders involved in the recognition process (Jacobsen, 2021). Within this process, information asymmetries can arise, because the competent bodies and the individuals each have information relevant to the procedure that is not known to the other side (Annen, 2012).

The public perception of recognised qualifications can represent a further barrier to labour market integration. Mergener and Maier (2019) show in a vignette study that qualifications acquired abroad are perceived more critically in the recruitment process. This can be interpreted in two ways: firstly, as evidence of discriminatory recruiting practices, and secondly, as an indication of potential reservations about the recognition system in general.

2.4 Educational Leadership in the Context of Recognition

In the long-term perspective, the focus in the context of migration should be on education, integration, language support, and the transfer of cultural knowledge. The term educational leadership is defined in this article with a focus on the leadership and management of organisational educational processes (Norberg, 2017). We argue that educational leadership plays a major role in ensuring the right to education and a right to equal opportunities for all people in Germany. Leadership represents an option to control the underlying processes to ensure this right, particularly for social organisations to which actors in the recognition process belong.

In addition to the existing rights of immigrants, the rights of the relevant actors to make decisions determine their educational and employment prospects to a considerable extent by affecting immigrants' educational and employment opportunities. The recognition process is complex, because different recognition bodies are responsible, depending on the type of qualification and region in Germany. They have extensive decision-making powers, especially if the documentation of qualifications is unclear. To make a decision, other factors are considered. For example, face to face interviews with applicants and in-depth information on their social integration and language skills can create inequality because the recognising actors can make subjective assessments. The principles of the two following leadership approaches, on the one hand contingency theory leadership and on the other hand situational leadership, can be used here to identify the decision-makers' opportunities for influencing and making decisions, as well as to ascertain their impact on the recognition process.

Contingency Theory

The first leadership approach is the contingency theory, which is task- and goal-oriented (Fiedler, 1978). This theory promotes dialogue and reflection in the organisation because it also has an open understanding of leadership and high adaptability in different contexts. However, this theory assumes that although the leadership and management style is basically stable and consistent, the task structure and the positional power of the leader play an important role, which is particularly relevant for the context of employees working in the recognition context. These employees are located in fixed structures but have decision-making powers that need to be controlled and, according to the assumptions of this theory, are closely dependent on the leadership culture. However, a comprehensive analysis of situational influence is necessary to identify the mechanisms and power relationships within organisations. A systematic literature review focusing on refugees summarises that educational leadership can both facilitate and hinder their integration. Moral action, awareness raising, and commitment emerge as success factors that must be implemented by the management level for the stakeholders involved (Arar & Orucu, 2022).

Situational Leadership

One leadership approach by Herzka (2013) emphasises that situational leadership, in particular due to its dynamic adaptability (Blanchard, Zigarmi & Nelson, 1993), is a suitable concept for managing legal organisations because effective leadership depends on the respective situation, which is why no rigid leadership style can be applied. Situational leadership enables flexible adaptation of the leadership and management style, making the approach particularly suitable for considering intercultural sensitivity as well as the necessary flexibility and crisis management. The approach aims to ensure that managers act in a way that is appropriate to the target group through dynamic customisability and adapt to constantly changing requirements and legal framework conditions. This is particularly important in the context of recognition procedures, as these are subject to complex and agile legal situations. However, rigid structures in educational organisations can make it more difficult to implement dynamic strategies in the long term.

The success of an open, reflective and situational leadership as mentioned above also occurs in empirical research studies, as shown e.g. in the context of forced migration in Greece. Sabchev (2022) demonstrates that the collaborative and situational approach employed by mayors significantly influenced the reception conditions for forced immigrants and led to better access to services for immigrants. Norberg (2017) hows a similar effect in the context of educational leadership in Sweden. The challenge for school principals is to create a supportive school structure and culture for newly arrived migrated students. Norberg concludes that a professional management style is required that includes openness and adaptability to the situation in the schools. This implies that a professional leadership style is necessary to include openness and adaptability to the situation in schools.

For the labour market, this means that companies, like schools, should develop an inclusive work culture and consider individual mentoring, the opportunity to participate in further language courses and individual management styles. However, to implement this openness and adaptability, it is essential to create transparency about qualifications so that companies can use the recognition decision as a basis for their recruitment decision-making. We therefore argue that increased management of the recognition process through educational leadership approaches has the potential to promote transparency and thus openness in companies.

3. Recognition Procedure: Legal Framework

The Recognition Act in Germany aims to simplify and improve the assessment of vocational qualifications acquired abroad. The aim is to harness existing qualification potential, promote employment in line with qualifications and support integration into the world of work (BMBF, 2012). A distinction is made between vocational, school and academic recognition, whereby vocational recognition is covered by the Professional Qualifications Assessment Act (Berufsqualifikationsfeststellungsgesetz, BQFG) and classifies the occupations into the categories of regulated occupations and non-regulated occupations. (Haag, 2022; Körtek, 2015). The BQFG introduced a separation of the recognition procedure from the respective nationality, thereby also granting immigrants from third countries a right to recognition (Haag, 2022). The BQFG applies to occupations regulated by federal law. Occupations that fall under the discretionary rights of the federal states are regulated by special recognition laws of these states (Körtek, 2015, p. 14). The equivalence for this process is determined by various stakeholders, such as chambers or state authorities (Körtek, 2015).

3.1 Recognition Opportunities

The opportunities for recognition can be classified into three categories: qualification recognition for regulated occupations, non-regulated occupations, and procedures for other qualifications (e.g. the assessment of academic qualifications).

Regulated occupations are those vocational activities whose labour market admission or practice is subject to legal or administrative requirements, necessitating specific professional qualifications (BMBF, 2012; Körtek, 2015). In principle, the relevant specialist law applies to the respective regulated occupations (e.g. the Federal Medical Practitioners' Code [Bundesärzteordnung] for doctors); the BQFG only applies if explicit reference is made to it or in the absence of specific regulations. Equivalence is considered to be established when the qualifications obtained abroad demonstrate a comparable level of vocational training to the corresponding German reference occupation, with no significant differences between the foreign qualification and the German standard (BMBF, 2012). Due to the large number of German training occupations, the reference occupation must be determined by agreement between the different competent bodies, such as chambers of crafts and trades (Handwerkskammern bzw. Industrie- und Handelskammern) and the applicant. The competent bodies serve an advisory role in this context and are expected to provide insights into the likelihood of success in the equivalence assessment. Criteria considered in such an assessment include how closely the professional profiles align, the relevance of prior work experience, and the emphasis of the intended professional activity (BMBF, 2012). If the equivalence assessment reveals differences that cannot be covered by additional relevant work experience, the respective body must identify binding compensatory measures. These measures, which usually take the form of courses or examinations, are intended to certify the applicants' lack of knowledge and skills (BMBF, 2012).

Vocational training occupations within the German dual system are mainly non-regulated occupations (Körtek, 2015). The recognition is usually carried out directly by the BQFG and if significant differences to the reference occupation are identified, it is checked whether this can be compensated for by relevant work experience (BMBF, 2012).

In the case of regulated occupations, the professional license is a decisive factor. This must be determined together with the equivalence and contains additional requirements that go hand in hand with the professional law (e.g. doctors also need a health aptitude in addition to the professional equivalence) (BMBF, 2012). Recognition is therefore mandatory to be able to work in a regulated occupation. In contrast, equivalence for non-regulated occupations primarily serves to improve transparency on the labour market (Haag, 2022).

In addition, there are projects that got initiated after the Recognition Act (Anerkennungsgesetz) and cover applicants who do not fit into the two above procedures. The project Prototyping Transfer aims to improve the recognition of professional qualifications acquired abroad. Instead of carrying out a pure document check, the qualification analysis enables a practice-oriented assessment of vocational skills through work samples, technical discussions, or presentations. This allows a well-founded assessment of the immigrants' skills, even if individual documents confirming the qualification are incomplete or missing (Raskopp, 2015) but is highly subjective. Building on the prototype approach, the project NetQA – Network Qualifications Analysis – aims to establish a network between the competent bodies in the recognition procedure. This structure supports the exchange of information on qualifications analysis and the Professional Qualifications Assessment Act (Wiemers, 2019) and shows first linking points for the necessity of cross-organisational control through educational leadership.

3.2 Barriers to Access

Despite the many opportunities to have qualifications recognised in Germany, the requirement processes lack standardisation and concrete description (Haag, 2022). The lengthy recognition procedures mean that many immigrants are unable to gain access to the German labour market. Stakeholders from business, politics and academia are therefore increasingly calling for the criterion of vocational equivalence to be made more flexible or even abolished (Angenendt, Knapp & Kipp, 2023). Mostly highly analogue processes, understaffing of the departments involved and cumbersome administrative structures compound these problems.

4. Gatekeepers in the Recognition Procedure: Leadership for Structured Control Within and Between Organisations

The recognition procedure is carried out and accompanied by various institutions and stakeholders, all acting in accordance with their organisational structure and legal requirements. Nevertheless, the decision-making process allows for flexibility and consideration of socio-cultural factors that have been empirically validated in prior studies (Jacobsen, 2021). In the following, we show how leadership in organisations and in political discourse can help establish a structured and transparent recognition practice and can thus lead to fairer recognition processes. The situational leadership approach and contingency theory are used to consider the benefits of an agile and situational leadership culture, as well as the challenges posed by positions of power and the importance of the organisation-employee relationship.

Initially, leadership generally describes the management of teams and individuals. In the context of leadership in state organisations the high degree of bureaucracy and rule-bondedness must be emphasised, which is always politically influenced and therefore situational (Hill, 2006; Yukl, 2006). In contrast to management, situational leadership entails the involvement of other participants in the decision-making process, with the objective of establishing legitimate conditions within organisational structures (Herzka, 2013). The recognition of qualifications acquired abroad is characterised by complex interactions between the stakeholders involved and their individual decision-making basis, which must be dynamically adapted to the current political situation and underlying legal situation, as explained in chapter 2.4. If intersubjective traceability of the recognition decision is guaranteed within the context of comprehensive leadership, any potential reservations regarding the recruitment of individuals with skills acquired abroad can be mitigated, thereby facilitating immigrants' long-term economic stability, self-sufficiency, social integration, and well-being.

One promising possibility of establishing a structured and transparent recognition practice is the idea of a European Qualifications Passport, which is intended to facilitate mobility, employability, and access to higher education within Europe (Mørland & Skjerven, 2017). This concept is accompanied by the mandatory prerequisite of overarching leadership at the legal and political level to create uniform framework conditions, which can then be used by the various stakeholders to ensure a standardised national process. The project demonstrates the importance of active leadership in guiding the stakeholders involved to ensure that the concept is implemented consistently across the various national offices. To achieve this, comprehensive guidance and national and cross-national exchange between managers and executive offices are essential.

The leadership concept therefore ties in with the political discourse on the recognition of qualifications from a meta-perspective at various points: in addition to the management of employees directly involved in the process, the coordination of various specialist areas and the management of the respective organisation, the level of social policy must also be emphasised. The concept of management is evolving beyond its traditional connotation of a dialogue between managers and employees.

Instead, there is a growing emphasis on guidance and shaping as key aspects of the management process.

5. Current Implications and Need for Further Research

The right to have qualifications acquired abroad recognised is a crucial aspect of immigrant integration, as it enables immigrants, and their children, to participate fully in society and to achieve their potential (Englmann, 2010). Nevertheless, currently only a moderate proportion of immigrants avail themselves of the opportunities for recognition. Furthermore, the success of recognition processes varies according to the groups of origin, political influence and whether the information asymmetries between the immigrants and the recognising bodies can be overcome. As research repeatedly shows that children from families with a migration background experience educational disadvantage (e.g. Gries et al., 2022; Sudheimer & Buchholz, 2021), this situation also has an impact on their right to education. To promote fair access to recognition procedures in the long term and to reduce (educational) inequalities and barriers in the labour market in the context of the recognition of qualifications, structured and situational management from a meta-perspective is required. The stakeholders and organisations involved in the recognition procedure, which have a gatekeeper function, play a central role here.

This article shows that a structured and centrally managed expansion of recognition options has the potential to encourage the use of fair, transparent and standardised recognition procedures. Practical qualification analyses, such as the prototyping transfer and NetQA projects presented here, are a useful but subjective complement to document review. If the process is centrally managed and quality-controlled, this represents a promising approach. The key challenge is to develop and monitor the intercultural sensitivity and leadership skills of the stakeholders involved, so that they exercise their decision-making powers fairly and transparently. Centrally managed training for employees of the recognition bodies and intensive programs on educational leadership can reduce power mechanisms in the context of contingency theory, strengthen transparency and sensitivity, and reduce companies' reservations about recognised qualifications. In particular, the comprehensive introduction of a structured, situational leadership approach can also take into account the dynamics of the processes.

As a research desideratum, it is necessary to gain insight into how the stakeholders involved in the recognition procedure perceive their own decision-making basis in the complex recognition process. This will enable the derivation of specific recommendations for action for the development of a comprehensive leadership approach. In order to establish an evidence-based foundation, it is also essential to determine which recognition procedures and successful labour market integration can be observed, e.g. for certain groups. Moreover, it would be beneficial to examine the potential for these findings to be applied to other groups of origin as a best practice strategy within the legal framework. Only fair recognition processes can assure the welfare of Germany in times of skill shortage and the social integration, social participation, and self-realisation of individuals. This also implicitly contributes to ensuring that children from migrant families can fully exercise their right to education.

References

Angenendt, S., Knapp, N., & Kipp, D. (2023). *Germany is looking for foreign labour: how to make recruitment development-orientated, sustainable and fair. SWP Research Paper.* Stiftung Wissenschaft und Politik (SWP). German Institute for International and Security Affairs. https://doi.org/10.18449/2023RP03

Anger, S., Bassetto, J., & Sandner, M. (2018). Anerkennung ausländischer Abschlüsse: Bürokratieabbau und bessere Informationen könnten die Antragsquote erhöhen [Recognition of Foreign Qualifications: Reducing Bureaucracy and Providing Better Information Could Increase the Application Rate]. *IAB-Forum: das Magazin des Instituts für Arbeitsmarkt- und Berufsforschung der Bundesagentur für Arbeit, 14.*

Annen, S. (2012). *Anerkennung von Kompetenzen: kriterienorientierte Analyse ausgewählter Verfahren in Europa [Recognition of competences: criteria-oriented analysis of selected procedures in Europe].* Bertelsmann.

Annen, S. (2021). Relevance of qualifications and work experience in the recruiting of foreign-trained immigrants – comparative insights from the Health and ICT Sectors in Germany and Canada. *International Journal of Training and Development, 25*(1), 3–22.

Annen, S., & Eberhardt, C. (2015). Recognising foreign qualifications and competences: An area of conflict between labour market, education and migration policy. *International Journal for Cross-Disciplinary Subjects in Education. Special Issue, 5*(1), 2437–2447.

Arar, K., & Orucu, D. (2022). The research on educational leadership for refugees since 2009: An international systemic review of empirical evidence. *International Journal of Leadership in Education*, 1–37. https://doi.org/10.1080/13603124.2022.2068190

Blanchard, K. H., Zigarmi, D., & Nelson, R. B. (1993). Situational Leadership after 25 years: A retrospective. *Journal of Leadership Studies, 1*(1), 21–36.

Böse, C., Schmitz, N., Zorner, J., & Ord, K. (2023). *Auswertung der amtlichen Statistik zum Anerkennungsgesetz des Bundes für 2022 [Analysis of Government Statistics on the Federal Recognition Act for 2022].* Bundesinstitut für Berufsbildung.

Brücker, H., Glitz, A., Lerche, A., & Romiti, A. (2021). Occupational Recognition and Immigrant Labour Market Outcomes. *Journal of Labour Economics, 39*(2), 497–525. https://doi.org/10.1086/710702

Brücker, H., Liebau, E., Romiti, A., & Vallizadeh, E. (2014). Anerkannte Abschlüsse und Deutschkenntnisse lohnen sich [Recognised Qualifications and Knowledge of German are Rewarded]. *DIW Wochenbericht, 81*(43), 1145–1151.

Brücker, H., Rother, N., & Schupp, J. (Eds.). (2018). *IAB-BAMF-SOEP-Befragung von Geflüchteten 2016: Studiendesign, Feldergebnisse sowie Analysen zu schulischer wie beruflicher Qualifikation, Sprachkenntnissen sowie kognitiven Potenzialen [IAB-BAMF-SOEP Survey of Refugees 2016: Study Design, Field Results and Analyses of Educational and Vocational Qualifications, Language Skills and Cognitive Potentials].* https://doku.iab.de/forschungsbericht/2017/fb1317.pdf

Bundesministerium für Bildung und Forschung. (BMBF). (2012). *Erläuterungen zum Anerkennungsgesetz des Bundes. Gesetz zur Verbesserung der Feststellung und Anerkennung im Ausland erworbener Berufsqualifikationen [Explanations on the Federal Recognition Act. Law to Improve the Assessment and Recognition of Professional Qualifications Acquired Abroad].* https://www.anerkennung-in-deutschland.de/assets/content/Medien_Dokumente-Fachpublikum/20120320_erlaeuterungen_zum_anerkennungsg_bund.pdf.

Bundesministerium für Bildung und Forschung. (BMBF). (2024). *Bericht zum Anerkennungsgesetz 2023 [Report on the Recognition Act 2023].*

Butterwegge, C. (2010). *Armut von Kindern mit Migrationshintergrund [Poverty of Immigrants' Children].* Springer VS. https://doi.org/10.1007/978-3-531-92316-1

Destatis. (2023, 16th February). *1,1 Millionen Zuzüge von Menschen aus der Ukraine im Jahr 2022. Pressemitteilung Nr. N010 [1.1 Million Immigrants from Ukraine in 2022].*

Englmann, B. (2010). Anerkennungsverfahren für ausländische Qualifikationen: im Kontext des lebenslangen Lernens [Recognition Procedures for Foreign Qualifications: in the Context of Lifelong Learning]. *REPORT-Zeitschrift für Weiterbildungsforschung, 33*(1), 11–20.

Etzel, M. (2022). New models of the "Good refugee" – bureaucratic expectations of Syrian refugees in Germany. In A. Hackl (Ed.), *Permitted Outsiders* (S. 127–146). Routledge. https://doi.org/10.4324/9781003342434-7

Fiedler, F. E. (1978). The Contingency Model and the Dynamics of the Leadership Process. In L. Berkowitz (Ed.), *Advances in Experimental Social Psychology* (vol. 11, pp. 59–112). Academic Press. https://doi.org/10.1016/S0065-2601(08)60005-2

Geiger, S., Müller, M., Schmidt-Hertha, B., & Faas, S. (2019). Professionalization and change: Recognition of qualifications, educational processes and competencies in Germany. In S. Faas, D. Kasüschke, E. Nitecki, M. Urban & H. Wasmuth (Eds.), *Globalization, Transformation, and Cultures in Early Childhood Education and Care: Reconceptualization and Comparison* (pp. 235–256). Springer.

Gries, T., Redlin, M., & Zehra, M. (2022). Educational assimilation of first-generation and second-generation immigrants in Germany. *Journal of International Migration and Integration, 23*(2), 815–845. https://doi.org/10.1007/s12134-021-00863-9

Haag, A. (2022). *Die Liberalisierung der bundesdeutschen Migrationspolitik am Beispiel des Anerkennungsgesetzes [The liberalization of German migration policy using the Recognition Act as an example].* Springer VS. https://doi.org/10.1007/978-3-658-37292-7

Herzka, M. (2013). *Führung im Widerspruch: Management in Sozialen Organisationen [Leadership in Contradiction: Management in Social Organisations].* Springer.

Hill, H. (2006). Von Good Governance zu Public Leadership [From Good Governance to Public Leadership]. *VM Verwaltung & Management, 12*(2), 81–84.

Jacobsen, J. (2021). An investment in the future: institutional aspects of credential recognition of refugees in Germany. *Journal of Refugee Studies, 34*(3), 3000–3023.

Körtek, Y. (2015). Rechtlicher Rahmen der Anerkennung [Legal framework of recognition]. In T. Ayan (Ed.), *Anerkennung ausländischer Qualifikationen: Forschungsergebnisse und Praxisbeispiele* (pp. 13–24). Springer. https://doi.org/10.1007/978-3-658-24676-1_2

Kracke, N., & Klug, C. (2021). Social Capital and Its Effect on Labour Market (Mis)match: Migrants' Overqualification in Germany. *Journal of International Migration and Integration, 22*(4), 1573–1598. https://doi.org/10.1007/s12134-021-00817-1

Lancee, B., & Bol, T. (2017). The transferability of skills and degrees: Why the place of education affects immigrant earnings. *Social Forces, 96*(2), 691–716.

Leschke, J., & Weiss, S. (2020). With a Little Help from My Friends: Social-Network Job Search and Overqualification among Recent Intra-EU Migrants Moving from East to West. *Work, Employment and Society, 34*(5), 769–788. https://doi.org/10.1177/0950017020926433

Liebau, E., & Salikutluk, Z. (2016). Many refugees have work experience but a smaller share possess formal vocational qualifications. *DIW Economic Bulletin, 6*(34/35), 392–399.

Menke, K. (2024). Between life course regimes and biographical orientations: labour market trajectories of refugee mothers in Germany from a gendered perspective. *Zeitschrift für Sozialreform, 70*(1), 101–120.

Mergener, A., & Maier, T. (2019). Immigrants' chances of being hired at times of skill shortages: results from a factorial survey experiment among German employers. *Journal of International Migration and Integration, 20*, 155–177.

Mørland, T., & Skjerven, S.A. (2017). Europe: a European Qualifications Passport for Refugees. In G. Mihut, P. G. Altbach & H. D. Wit (Eds.) *Understanding Global Higher Education. Global Perspectives on Higher Education.* Sense Publishers. https://doi.org/10.1007/978-94-6351-044-8_25

Norberg, K. (2017). Educational leadership and im/migration: preparation, practice and policy – the Swedish case. *International Journal of Educational Management, 31*(5), 633–645. http://dx.doi.org/10.1108/IJEM-08-2016-0162

Raskopp, K. (2015). *Prototyping Transfer. Berufsanerkennung mit Qualifikationsanalysen [Prototyping Transfer. Professional recognition with qualification analyses].* Bundesinstitut für Berufsbildung (BIBB). https://www.bibb.de/.

Rohrbach-Schmidt, D., & Tiemann, M. (2016). *Limited transferability of human capital across countries-the case of workers with foreign qualifications in Germany. Wissenschaftliche Diskussionspapiere.* Bundesinstitut für Berufsbildung (BIBB).

Sabchev, T. (2022). The role of local political leadership in the reception of forced migrants: evidence from Greece. *Territory, Politics, Governance, 10*(3), 306–326. https://doi.org10.1080/21622671.2021.1927815

Sudheimer, S., & Buchholz, S. (2021). Muster migrationsspezifischer Unterschiede unter Studienberechtigten in Deutschland: Soziale Herkunft – Schulische Leistungen – Bildungsaspirationen [Migration-specific differences among school leavers in Germany: social origin, academic performance and educational aspirations]. *Migration, Mobilität und soziale Ungleichheit in der Hochschulbildung*, 27–58. https://doi.org/10.1007/978-3-658-31694-5_2

Wiemers, D. (2019). *Projektbeschreibung Netzwerk Qualifikationsanalyse (NetQA) [Project description Network Qualification Analysis (NetQA)].* Bundesinstitut für Berufsbildung (BIBB).

Will, A.-K. (2018). On Genuine and Illegitimate Refugees: New Boundaries Drawn by Discriminatory Legislation and Practice in the Field of Humanitarian Reception in Germany. *Social Inclusion, 6*(3), 172–189.

Worbs, S., & Bund, E. (2016). *Asylberechtigte und anerkannte Flüchtlinge in Deutschland: Qualifikationsstruktur, Arbeitsmarktbeteiligung und Zukunftsorientierungen [Asylum Seekers and Recognised Refugees in Germany: Qualification Structure, Labour Market Participation and Future Orientations].* https://nbn-resolving.org/urn:nbn:de:0168-ssoar-67441-2.

Yukl, G. (2006). *Leadership in Organizations.* Prentice Hall.

Further Contributions in the Volume

Another article focusing on leadership at the system level is authored by *Robert Pham Xuan* and *Dong Nguyen* on the German tracking system as an issue regarding children's rights (pp. 53–64).

For a switch onto the international context, we recommend the article by *Carolina Dahle* and *Tine Sophie Prøitz* on the Norwegian zero-tolerance-policy against bullying in schools (pp. 89–101).

Julia Hugo, Charlotte Assmann, Andreas Schmidt (Eds.)
Educational Leadership and Children's Rights?/
Kinderrechte als Führungsaufgabe?
© 2025, Waxmann. https://doi.org/10.31244/9783830998259_6

Antonia Bongen

Diversitätsmanagement zur Diskriminierungsprävention als Führungsaufgabe in Kindertageseinrichtungen

Zusammenfassung
In Deutschland ist der Bildungserfolg von Kindern nach wie vor stark durch ihre soziale Herkunft geprägt. Kindertageseinrichtungen kommt bzgl. der Aufgabe, Bildungsungleichheiten frühzeitig abzubauen und einen diskriminierungsfreien Zugang zu Bildungsressourcen zu gewährleisten, eine Schlüsselrolle zu. Der Umgang mit der Diversität der Kinder hält jedoch besondere Herausforderungen für pädagogische Fach- und Führungskräfte bereit. Dieser Beitrag beleuchtet, welche Chancen ein Transfer des betriebswirtschaftlichen Diversitätsmanagements zur Vorbeugung von Diskriminierung i. S. v. Art. 2 Abs. 1 UN-KRK als Führungsaufgabe in Kindertageseinrichtungen bietet. Dabei wird die Bedeutung von Führung für das Anstoßen langfristiger und strategischer Veränderungen im Kontext von Diversität hervorgehoben. Es wird dargelegt, wie die mit Diversitätsmanagement einhergehenden Maßnahmen zur Stärkung von Bildungsteilhabe dazu beitragen können, Diskriminierung effektiv vorzubeugen.

Schlüsselbegriffe
Diversitätsmanagement, Frühe Bildung, Führung, Diskriminierung, UN-Kinderrechtskonvention

Diversity Management for Discrimination Prevention

A Leadership Task in Daycare Centers

Abstract
In Germany, children's educational success is strongly influenced by their social background. Daycare centers are crucial in reducing educational inequalities and ensuring non-discriminatory access to educational resources. However, dealing with the diversity of children poses challenges for educational professionals and leaders. This article highlights the leadership opportunities offered by the transfer of diversity management as an economic concept to prevent discrimination according to Art. 2 Para. 1 UN CRC in child daycare centers. The importance of leadership for initiating long-term and strategic changes in the context of diversity is emphasized. It is shown how the measures associ-

ated with diversity management can contribute to strengthening educational equity, and effectively preventing discrimination.

Keywords
Diversity Management, Early Childhood Education, Leadership, Discrimination, UN Convention on the Rights of the Child

1. Einleitung

In Deutschland wird der Bildungserfolg eines Kindes weiterhin maßgeblich durch seine soziale Herkunft und den familiären Hintergrund beeinflusst (Ruppin, 2017; Walgenbach, 2017; Fischer & Gramelt, 2021a). Ungleiche Startchancen, bedingt durch unterschiedliche sozioökonomische Verhältnisse, führen zu Benachteiligungen beim Zugang zu Bildungsressourcen und Fördermöglichkeiten. Kindertageseinrichtungen spielen als erste institutionelle Bildungsinstanz eine entscheidende Rolle, Bildungsungleichheiten frühzeitig zu durchbrechen und den Grundstein für eine gerechte Bildungsbiografie zu legen. Diese Verantwortung wird auch durch die UN-Kinderrechtskonvention (UN-KRK) unterstrichen, die u.a. das Diskriminierungsverbot in Artikel 2 Abs. 1 festschreibt. Wenngleich diese völkerrechtlich bedingten Rechtspositionen eine wesentliche Grundlage für die Tätigkeit an allen pädagogischen Institutionen darstellen, ergibt sich auch in Kindertageseinrichtungen für pädagogische Fachkräfte allgemein und Leitungskräfte speziell daraus die wichtige Aufgabe, einen sensiblen und bewussten Umgang mit Vielfalt zu fördern. Sie tragen eine besondere Verantwortung dafür, sicherzustellen, dass alle Kinder unabhängig von Herkunft, Geschlecht oder anderen Merkmalen vor Benachteiligung geschützt werden.

Gleichzeitig sind sowohl pädagogische Fachkräfte als auch Leitungskräfte in einer von struktureller Diskriminierung geprägten Gesellschaft sozialisiert und tragen so zur Reproduktion von Ungleichheit in Kindertageseinrichtungen bei (Simon, Kerle & Prigge, 2022, S. 93–94). Zudem besteht bei vielen Fachkräften noch Entwicklungsbedarf im Umgang mit Diversität (Menz & Abdessadok, 2022; Betz & Bischoff, 2017; Steiner-Khamsi, 2010), was ihre Möglichkeiten zur vollständigen Umsetzung einer diversitätsbewussten Pädagogik herausfordert. Nachdem bisher vor allem die pädagogischen Fachkräfte im Zentrum des Diversitätsdiskurses standen, sollte die Rolle von Leitungskräften zur Bewältigung dieser Herausforderungen stärker berücksichtigt werden. Ansätze wie *inclusive Leadership*, das wie das Diversitätsmanagement auf die Förderung von Teilhabe und Chancengerechtigkeit abzielt, verdeutlichen die Bedeutung einer stärkeren Einbindung von Leitungskräften, um langfristige und strategische Veränderungen in diesem Bereich anzustoßen. Nachfolgend soll daher ausgelotet werden, welche Chancen ein Transfer des betriebswirtschaftlichen Diversitätsmanagements zur Vorbeugung von Diskriminierung im Sinne eines *inclusive Leaderships* in Kindertageseinrichtungen bietet.

Dazu wird zunächst die Rolle der UN-KRK für den Umgang mit Diversität erläutert (Kapitel 2). Im Anschluss wird der aktuelle Stand hinsichtlich des Umgangs mit Diversität in Kindertageseinrichtungen abgebildet (Kapitel 3) und der Ansatz des Diversitätsmanagements vorgestellt (Kapitel 4). Abschließend werden die Implikationen eines Transfers des Diversitätsmanagements auf den Bereich der frühen Bildung diskutiert (Kapitel 5).

2. Rolle der Kinderrechtskonventionen für den Umgang mit Diversität in der frühen Bildung

Artikel 2 Abs. 1 UN-KRK fordert, dass die Gewährleistung der Kinderrechte „ohne jede Diskriminierung unabhängig von der Rasse [sic!], der Hautfarbe, dem Geschlecht, der Sprache, der Religion, der politischen oder sonstigen Anschauung, der nationalen, ethnischen oder sonstigen Herkunft, des Vermögens, der Behinderung, der Geburt oder des sonstigen Status des Kindes, seiner Eltern oder seines Vormunds" erfolgen muss.

Entsprechend braucht es in Kindertageseinrichtungen einen konstruktiven Umgang mit der Vielfalt der Kinder. Auf der Interaktions- und Handlungsebene begegnen diesem Anspruch bereits bestehende Konzepte wie der Anti-Bias-Ansatz[1], die vorurteilsbewusste Bildung und Erziehung[2] oder die diversitätsbewusste Perspektive[3]. Dieser Beitrag basiert auf der Grundannahme, dass das aus der Betriebswirtschaft stammende Diversitätsmanagement (Loden & Rosener, 1991) ein geeigneter Ansatz für pädagogische Führungskräfte ist, um einen konstruktiven Umgang mit Diversität in der frühkindlichen Bildung zu gestalten.

3. Ausgangslage: Diversität in der frühen Bildung

Der Diversitätsdiskurs in der frühen Bildung wird maßgeblich von den Auswirkungen von sozialer Vielfalt auf die Bildungschancen der Kinder beeinflusst (Ruppin, 2017; Walgenbach, 2017; Fischer & Gramelt, 2021a). Besonders prägend waren die Ergebnisse der PISA-Studie aus dem Jahr 2001, welche die strukturelle Bildungsungerechtigkeit im deutschen Bildungssystem entlang verschiedener Differenzachsen wie dem Geschlecht, der ethnischen Herkunft oder dem sozialen Status aufzeigten (Walgenbach, 2017, S. 22). Die Benachteiligung bestimmter sozialer Gruppen im Bildungssystem war zuvor zwar bekannt und fand in spezifischen Ansätzen wie der interkulturellen, feministischen oder integrativen Pädagogik Berücksichtigung (Prengel, 2019),

1 Der Anti-Bias-Ansatz ist ein intersektionales, proaktives und anwendungsbasiertes Konzept mit dem Ziel, eine vorurteilsbewusste und machtsensible Gesellschaft zu fördern (Derman-Sparks & Edwards, 2010).

2 Die Vorurteilsbewusste Bildung und Erziehung verbindet den Anti-Bias-Ansatz mit dem elementarpädagogischen Situationsansatz und fokussiert die Entwicklung einer diversitätsbewussten und diskriminierungskritischen Haltung (Wagner, 2018; Richter, 2022).

3 Die diversitätsbewusste Perspektive stellt einen multifaktoriellen Ansatz dar, in dem den Interdependenzen der Zugehörigkeiten von Kindern und Familien ganzheitlich begegnet wird. Dazu gehört, sich von normativen Kategorien wie Gender oder Migration zu lösen und stattdessen übergeordnete Strukturen, wie die soziale Herkunft oder die Bildungsvoraussetzungen der Eltern und Kinder, zu nutzen (Fischer & Gramelt, 2021b).

allerdings verschob sich der wissenschaftliche Fokus in den letzten zwei Jahrzehnten von einer isolierten Betrachtung der Diversitätsdimensionen hin zu einer intersektionalen[4] Analyse von Vielfalt.

Als Konsequenz geriet die frühe Bildung als bisher vernachlässigter Bereich in das Blickfeld von Politik und Forschung, mit dem Ziel, die Chancen und Herausforderungen von Diversität für Kinder, Familien, pädagogische Fachkräfte und Einrichtungsleitungen adäquat adressieren zu können (Walgenbach, 2017, S. 23). Viele Kindertageseinrichtungen haben das Thema erkannt und bemühen sich um eine bewusstere Herangehensweise an Diversität, die sich jedoch sehr unterschiedlich gestaltet. Ein wesentlicher Entwicklungsbereich liegt in der Diversitätskompetenz der pädagogischen Fachkräfte (Menz & Abdessadok, 2022; Betz & Bischoff, 2017; Steiner-Khamsi, 2010).

Damit ist im Diversitätsdiskurs bisher vorwiegend die Rolle der pädagogischen Fachkräfte als zentrale Handlungsträger fokussiert worden. In der Unternehmensforschung konnte gezeigt werden, dass *inclusive Leadership* über eine hohe Wirkmacht verfügt (Jin, Lee & Lee, 2017, S. 304). Diese Ergebnisse sind zwar nicht uneingeschränkt auf die frühe Bildung übertragbar, legen allerdings nahe, dass Führungskräfte in Kindertageseinrichtungen eine ähnliche Schlüsselfunktion einnehmen könnten, um Diversitätsbewusstsein strukturell und nachhaltig zu fördern. Führung wurde in Kindertageseinrichtungen jedoch ebenfalls lange wenig Bedeutung beigemessen, da die pädagogische Arbeit mit den Kindern und Familien im Vordergrund stand (Beher & Lange, 2014, S. 95). Im Zuge der zunehmenden Fokussierung auf Qualitätsentwicklung und dem damit einhergehenden Professionalisierungsdiskurs der letzten zwanzig Jahre wurde die Bedeutung von Kitaleitungen als Schnittstelle zwischen Träger und pädagogischen Fachkräften für die Organisationsentwicklung deutlicher. Diese Schnittstellenposition verfügt über noch ungenutzte Potenziale. Allerdings herrscht in Kindertageseinrichtungen oftmals ein „implizites und intuitives Konzept von Führung“ (Ballaschk, Anders & Flick, 2017, S. 686), welches zudem von „Unsicherheit im Umgang mit Entscheidungsmacht“ (ebd.) geprägt ist. Gerade deshalb können Kitaleitungen von einem strukturierten Managementkonzept profitieren, besonders in noch wenig etablierten Bereichen wie der diversitätsbewussten Pädagogik.

4. Was ist Diversitätsmanagement?

Um Führungskräfte stärker in den Diversitätsdiskurs einzubinden und die Relevanz ihrer Handlungsperspektiven hervorzuheben, lohnt sich ein Blick auf das Diversitätsmanagement. Hierbei handelt es sich um einen ursprünglich betriebswirtschaftlichen Ansatz aus den USA, der zunehmend in Unternehmen etabliert ist (Bührmann, 2020, S. 57). Unter Diversitätsmanagement werden organisationale Maßnahmen gefasst, die sich mit der Heterogenität der Stakeholder einer Institution befassen (Fujimoto, Härtel & Azmat, 2013, S. 148). Diversitätsmanagement kann als „Lern- und Verän-

4 Intersektionalität beschreibt die Verwobenheit von Diskriminierungs- und Privilegierungsstrukturen (Crenshaw, 1989).

derungsstrategie von Organisationen" (Hanappi-Egger & Hofmann, 2012, S. 328) begriffen werden, wobei das Lernen auf individueller, kollektiver und organisationaler Ebene vollzogen wird. Die Motivation für eine Einführung dieses Ansatzes war zu Beginn oftmals zweckrational an ökonomischen Profitlogiken ausgerichtet (Bührmann, 2020, S. 95). Dieser humankapitalistischen Orientierung des Diversitätsmanagements wird der machtsensible Ansatz entgegengestellt, der auf die Steigerung von Teilhabe und Chancengerechtigkeit abzielt. Dazu werden über die Kritik an Vorurteilen und deren Abbau hinaus vor allem die dahinter liegenden sozialen Strukturen angesteuert (Walgenbach, 2017, S. 104).

Konkrete Maßnahmen, für welche die Führungskräfte im Rahmen von Prozessbegleitung Verantwortung übernehmen, sind beispielsweise die *Entwicklung diversitätssensibler Leitlinien*, die *Sensibilisierung von Mitarbeiter*innen*, der *Aufbau von diversitätsbezogenem Wissen* und die *stetige Reflexion eigener Vorurteile und Handlungen* (Warmuth, 2012; Franken, 2015). Kurzgefasst: Diversität soll als Querschnittsaufgabe in der Organisation implementiert werden (Walgenbach, 2017, S. 114).

Kindertageseinrichtungen sind aufgrund ihrer Organisationsstruktur, die sie an das Mehrebenensystem des Bildungswesens bindet, sowie ihrer starken Abhängigkeit von politischen Entscheidungsträgern und der kommunalen Verwaltung nicht mit betriebswirtschaftlichen Organisationen gleichzusetzen (Stiftung Haus der kleinen Forscher, 2023, S. 36). Dennoch haben die oben genannten Maßnahmen des unternehmerisch ausgerichteten Diversitätsmanagements Übertragungspotenzial.

5. Implikationen für Kindertageseinrichtungen

Vor dem Hintergrund, dass Bildungsungerechtigkeit ein strukturelles Problem darstellt, bietet das Diversitätsmanagement gegenüber reinen Handlungskonzepten den Vorteil, dass es auf eine *strukturelle Verankerung* von Diversitätsbewusstsein abzielt. In diesem Prozess nimmt die Leitung eine zentrale Rolle ein, in Zusammenarbeit mit den pädagogischen Fachkräften Diversität in den Leitlinien und in der pädagogischen Arbeit zu integrieren.

Ein erster Schritt im Rahmen der Organisationsentwicklung ist die Überarbeitung der Kita-Konzeption als *Leitlinie*, welche die Werte, Ziele und Prozesse der Einrichtung abbilden soll. Hier bietet sich auch die Möglichkeit, konkrete Handlungskonzepte zu evaluieren und in die Konzeption aufzunehmen. Um eine gemeinsame Arbeitsgrundlage im Sinne einer diversitätsbewussten Wertebasis zu schaffen, bedarf es einer kontinuierlichen *Sensibilisierung der pädagogischen Fachkräfte*. Dies wiederum erfordert eine kritische *Reflexion* der eigenen Vorurteile und eine Positionierung im gesellschaftlichen und institutionellen Machtgefüge. Das regelmäßige Anstoßen und Ermöglichen von Reflexionen liegen in der Verantwortung der Leitung. Reflexionen können in unterschiedlichen Gruppenzusammensetzungen erfolgen und Faktoren, wie das eigene Verhalten in konkreten Situationen oder Einstellungen zu Diversität, behandeln. Auch Fallanalysen und Rollenspiele können genutzt werden, um die Perspektive beteiligter Kinder und Familien nachzuvollziehen. Externe Expert*innen können in diesem Rahmen durch Fortbildungen oder Supervision unterstützend wirken und Leitungen entlasten. Gleichzeitig helfen sie dabei, die Auswirkungen von Hierarchien innerhalb des Teams besser zu berücksichtigen.

Neben Reflexionsrunden nimmt auch das Erweitern von *Wissen* über Diversität einen zentralen Stellenwert ein. Dazu gehört das Verständnis theoretischer Grundlagen, denn fundiertes Wissen über Diversität hilft dabei, die unterschiedlichen Hintergründe, Erfahrungen und Bedürfnisse von Individuen zu verstehen. Der Ausbau von Methodenkompetenz durch praxisorientierte Übungen kann Fachkräfte darin schulen, Vorurteile zu erkennen und zu hinterfragen.

Aufgrund ihrer Schnittstellenpositionierung können Leitungen *Veränderungen initiieren* und tragen im weiteren Verlauf die Verantwortung, die gesetzten Impulse langfristig zu sichern. Im Rahmen der fortlaufenden Prozessbegleitung erfordert dies eine kontinuierliche Auseinandersetzung mit Diversität sowie eine regelmäßige Evaluation von Entwicklungs- und Handlungsbedarfen. Auch hier können externe Expert*innen helfen, passende Maßnahmen und Handlungskonzepte zu identifizieren und zu etablieren. Im weiteren Verlauf sollte gemeinsam mit den pädagogischen Fachkräften evaluiert werden, welche Maßnahmen Wirkung entfalten und wo noch Anpassungsbedarf besteht. So kann sich beispielsweise herausstellen, dass die Inklusion von Kindern mit Behinderung schon sehr gut gelingt, Kinder mit Deutsch als Zweitsprache jedoch noch stärker unterstützt werden müssen. Solche Erkenntnisse tragen dazu bei, die Praxis gezielt weiterzuentwickeln.

Ein weiterer, bisher unbeachteter Vorteil des Diversitätsmanagements liegt in der Reduktion von *Decoupling*, also der Entkopplung bzw. Diskrepanz zwischen konzeptionell verankerten Leitlinien und der tatsächlichen Praxis (Bromley & Powell, 2012, S. 483). Durch die aktive Einbindung der Leitungen in die Umsetzung pädagogischer Konzepte kann dieser Bruch zwischen Anspruch und Wirklichkeit reduziert und eine als von den beteiligten Akteur*innen kohärenter wahrgenommene pädagogische Praxis entwickelt werden.

6. Resümee

Abschließend lässt sich festhalten, dass Diversitätsmanagement eine wertvolle Grundlage bietet, um nicht nur der strukturellen Bildungsungerechtigkeit entgegenzuwirken, sondern auch nachhaltige Veränderungen in den pädagogischen Alltag zu integrieren, die sowohl den Kinderrechten als auch den Bedürfnissen diverser Gesellschaften gerecht werden. Konkret ließe sich so Diskriminierungen i. S. v. Art. 2 Abs. 1 UN-KRK vorbeugen. Dies erfordert eine Orientierung am machtkritischen Diversitätsmanagementansatz, um sicherzustellen, dass die Rechte von Minderheiten gestärkt und nicht nur ihre Potenziale in den Vordergrund gerückt werden (Walgenbach, 2017, S. 122).

Literatur

Ballaschk, I., Anders, Y., & Flick, U. (2017). Führung als Thema deutscher Kindertageseinrichtungen: Welches Führungsverständnis zeigen pädagogische Fachkräfte mit Leitungsfunktion? *Zeitschrift für Erziehungswissenschaft, 20*(4), 670–689. https://doi.org/10.1007/s11618-017-0761-3

Beher, K., & Lange, J. (2014). Empirische Befunde zu den Leitungstätigen in Kindertageseinrichtungen Qualifikation – Qualifizierung – Kompetenzen. In R. Schelle (Hrsg.), *WiFF-Wegweiser Weiterbildung. 10: Leitung von Kindertageseinrichtungen: Grundlagen für die kompetenzorientierte Weiterbildung* (S. 95–108). DJI.

Betz, T., & Bischoff, S. (2017). Heterogenität als Herausforderung oder Belastung? Zur Konstruktion von Differenz von frühpädagogischen Fachkräften in Kindertageseinrichtungen. In U. Stenger, D. Edelmann, D. Nolte & M. Schulz (Hrsg.), *Diversität in der Pädagogik der frühen Kindheit: Im Spannungsfeld zwischen Konstruktion und Normativität* (S. 101–118). Beltz Juventa.

Bromley, P., & Powell, W. W. (2012). From Smoke and Mirrors to Walking the Talk: Decoupling in the Contemporary World. *Academy of Management Annals, 6*(1), 483–530. https://doi.org/10.5465/19416520.2012.684462

Bührmann, A. D. (2020). Diversitätsmanagement als „traveling concept". Prinzipielle Überlegungen zur Erforschung der Translation des Diversitätsmanagements aus der Perspektive einer reflexiben Diversitätsforschung. In H. Leontiy & M. Schulz (Hrsg.), *Ethnographie und Diversität: Wissensproduktion an den Grenzen und die Grenzen der Wissensproduktion* (S. 55–91). Springer. https://doi.org/10.1007/978-3-658-21982-6

Crenshaw, K. (1989). Demarginalizing the Intersection of Race and Sex: A Black Feminist Critique of Antidiscrimination Doctrine, Feminist Theory and Antiracist Politics. *University of Chicago Legal Forum, 139*(1), 139–167.

Derman-Sparks, L., & Edwards, J. O. (Hrsg.). (2010). *Anti-bias education for young children and ourselves.* National Association for the Education of Young Children.

Fischer, V., & Gramelt, K. (Hrsg.). (2021a). *Diversity in der Kindheitspädagogik und Familienbildung.* UTB.

Fischer, V., & Gramelt, K. (2021b). Handlungsanregungen für eine diversitätsbewusste Kindheitspädagogik und Familienbildung. In V. Fischer & K. Gramelt (Hrsg.), *Diversity in der Kindheitspädagogik und Familienbildung* (Bd. 2, S. 193–234). UTB.

Franken, S. (2015). *Personal: Diversity Management.* Springer Gabler.

Fujimoto, Y., Härtel, C. E. J., & Azmat, F. (2013). Towards a diversity justice management model: Integrating organizational justice and diversity management. *Social Responsibility Journal, 9*(1), 148–166. https://doi.org/10.1108/17471111311307877

Hanappi-Egger, E., & Hofmann, R. (2012). Diversitätsmanagement unter der Perspektive organisationalen Lernens: Wissens- und Kompetenzentwicklung für inklusive Organisationen. In R. Bendl, E. Hanappi-Egger & R. Hofmann (Hrsg.), *Diversität und Diversitätsmanagement* (S. 327–350). facultas.

Jin, M., Lee, J., & Lee, M. (2017). Does leadership matter in diversity management? Assessing the relative impact of diversity policy and inclusive leadership in the public sector. *Leadership & Organization Development Journal, 38*(2), 303–319. https://doi.org/10.1108/LODJ-07-2015-0151

Loden, M., & Rosener, J. B. (1991). *Workforce America! Managing employee diversity as a vital resource.* Irwin.

Menz, M., & Abdessadok, L. (2022). Chancengleichheit als politische Aufforderung und pädagogische Praxis. Positionierungen von Eltern und Familien durch Kita-Leitungen. In S. Geiger, S. Dahlheimer & M. Bader (Hrsg.), *Heterogenität und Differenz in Kindheits- und Sozialpädagogik: Theoretische und empirische Beiträge* (S. 194–208). Beltz Juventa.

Prengel, A. (2019). *Pädagogik der Vielfalt: Verschiedenheit und Gleichberechtigung in Interkultureller, Feministischer und Integrativer Pädagogik.* Springer. https://doi.org/10.1007/978-3-658-21947-5

Richter, S. (2022). *Vorurteilen und Diskriminierung in der Kita begegnen: Vorurteilsbewusste Bildung und Erziehung als inklusives Praxiskonzept.* Herder.

Ruppin, I. (Hrsg.). (2017). *Diversity Management in Kindertagesstätten.* Beltz Juventa.

Simon, S., Kerle, A., & Prigge, J. (2022). „In ner Kita gibt's erst mal keinen Stempel". Sprechen über (Kinder-)Armut und strukturellen Benachteiligungen als Herausforderung im Umgang mit Heterogenität. In S. Geiger, S. Dahlheimer & M. Bader (Hrsg.), *Heterogenität und Differenz in Kindheits- und Sozialpädagogik: Theoretische und empirische Beiträge* (S. 89–108). Beltz Juventa.

Steiner-Khamsi, G. (2010). Wieviel Heterogenität erträgt eine Lehrperson? Über den Zusammenhang zwischen Belastungsebenen und Verfügbarkeit von interkulturellen Fachleuten. In M. Krüger-Potratz, U. Neumann & H. H. Reich (Hrsg.), *Bei Vielfalt Chancengleichheit: Interkulturelle Pädagogik und durchgängige Sprachbildung* (S. 24–35). Waxmann.

Stiftung Haus der Kleinen Forscher. (Hrsg.). (2023). *Kita-Entwicklung – Organisationsentwicklung als Chance für die frühe Bildung.* Barbara Budrich. https://doi.org/10.3224/84742700

Wagner, P. (2018). *Vorurteilsbewusste Bildung und Erziehung als inklusives Praxiskonzept in der Kita.* Fachstelle Kinderwelten für Vorurteilsbewusste Bildung und Erziehung.

Walgenbach, K. (2017). *Heterogenität – Intersektionalität – Diversity in der Erziehungswissenschaft* (2., durchges. Aufl.). Barbara Budrich.

Warmuth, G.-S. (2012). Die strategische Implementierung von Diversitätsmanagement in Organisationen. In R. Bendl, E. Hanappi-Egger & R. Hofmann (Hrsg.), *Diversität und Diversitätsmanagement* (S. 203–236). facultas.

Further Contributions in the Volume

Further practical implications of children's rights are discussed in *Thea Jenners* focus article on the German "Ganztagsförderungsgesetz" (pp. 139–145).

Another discrimination-related article is authored by *Robert Pham Xuan* and *Dong Nguyen* on the German tracking system as an issue regarding children's rights to school education (pp. 53–64).

Children's Rights – and Educational Leadership?

Julia Hugo, Charlotte Assmann, Andreas Schmidt (Eds.)
Educational Leadership and Children's Rights?/
Kinderrechte als Führungsaufgabe?
© 2025, Waxmann. https://doi.org/10.31244/9783830998259_7

Carolina Dahle & Tine Sophie Prøitz

School Principals and the Obligation to Act Under a Zero-Tolerance Policy Against Bullying in Schools[1]

Abstract

Equity and inclusion in education are emphatic elements of the Convention on the Rights of the Child in many countries. This study explores Norway as an example of what happens to the autonomy of school principals under a zero-tolerance policy against bullying in schools. In Norway, principals are obligated by law to act while facing the dilemma of contradicting legislation and the possibility of being personally sanctioned for not acting. Drawing on an analysis of national regulations and a school leader union magazine, this study discusses the changing discourse on principals' obligations in the execution of a national law. The analysis reveals that principals are being assigned significant responsibilities, leading to a heightened need for greater competence and supervision, while at the same time, their given autonomy to act does not match their responsibilities. Regarding changes in the discourse, successful examples of the handling of the Norwegian Education Act, particularly the school environment act, have been highlighted increasingly, just as a further discussion has emerged about how to define bullying and the role of principals in addressing it.

Keywords

School Environment Act, School Principals' Obligations, Foregrounded and Modification Work Discourses, Children's Rights

Schulleitende und die Verpflichtung zum Handeln im Rahmen einer Null-Toleranz-Politik gegen Mobbing an Schulen

Zusammenfassung

Chancengleichheit und Inklusion im Kontext von Bildung, wie sie in der Kinderrechtskonvention verankert sind, werden in vielen Ländern betont. Diese Studie untersucht anhand des Länderbeispiels Norwegen, was mit der Autonomie von Schulleitenden unter einer Null-Toleranz-Politik gegen Mobbing in Schulen geschieht. In Norwegen sind Schulleitende gesetzlich verpflichtet zu handeln, während sie vor dem Dilemma wider-

1 Funding: This work has been funded by the Research Council of Norway under Grant Agreement #315147 in the research project CLASS-Comparisons of Leadership Autonomy in School districts and Schools.

sprüchlicher Gesetze stehen und bei unterlassenen Handlungen möglicherweise persönlich sanktioniert werden. Basierend auf einer Analyse nationaler Vorschriften sowie des Magazins des norwegischen Schulleitungsverbandes diskutiert diese Studie den sich wandelnden Diskurs über die Verpflichtungen von Schulleitenden in der Umsetzung eines nationalen Gesetzes. Die Analyse zeigt, dass Schulleitende erhebliche Verantwortlichkeiten zugewiesen bekommen, was zu einem erhöhten Bedarf an Kompetenz und Supervision führt. Gleichzeitig stimmt die den Schulleitenden gewährte Autonomie nicht mit den ihnen zugewiesenen Verantwortlichkeiten überein. In Bezug auf Veränderungen im Diskurs werden erfolgreiche Beispiele für den Umgang mit dem norwegischen Bildungsgesetz, insbesondere dem sogenannten Schulmilieugesetz, zunehmend hervorgehoben. Es ist außerdem eine weitere Diskussion darüber entstanden, wie Mobbing zu definieren ist und welche Rolle Schulleitende bei der Thematisierung spielen.

Schlüsselbegriffe
norwegisches Schulmilieugesetz, Schulleiterverpflichtungen, hervorgehobene und modifizierte Diskurse

1. Principals' Obligation to Act

The *Convention on the Rights of the Child* (UN CRC) was adopted in 1989 and has as a legally binding agreement influenced many countries. Norway, for example, ratified the UN CRC in 1991. Both the *Norwegian Education Act* and the UN CRC emphasise individual rights and the importance of the subjective experience of pupils (Roland, 2020). The *Norwegian Education Act* has been revised several times in the last decades. For example, the regulations have shifted focus from collective rights to individual rights, from pupils' working environment to their learning and school environment and from defining the legal responsibility of the school to define the individual right of the pupil, all with several administrative consequences (Hall & Johansson, 2023).

The *Norwegian Education Act* with its section on pupils' school environment states: "All pupils are entitled to a safe and good physical and psychosocial environment conducive to health, inclusion, well-being and learning" (Education Act, 2024, §12-2)[2]. The paragraph mainly mandates zero tolerance against bullying and includes that school staff has an "obligation to act", as stated in Section 12-4: "Everyone working at the school must keep an eye on the pupils to ensure they have a safe and good psychosocial school environment, and if possible, intervene if someone offends a pupil" (Education Act, 2024, §12-4). The explication of this obligation has been clarified and has exerted significant influence on constructing the responsibilities of the school as a legal unit, with a special focus on principals. Section 12-9 on criminal liability describes how anyone who "wilfully or negligently [...] violates the obligation [...] is subject to fines or imprisonment" (Education Act, 2024, §12-9). Researchers have characterised this responsibility by positioning educational leaders to ensure that the rights of children are maintained (Hall & Johansson, 2023; Roland, 2020). Further,

2 For the expired version, see chapter 9A: https://lovdata.no/NLEO/lov/1998-07-17-61.

principals are also expected to balance the individual rights of one pupil with the collective needs of other pupils (Gunnulfsen & Hall, 2024), as expressed in the UN CRC and articulately emphasised in the *Norwegian Education Act*. The challenges and inherent tension for educational leaders in handling the legislation are evident in the fact that principals and other leaders in education can personally face a penalty if they fail to apply the law correctly.

With this point of departure, this article aims to outline principals' individual obligations in the execution of chapter 12 (previously section 9A) of the *Norwegian Education Act* and analyses changes in the discourse about individual obligations. The study focuses on the legal text in the *Norwegian Education Act*, which defines principals' obligation to act to ensure pupils a good psychosocial school environment and how this obligation is interpreted, discussed, and acted upon in the Norwegian school leader magazine *Skolelederen* since its major revision in 2017.

2. The Norwegian Context

Norway is considered a pioneer in the implementation of children's rights, as the first country to have a children commissioner (Smith & Brain, 2000) and the first to enact social policy measures for the rights of children (Ingebritsen, 2006). Norway has been widely regarded to have a promising legal framework, especially concerning articles 3 and 12 of the UN CRC (Lundy et al., 2012). The Norwegian section 9A is considered as the working environment act of pupils and was incorporated into the Education Act in 2002[3]. Zero tolerance against bullying, violence, discrimination and harassment has been added in 2017, and schools must continuously work preventatively by including pupils in this work. Next to observations from school staff, the subjective experience of pupils and/or legal guardians is decisive for the execution of the section. If a pupil does not feel safe at school and expresses this to a teacher or legal guardian, the school must develop a written plan with a description of the problem, measures that are going to be implemented and a distribution of tasks. The plan is an essential document as it serves as proof of adherence to the legal obligation to act. The law explicitly states that the pupils involved are to be heard and that the best interest of the pupils must "be a fundamental concern in the school's work" (Education Act, 2017, §9A-4). In the newly revised law, a general right of the pupil to be heard in all matters that concern them has been added (Education Act, 2024, §10-1, §10-2) (see section 6.1 for more details on the changes of the law).

If a pupil does not experience an improved situation after one week of notifying the principal, the pupil or legal guardians can report the case to the county governor on low threshold. A phone call or filling out an online scheme is adequate[4]. The county governor must ensure that the pupil is heard and must investigate whether school

3 Until August 1st, 2024, the law has been referred to as section 9A and is now covered by the new chapter 12.

4 Melde fra om mobbing eller dårlig skolemiljø [Report on bullying or bad school environment]: https://skjema.no/SF/mobbing?noprompt=true.

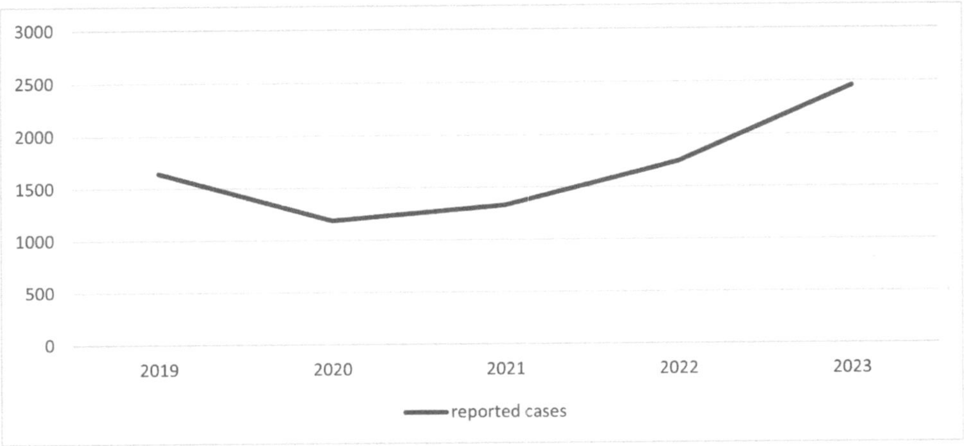

Figure 1: Cases reported to the county governor about the school environment.

staff fulfilled their obligation to act. As figure 1 shows, the number of reported cases has been steadily rising since the introduction of the law (Directorate for Education and Training, 2024a).

3. Previous Research on the School Environment Act

Even though section 9A is widely discussed among principals and at the local authority level in Norway, limited research exists on how to act in accordance with it (Roland, 2020). Few studies have investigated principals' experiences and how they handle the diverse situations that emerge in the school setting in relation to the law.

Hall and Johansson (2023) analysed key changes in pupils' school environments after the phrase "best for children" was added to the Norwegian curriculum. They conclude that these changes have led to a shift "from defining the legal *responsibility of the school* to defining the *individual right of the student*" (Hall & Johansson, 2023, p. 505). Further, the shift will increase bureaucratization and impact principals, who as a result will need to adapt to new regulations and gain knowledge on how to practice such legal mandates (Hall & Johansson, 2023).

Støen and Gutzwiller-Helfenfinger (2023), in contrast, assert that section 9A provides a clear definition of the responsibilities and accountabilities of principals, teachers and legal guardians. They highlight Norway as an inspirational example for other countries. Clark (2017), however, criticises the Norwegian legislation for failing to uphold children's rights adequately, especially regarding the right of the child to be heard, as Norway has not agreed on the third optional protocol of the UN CRC which emphasises the right of the child to file a complaint to the UN directly. Clark concludes that "the voices of children subjected to bullying in schools have not been heard; though the law in section 9a provides for some form of agency, it has been grossly underused by children" (2017, p. 144).

Gunnulfsen and Hall (2024) explore the question of whether the rights of pupils, based on their subjective experience, outranks the rights of, for example, teachers. The authors stress the possibility that the normative request of the law can cause pressure, both for teachers and principals.

Roland (2018) emphasises that a successful approach to 9A-related cases is dependent on principals. Based on a study and a categorization of schools according to their handling of the law, good practice regarding 9A-cases emerges from a division of tasks and effective communication, active listening to pupils and legal guardians and the demonstration of real care and empathy (Roland, 2020, p. 83).

A recent survey reveals that principals consider section 9A as the one factor with the biggest impact on their workload. The principals in this study report that section 9A entitles too many rights to pupils and legal guardians, leading to overly high expectations from society of what schools can solve. "On this basis, critical factors for effective leadership are that the goals are clear, resources are sufficient and the autonomy for local leaders is sufficient" (Baldersheim, Øgård & Hye, 2023, p. 14). The scope for action regarding section 9A has also been raised in an interview study, with principals experiencing 9A-cases as interminable and sharing that they are working under serious time pressure, emotional pressure, and institutionalised pressure (Skutlaberg, 2024, p. 196).

Previous studies on principals and their handling of section 9A illustrate the high degree of complexity that principals must navigate in securing pupils' rights in schools. The research displays variations in how the law's clarity is evaluated, from unclear to admirably clear. Further studies emphasise that the law places high expectations on principals to be able to handle the law, confers a heavy workload and exerts high pressure on principals to act on complicated cases with high degrees of normativity. Yet another aspect raised is how the law has administrative and bureaucratic consequences for principals and will impact their autonomy in relation to both pupils and legal guardians as well as the county governor.

Considering the limited corpus of previous research there seems to be a need for more research along several dimensions on how pupils' school environment is regulated and understood along with its potential consequences for all actors in schools. In the Norwegian context school staff has a particular obligation to act leading us to focus on how the *Education Act* defines a principals' obligation to act to ensure pupils a good psychosocial school environment and how this obligation is interpreted, discussed, and acted upon since its major revision in 2017.

4. Theoretical Concepts for the Analysis – Foregrounding and Modifying Work

In this study, we employ the theoretical concepts of *foregrounding* described by Saarinen (2008) in combination with the concept of *modifying work* described by Asdal (2015). Saarinen's work, which uses policy documents as a source of data, underscores that policy texts "tell us which policy problems and goals [...] are brought to the fore and which are left aside" (Saarinen, 2008, p. 719). This paper follows this perspective's assumptions that any use of language has political implications and underlines that the definition of words involves prescriptive claims. Furthermore, according to Saarinen's work on policy construction, actors such as principals and teachers may present varying and competing conceptualizations based on their roles, backgrounds, and understanding of society. It also follows that actors may foreground certain views, emphasising concepts through textual prominence while narrowing the space for competing views by backgrounding other concepts, giving them limited space in texts. As this study aims to study how school leaders' obligation to act is defined in the current legislative documents, this analysis focuses on what is foregrounded more than what is backgrounded. Emphasising what is foregrounded is particularly relevant considering our aim to analyse how the legal text is interpreted in the discourse in the school leader union magazines over time. This approach emphasises the policy messages themselves as well as that the understanding and interpretation of these has the potential to change over time (Prøitz, 2015; Stenersen & Prøitz, 2022; Dieudè & Prøitz, 2022). To analyse these potential changes in the discourse, we employ the concept of *modifying work* by Asdal (2015). According to Asdal, modifying work happens when a document may transform issues as part of text relations to reality. In her words, "texts do not stand in a random relation to reality but are already part of reality, and textual work helps different actors renegotiate and modify that reality" (Asdal, 2015, p. 88). Asdal argues that one need to analyse both how issues emerge, what kind of issue it is and with which it effects the object or issue in question (Asdal & Marres, 2014). Further, what follows from this is that we need to be aware that issues in themselves may be modified and transformed across texts such as policy documents and school leader magazines and that issues also can mean different things and be translated in different ways.

5. Material and Method

For the study of how the *Norwegian Education Act* defines principals' obligation to act and how this obligation is interpreted, discussed and acted upon since its major revision in 2017, the study draws on a qualitative content analysis (Bowen, 2009) of legislation and accompanying documents and articles from the Norwegian School Leader Union magazine. For the analysis of legislation, section 9A (legal from 2017 until July 31, 2024) and chapter 12 (legal since August 1, 2024), with its accompanying document explaining the most important revisions, published by the Norwegian Directorate for Education and Training, were juxtaposed with each other, as presented in chapter 6. Chapter 6.1 to 6.2 present the foregrounded and modifying discourse, derived from the magazines. The articles from this magazine serve as rich material for the analysis of changes in the discourse. Editors from the magazine, researchers and educational leaders on all levels regularly publish in this magazine, with a focus on school management. The most current discourse can be found in its pages and, thus, changes in the understanding of the law, difficulties, different approaches, and cogitations from different actors become comprehensible.

The initial sample of magazines selected for the analysis were analysed from the first issue of 2017 to the first issue of 2024, as 2017 signifies the year when section 9A was introduced in its current format. The total document corpus of 62 issues was filtered using word searches facilitated by the word search function in the Adobe Acrobat Reader software, focusing on articles containing the terms '9A' and/or 'mobbelov' (the bully law) the Norwegian colloquial term for section 9A. This screening process resulted in the identification of 42 relevant articles, distributed across 32 issues, deemed appropriate for the analysis (see tab. 1).

Following a systematic reading, the articles were mapped and coded in an Excel chart according to the tabs *year, volume, title, text type, ingress, description of contents, understanding of contents* and *topics for discussion*.

Table 1: Referenced articles in the Norwegian School Leader Union magazine (2017–2024).

Volume	**Original title/translated title**
Vol. 2017/2	Nulltoleranse lovfestes/Zero tolerance is legislated
Vol. 2017/3	Leder/Leader
Vol. 2017/6a	Leder/Leader
Vol. 2017/6b	Kurs i hvordan behandle elevsaker/Course in handling student cases
Vol. 2017/9	Aktivitetsplikten er også et personlig ansvar/The obligation to act is also a personal responsibility
Vol. 2018/3	Son-konferansen/The Son-conference
Vol. 2018/4a	En rektors dilemmaer med Paragraph 9A/A principal's dilemmas with section 9A
Vol. 2018/4b	Hva betyr Paragraph 9a for skoleledere?/What does section 9a mean for school leaders?
Vol. 2018/4c	Si fra til fylkesmannen/Tell the county governor
Vol. 2018/5	Når gode intensjoner kolliderer/When good intentions collide
Vol. 2018/7a	Erfaringer med nytt regelverk mot mobbing/Experiences with new regulations against bullying
Vol. 2018/7b	"Byggeleder" og rektor/"Construction manager" and school principal
Vol. 2018/7c	En god kultur gir godt læringsmiljø/A good culture provides a good learning environment
Vol. 2018/8	MOT, fagfornyelsen og nasjonale føringer/MOT, the curriculum renewal and national guidelines
Vol. 2018/9	Et offensivt miljøteam/A proactive environmental team
Vol. 2018/10	Lederutvikling – en naturlig del av kvalitetsutvikling/Leadership development – a natural part of quality improvement
Vol. 2019/2	Skolelederkonferansen på Sola/School leader conference at Sola
Vol. 2019/4	Elevenes rett til å bli hørt/Pupils' right to be heard
Vol. 2019/6	Flere elever blir hørt og får hjelp/More pupils are being heard and receive help
Vol. 2019/7	Tilhørighet er mer enn inkludering/Belonging is more than inclusion
Vol. 2019/10	Systematisk arbeid med fagfornyelsen/Systematic work with the curriculum renewal
Vol. 2020/1a	Når laget rundt eleven kun består av målvakter/When the team around the pupil only consists of goalkeepers
Vol. 2020/1b	Fra gallionsfigur til overarbeidet altmuligmann?/From figurehead to overworked jack-of-all-trades?

Volume	Original title/translated title
Vol. 2020/2	Help til å se helhelten/Help to see the big picture
Vol. 2020/4a	Ansattes rettigheter i 9A-saker/Employees' rights in 9A-cases
Vol. 2020/4b	Krevende krysspress/Challenging cross-pressure
Vol. 2020/6	Barns rett til å bli hørt/Children's rights to be heard
Vol. 2020/7	Nye juridiske kurs/New legal courses
Vol. 2020/8	Skolesymfonien/The School Symphony
Vol. 2021/1a	Webinarer på skolelederforbundet.no/New webinars at skolelederforbundet.no
Vol. 2021/1b	Hva sier lovverket om foreldrenes rett til å være til stede i klasserommet?/What does the legislation say about parents' right to be present in the classroom?
Vol. 2021/2	Meld deg på kurs hos Skolelederforbundet/Sign up for a course at the School Leaders' Association
Vol. 2021/6	Elever som blir utsatt for mobbing trenger en lærer som beskytter dem/Pupils who are subjected to bullying need a teacher who protects them
Vol. 2022/2	Hvorfor har internkontroll betydning for elevenes skolemiljø?/Why is internal control important for pupils' school environment?
Vol. 2022/3a	Stort fokus på opplæringslovens §9a/Significant focus on section 9a of the Education Act
Vol. 2022/3b	Fylkeslederen har ordet/The county leader has the word
Vol. 2022/7	Mobbing oppstår i felleskap og er ikke et individuelt fenomen/Bullying arises in communities and is not an individual phenomenom
Vol. 2023/2a	Jobber for å få en mer inkluderende russetid/Work towards a more inclusive pupils' celebration of final graduation
Vol. 2023/2b	Russetiden er ikke en losløs tid/Pupils' celebration of final graduation is not a time without a pilot
Vol. 2023/5	Ny rapport om skolelederrollen: Høye krav, stort ansvar og lite handlefrihe/New report about the role of school leaders: high demands, great responsibility and little autonomy
Vol. 2023/6	Rektor med arbeidsglede og handlingsrom-styrt eller støttet?/Principals with job satisfaction and scope of action-ruled or supported?
Vol. 2024/1	Skolen trenger et krafttak/The school need a major effort

6. Changes in School Principals' Obligations

Even though section 9A has undergone several changes in its placement and is now found under chapter 12, there are minor but still important content-related changes regarding the obligations of principals.

Little has changed regarding principals' duty to inform the leader on the municipal level if a serious case of a pupil not experiencing a good and safe school environment has been reported to them. However, the wording in the legal text has changed from "alerting the leader on municipal level" (School Environment, 2017, §9A-4) to "give notice to the municipality or the county council" (Education Act, 2024, §12-4). The change cannot be considered as significant, but it can be interpreted to signify a change in the relation between municipal leaders and principals. The former section describes how principals are required to alert or warn the municipal leader about a serious situation while in the latter principals must make the municipal aware of or orient about a serious situation. While section 9A gave no limitations to reported incidents, the new chapter 12 leaves room for consideration. For example, if the case is "manifestly unfounded" (Education Act, 2024, §12-5), no need for reporting is given. The legislation itself does not provide further information on how to investigate such a case. Nevertheless, the accompanying document states that a case is manifestly unfounded if it is apparent that it could not have happened as described, for instance, because the accused teacher was not present at that moment. An incident is further not classified as a chapter 12-case if it is not defined as an infringement. "The threshold is high for the principal to be able to say that a report is unfounded" (Directorate for Education and Training, 2024b). Under the new law, schools, represented by principals, still must document the work that has been done to follow the obligation to act, but since August 2024, just "in the form and to the extent that is necessary" (Education Act, 2024, §12-4). While in the prior legislation, the county governor could enforce concrete tasks upon single schools after a case has been brought forward, the new law enables the county governor to prompt municipalities to generally improve or correct the situation.

6.1 Foregrounded Discourse

Three foregrounded aspects can be found in the Norwegian School Leader Union magazines in the period studied. Prominent in the texts are the many possibilities to use *discretion*, the need for *competence* in principals and other school staff and an emphasis on the *demanding challenges* associated with section 9A, now chapter 12.

Regarding *discretion*, some articles suggest examples of how principals solved the issue of enacting adequate measures without clear definitions in the legislation (Vol. 2018/4a). The question of how to balance the individual and subjective experience of one child with central management from the municipality is also explored (Vol. 2018/7a). While the law has narrowed the room for discretion (Vol. 2018/5), budget cutbacks have led to the "impossible task of prioritizing between an environmental worker or a health nurse left to principals" (Vol. 2020/1a).

Another foregrounded aspect is the need for competence in how to handle cases of infringement. This is visible through a series of courses and conferences advertised over the years which refer to the section 9A (Vol. 2017/6b; Vol. 2018/3; Vol. 2019/2; Vol. 2020/7; Vol. 2021/1a). The uncertainty surrounding its implementation and the need for more knowledge led to articles asking lawyers to clarify the law and provide concrete instructions and formulations in the event of an indictment: "Use the criterion of reasonableness and argue that these measures 'in my opinion' are reasonable, encourages Eriksen [lawyer]" (Vol. 2018/4b). In addition, principals are supposed to learn about the content of the UN CRC and how to "really" listen to and include children (Vol. 2019/4; Vol. 2020/6). Since there are many factors adversely contributing to an incident, the need for greater competence is ongoing (Vol. 2022/3a).

These two aspects are reflected in the third foregrounded discourse, namely the emphasis on demanding challenges and the "enormous obligations that the law places on them [the principals]" (Vol. 2017/3). It is emphasised throughout the years that a safe and good school environment must be included in all aspects of work, with principals as one of the responsible actors. Several research reports are summarised, illustrating that principals' responsibility mismatches their autonomy, that reporting and documenting cases consumes unnecessary amounts of time, and that county governors possibly intervene too much, leading to "demanding cross pressure" (Vol. 2019/6; Vol. 2020/4b; Vol. 2024/1). Words like this continue to be mentioned: "enormous expectations", "total responsibility", "dilemma" and "conflicting considerations" (Vol. 2023/5). Principals are further advised "not to go home" before they have started processing a case that has been brought forward (Vol. 2018/4).

6.2 Modifying the Discourse

The foregrounded aspects identified in the analysis also provide a preeminent vantage point to observe two overall changes in the discourse that can be interpreted as modifying work (Asdal, 2015).

The uncertainty regarding the former section 9A, explicitly expressed at first, changed over the course of the examined years. In 2018, model examples of how to deal with this section gradually began to be presented (Vol. 2018/4; Vol. 2018/7b; Vol. 2018/7c; Vol. 2018/9; Vol. 2018/10). Towards the end of the analysed period, the need for more competence on the part of principals is still present, but expanded thoughts on the topic of bullying are gaining influence (Vol. 2022/3b; Vol. 2022/7; Vol. 2023/6). Beginning with section 9A from 2017, principals are asking themselves in the magazine if and how they can fulfil the great expectations and obligations placed on them (Vol. 2017/9a). Later, examples presented in the magazines relate to how principals across the country manage to handle the law section (Vol. 2018/7b; Vol. 2018/7c; Vol. 2018/8; Vol. 2019/10), that county governors support rather than control principals' work (Vol. 2018/4c) and that several programs further support the work of schools (Vol. 2018/7c; Vol. 2018/10). Finally, section 9A is included in discussions about schoolwork and is used to address questions about everyday school life. In 2021, for example, the question arose if parents are allowed to attend lessons and how this can influence the subjective assumption of a safe school environment (Vol. 2021/1b). Focus is also set on how to create a more inclusive graduation celebration in upper secondary school (Vol. 2023/2a; Vol. 2023/2b).

The second modified discourse addresses the topic of bullying itself. When the new law chapter was introduced in 2017, school employees, especially principals, expressed their concerns about having the great responsibility to solve the issue of bullying in schools. However, in 2018, the leader of the Norwegian School Leader Union accentuated that bullying is not just an individual problem happening here and there to single pupils at school but rather a social dynamic (Vol. 2018/7a). The discussion advanced, concluding in 2019 that the "bullying section [the law] is about more than bullying" (Vol. 2019/7), and that well-being, which has been seen as the most important aspect in school, not only promotes learning but that both well-being and learning positively influence each other (Vol. 2019/7). In the ongoing discussion, principals are once again given an important role. Since bullying is not simply an individual, but a social phenomenon, changes in the understanding of basic values are required, with "principals as the starting point for those changes" (Vol. 2022/7).

7. Conclusion – High Expectations and Autonomy

The analysis has shown that section 9A of the *Norwegian Education Act* emphasises the subjective perception of pupils in relation to what constitutes a good and safe physical and psychosocial environment, and it applies zero tolerance against bullying. The expectations outlined in the *Norwegian Education Act* go hand in hand with great responsibility on the part of principals, who face the risk of being punished for insufficient action. In line with previous research, the analysis indicates that principals' level of responsibility not only mismatches their level of autonomy but also sets high expectations for principals' ability to act autonomously in these highly complex matters. Paralleled with this is the fact that county governors could intervene directly in school administration with precisely defined instructions for actions leading to demanding challenges for principals of cross-pressure in the execution of the law.

The recent changes from August 1st, 2024 widened the scope of action regarding decisions about infringements. Pupils' subjective experiences are no longer the only deciding factor, but principals must decide as to whether the situation in question is an infringement or not and whether the information needs to be passed on to the municipal leader. County governors can no longer intervene directly in schools and assign concrete tasks. In the event of an accusation, the county governor can now only turn to the municipality and instruct them to change the situation, illustrating a modification in responsibility and autonomy that places more expectations on principals' ability to handle the situation, but now with greater support and supervision from the county governor.

Whether these discursive changes can reduce cross-pressure and further contribute to a reduction in the "great expectations and obligations" (Vol. 2023/6) of principals, due to the topicality of the changes in the law in real-life principalship, is still an empirical question for further research.

References

Asdal, K. (2015). What is the issue? The transformative capacity of documents, *Distinktion: Scandinavian Journal of Social Theory, 16*(1), 74–90. https://doi.org/10.1080/1600910X.2015.1022194

Asdal, K., & Marres, N. (2014). Performing environmental change: The politics of social science methods. *Environment and Planning, 49*(9), 2055–2064. https://doi.org/10.1068/a140292e

Baldersheim, H., Øgård, M., & Hye, L. (2023). *Rektors handlingsrom: Er vi styrt eller støttet? Research report [Principal's scope of action: are we controlled or supported? Research Report]*. Skolelederforbundet. https://www.skolelederforbundet.no/wp-content/uploads/2023/08/skolelederen_rapport_2023-web.pdf.

Bowen, G. A. (2009). Document analysis as a qualitative research method. *Qualitative Research Journal, 9*(2), 27–40. https://doi.org/10.3316/QRJ0902027

Clark, S. (2017). Voice or voice-over? Harnessing the relationship between a child's right to be heard and legal agency through Norwegian bullying cases. *Social Inclusion, 5*(3), 131–147. http://dx.doi.org/10.17645/si.v5i3.970

Dieudè, A., & Prøitz, T. S. (2022). Curriculum policy and instructional planning: Teachers' autonomy across various school contexts. *European Educational Research Journal, 23*(1), 28–47. https://doi.org/10.1177/14749041221075156

Directorate for Education and Training. (2024a). *Saker meldt til statsforvalterne om skolemiljø [Cases reported to the County Governors about the school environment]*. https://www.udir.no/tall-og-forskning/finn-forskning/tema/saker-meldt-til-fylkesmennene-om-skolemiljo/#a159291.

Directorate for Education and Training. (2024b). *Retten til et trygt og godt skolemiljø [The right to a safe and good school environment].* https://www.udir.no/regelverk-og-tilsyn/skole-og-opplaring/ny-opplaringslov/hva-er-nytt-i-ny-opplaringslov/retten-til-et-trygt-og-godt-skolemiljo/.

Education Act. (2017). *Lov om grunnskolen og den vidaregåande opplæringa (LOV-1998-07-17-61) [Act on Primary and Secondary Education]* (repealed). https://lovdata.no/dokument/NLO/lov/1998-07-17-61/KAPITTEL_10#KAPITTEL_10.

Education Act. (2024). *Lov om grunnskoleopplæringa og den vidaregåande opplæringa (LOV-2023-06-09-30) [Act on Primary and Secondary Education].* https://lovdata.no/dokument/NL/lov/2023-06-09-30.

Gunnulfsen, A. E., & Hall, J. B. (2024). *Rektor som rettsanvender: juridisk tenkning som verktøy for ledelse i skolen [The principal as a legal practitioner: legal thinking as a tool for leadership in schools].* Fagbokforlaget.

Hall, J. B., & Johansson, L. (2023). Shifting school environment policies: A Deleuzian problematisation of universal rights in Norwegian education. *Policy Futures in Education, 22*(4), 493–510. https://doi.org/10.1177/14782103231177614

Ingebritsen, C. (2006). Scandinavia's role in world politics. In C. Ingebritsen, I. Neumann, S. Gstöhl & J. Beyer (Eds.), *Small states in international relations* (pp. 273–285). University of Washington Press.

Lundy, L., Kilkelly, U., Byrne, B., & Kang, J. (2012). *The UN Convention on the Rights of the Child: A study of legal implementation in 12 countries.* Research report. UNICEF, United Nations Children's Fund. https://downloads.unicef.org.uk/wp-content/uploads/2012/11/UNICEFUK_2012CRCimplementationreport-FINAL-PDF-version.pdf?_ga=2.143449526.2074372114.1564059496-355458155.1563455639.

Prøitz, T. S. (2015). Uploading, downloading and uploading again – concepts for policy integration in education research. *Nordic Journal of Studies in Educational Policy, 2015*(1), 70–80. https://doi.org/10.3402/nstep.v1.27015

Roland, E. (2018). Type I- og Type II-skoler: problemløsing i mobbesaker [Type I and Type II schools: problem solving in bullying cases]. In J. Støen, H. Fandrem & E. Roland (Eds.), *Stemmer i mobbesaker: resultater og erfaringer fra Stigma-prosjektet* (pp. 157–172). Fagbokforlaget.

Roland, E. (2020). *Mobbeloven: opplæringslovens kapittel 9A og god praksis [The anti-bullying law: chapter 9A of the Education Act and good practices].* Fagbokforlaget.

Saarinen, T. (2008). Position of text and discourse analysis in higher education policy research. *Studies in Higher Education, 33*(6), 719–728. https://doi.org/10.1080/03075070802457090

School Environment. (2017). *Lov om endringer i opplæringslova og friskolelova (LOV-2017-06-09-38) [Act on amendments to the Education Act and the Independent Schools Act]*. https://lovdata.no/dokument/LTI/lov/2017-06-09-38.

Skutlaberg, K. B. (2024). *Å være rektor i arbeid med langvarige saker knyttet til elevers psykososiale skolemiljø – mellom pedagogikk, etikk og juss [Being a principal in dealing with long-term issues related to students' psychosocial school environment – between pedagogy, ethics, and law]* [Doctoral dissertation]. University of Oslo.

Smith, P. K., & Brain, P. (2000). Bullying in schools: Lessons from two decades of research. *Aggressive Behavior*, *26*(1), 1–9. https://onlinelibrary.wiley.com/doi/10.1002/(SICI)1098-2337(2000)26:1%3C1::AID-AB1%3E3.0.CO;2-7.

Stenersen, C. R., & Prøitz, T. S. (2022). Just a buzzword? The use of concepts and ideas in educational governance. *Scandinavian Journal of Educational Research*, *66*(2), 193–207. https://doi.org/10.1080/00313831.2020.1788153

Støen, J., & Gutzwiller-Helfenfinger, E. (2023). Addressing school bullying on the level of educational legislation: The example of Norway. *Bildung und Erziehung*, *76*(3), 265–274.

Further Contributions in the Volume

For complementary insights into the professionalization of teachers as change agents, the authors *Andreas Schmidt, Ruth Luzmore,* and *Colin Cramer* discuss the concept of meta-reflexivity in teacher education (pp. 41–51).

An additional insight into the realization of children's rights in German educational practice is offered by *Linn Behrendts* article, illustrating the concept 'nursery democracy' for early childhood education as an answer to Art. 12 UN CRC (pp. 131–138).

Julia Hugo, Charlotte Assmann, Andreas Schmidt (Eds.)
Educational Leadership and Children's Rights?/
Kinderrechte als Führungsaufgabe?
© 2025, Waxmann. https://doi.org/10.31244/9783830998259_8

Mirjam Maier-Röseler, Enkeleta Shtërbani & Gabriele Weigand

Begabungsentfaltung im Kontext von Kinderrechten

Ziel von Schulgestaltung und Leadership

Zusammenfassung
Gemäß Art. 29 Abs. 1a der UN-Kinderrechtskonvention (1989) steht jedem Kind das Recht auf Begabungsentfaltung zu. Der Beitrag argumentiert vor dem Hintergrund aktueller Befunde zur (inklusiven) Begabungsforschung dafür, *allen* Kindern die Entfaltung ihrer Begabungen in ihrer Vielfalt im Rahmen von schulischen Bildungsprozessen zu ermöglichen. Die Realisierung dieses Rechts – auch im Sinne von Bildungsgleichheit – geht in der Praxis mit komplexen Veränderungs- und Gestaltungsprozessen von Schule und Unterricht, aber auch mit der Professionalisierung der handelnden Akteur*innen und damit letztlich einer Veränderung der individuellen und kollektiven Praktiken in Schulen einher. Dabei nehmen Schulleitungen und Educational Leadership eine wesentliche Rolle ein. Im Beitrag wird zunächst die maßgebliche Forschung zum Begabungsbegriff und damit einhergehend die Notwendigkeit der schulischen Förderung dargelegt. Anschließend wird die Bedeutung einer begabungsfördernden Schulgestaltung im Zusammenhang mit dem Beitrag von Schulleitungen und Educational Leadership auf Grundlage aktueller Theorien und empirischer Befunde diskutiert. Ein kurzes Fazit mit Verweis auf Art. 29 Abs. 1a der UN-KRK schließt den Text ab.

Schlüsselbegriffe
Kinderrechte, Inklusive Begabungsentfaltung, Begabungsforschung, Schulleitung, Educational Leadership

Talent Development in the Context of Children's Rights

The Goal of School Design and Leadership

Abstract
According to Art. 29 Para. 1a of the UN Convention on the Rights of the Child (1989), every child has the right to develop their talents. The article argues, considering current findings on (inclusive) talent research, that all children should be enabled to develop their talents in their diversity within the framework of school educational processes. The realization of this right, which also contributes to educational equity, involves complex processes of change and design in schools and teaching, as well as the professional development of the actors involved, ultimately leading to changes in individual and collective

practices in schools. School and educational leadership play a significant role in this. The article first outlines the key research on the concept of giftedness and talent and, consequently, the need for educational support in schools. It then discusses the importance of a talent-promoting school design and addresses the contribution of school and educational leadership based on current theories and empirical findings. A short conclusion with reference to Art. 29 Para. 1a of the UN CRC completes the text.

Keywords
Children's Rights, Promotion and Research of Giftedness, Talents, School Leadership, Educational Leadership

1. Einleitung

Als gesellschaftliche und staatlich kontrollierte Bildungsinstitution sowie als Lern-, Lebens- und Erfahrungsraum von Kindern nehmen Schulen eine Vorrangstellung bei der Verwirklichung der UN-Kinderrechte ein. Darunter fällt auch die Entfaltung von Begabungen. So betont die Konferenz der Kultusminister der Länder (KMK) bereits 2006 die besondere Bedeutung von „[…] Maßnahmen zur Förderung von Begabungsvielfalt sowie zur Vermeidung sozialer Ausgrenzung […]" (KMK, 2006, S. 1). Der damit u.a. angesprochene Artikel 29 Abs. 1a der UN-Kinderrechtskonvention (UN-KRK, 1989) bildet auch den Bezugspunkt des vorliegenden Beitrags. Noch heute – fast 20 Jahre nach der Erklärung der KMK – besitzen beide Elemente besondere Brisanz, wie sich nicht zuletzt in der seit Jahrzehnten wiederkehrenden Identifikation sozialer Disparitäten zeigt (Ditton & Maaz, 2022). Kinder erfahren in Schulen nach wie vor Diskriminierung, die sich hemmend auf die Entfaltung ihrer individuellen Begabungen auswirkt (Horvath, 2018).

Im vorliegenden Beitrag wird deshalb argumentiert, dass sich Begabungsentfaltung gezielt auf *alle* Kinder richten muss, und es wird die Frage diskutiert, wie Schulen dies bewältigen können. Da es sich beim Begabungsbegriff um ein soziokulturelles Konstrukt handelt (Hoyer, Weigand & Müller-Oppliger, 2013), dessen Bedeutung sich historisch und gesellschaftlich wandelt, wird dieser Begriff in Abschnitt *zwei* näher beleuchtet und dessen Bedeutung für die Begabungsentfaltung als Element des Kinderrechts auf Bildung und Förderung thematisiert. Wir schließen uns dabei an das im Rahmen der Bund-Länder-Initiative ‚Leistung macht Schule' (KMK, 2016) vom gleichnamigen Forschungsverbund (kurz LemaS) erarbeitete Verständnis an. Daraus resultiert die Herausforderung einer begabungsfördernden Schulgestaltung. Abschnitt *drei* zeigt, dass Schulleitungen dabei eine herausragende Stellung als Visionär*innen und Change Agents einnehmen. Konkret wird der Frage nachgegangen, wie es Schulleitungen im Sinne von Educational Leadership gelingen kann, eine begabungsfördernde Schule und somit die Umsetzung von Begabungsentfaltung für *alle* Kinder zu ermöglichen. Das Fazit fasst den Text zusammen und unterstreicht als Ausblick die Bedeutung des Engagements weiterer Akteur*innen bei der Verwirklichung des Kinderrechts auf Begabungsentfaltung.

2. Zum Begabungsbegriff und zur Bedeutung von Begabungsentfaltung als Bestandteil der Kinderrechte

Die nachfolgenden Ausführungen akzentuieren Begabungsentfaltung als Element der Kinderrechte im Bereich Bildung und Förderung gemäß Artikel 29 Abs. 1a der UN-KRK (1989). Darin heißt es, „dass die Bildung des Kindes darauf gerichtet sein muss, (a) die Persönlichkeit, die Begabung und die geistigen und körperlichen Fähigkeiten des Kindes voll zur Entfaltung zu bringen".

2.1 Der Begabungsbegriff in seiner historischen Entwicklung

Beim Begabungsbegriff gab es immer wieder „Neubestimmungen und Kontroversen" (Weiand & Weigand, 2024, S. 232), was auch für die Überlegungen zur Begabungsentfaltung als Element der Kinderrechte von Belang ist.

Die Anfänge wissenschaftlicher Auseinandersetzungen finden sich vor mehr als 100 Jahren, in Zusammenhang mit der psychologischen Intelligenzforschung. Dabei wird das Phänomen (einer hohen) Begabung mit (außergewöhnlich hohen) kognitiven Fähigkeiten gleichgesetzt (Preckel, 2022) und mit besonderer (sichtbarer) Leistung verknüpft (Pflüger, 2022).[1] Mit der Betonung der dynamischen Entfaltung und Entwickelbarkeit von Begabung ab Mitte des 20. Jahrhunderts rückt gegenüber der vorwiegend psychologisch orientierten Diskussion die pädagogische Frage nach Möglichkeiten der Förderung von Begabung in den Vordergrund (Roth, 1952). Eine weitere Dynamik vollzieht sich im Hinblick auf die Bereiche, in denen sich Begabungen zeigen können: Seit den 1980er Jahren wird über die Vielfalt an möglichen Begabungsfeldern diskutiert, angeführt vom amerikanischen Begabungsforscher Howard Gardner und dessen „multiple Intelligenzen" (1983). Der Wandel bringt eine Öffnung für weitere Formen von Begabungen, etwa im sozial-emotionalen, ethisch-philosophischen und kreativen Bereich, mit sich. Mittlerweile ist der Begriff *Begabung* fester Bestandteil bildungswissenschaftlicher Arbeiten und pädagogischer Praxis, dabei weithin verbunden mit einer Anthropologie der Person, die wiederum auch den Menschen- und Kinderrechten zugrunde liegt (Weigand et al., 2014).[2]

Unterstützt wird die pädagogische Perspektive auf Begabungsförderung ab 2009 durch die Ratifizierung der UN-Behindertenrechtskonvention mit einer Hinwendung zu einem inklusiven Begabungsverständnis, welches Begabungsentfaltung als Kinderrecht impliziert (Weigand & Kaiser, 2021).

---

1 In Zusammenhang mit der Frage, wie man begabte Menschen identifizieren kann, wurden Messverfahren entwickelt, mit deren Hilfe der Intelligenzquotient (IQ) einer Person ermittelt werden kann. So wird etwa bei IQ-Tests, die auf einen Mittelwert 100 und eine Standardabweichung 15 normiert sind, eine Hochbegabung bei 130 und höher, also bei zwei Standardabweichungen nach oben, festgestellt.

2 Im Zuge dieser Entwicklungen wird zunehmend die schulische Förderung von Begabungen in den Blick genommen. Ab Ende der 1990er und während der 2000er Jahre hat sich zwar eine segregative Förderung in spezifischen Klassen und Schulen für als hochbegabt getestete Schüler*innen etabliert, ergänzend wurden aber bereits zu dieser Zeit auch integrative Methoden der Begabungs- und Begabtenförderung in Regelklassen umgesetzt.

Besonders relevant ist diese Entwicklung vor dem Hintergrund von Forschungserkenntnissen, wonach das Erkennen von Begabungen und die Begabungsentfaltung von soziokulturellen Hintergründen (Ehmke & Jude, 2010), dem Geschlecht (Macha, 2015) und/oder der Migrationsgeschichte (Preckel & Baudson 2013) der Kinder beeinflusst wird. Zahlreiche Studien zeigen, dass Kinder aus sozial benachteiligten Kontexten in spezifischen Begabtenförderprogrammen deutlich unterrepräsentiert sind und damit eine besondere Form der Diskriminierung erfahren (Borland, 2010; Stamm, 2007). Problematisch ist zudem, dass sich Unterschiede in der Leistungsentwicklung durch eine defizitär interpretierte Passung zwischen a) Vorwissen, Fähigkeiten, Erfahrungen, aber auch Bildungsaspiration sowie b) schulischen Inhalten und Praxis ergeben können – insbesondere bei Kindern aus herausfordernden Lagen (Drucks & Bremm, 2021). Im Bereich der Begabungsentfaltung kommt dies etwa darin zum Ausdruck, dass durch Klassifikationslogiken „inhärent gesellschaftliche Ungleichheiten" (Horvath, 2018, S. 259) reproduziert und Ungleichheitseffekte verstärkt werden. Eine konsequente Hinwendung zu den individuellen Begabungen *aller* Kinder (auch i. S. v. Art. 29 Abs. 1a UN-KRK) und eine damit einhergehende kritische Reflexion bestehender Mechanismen der Diskriminierung und Reproduktion sozialer Ungleichheiten stellen somit wichtige Voraussetzungen für eine gleichberechtigte Teilhabe an Bildungschancen und Anerkennungsgerechtigkeit (Bremm, 2021) dar.

2.2 Begabungsentfaltung als Element der Kinderrechte

Werden Begabungen im Kontext von Kinderrechten akzentuiert, wie es in Artikel 29 Abs. 1a der UN-KRK (1989) geschieht, so impliziert dies, dass das Recht für *alle* Kinder gleichumfänglich gilt. Das bedeutet im Umkehrschluss, dass entsprechende Möglichkeiten zu schaffen sind, um die Begabungen *aller* Kinder zu entfalten.

Die Definition von Begabung, wie sie auch der Initiative ‚Leistung macht Schule' zugrunde liegt, ist in hohem Maße anschlussfähig an dieses Postulat und daher Basis des vorliegenden Beitrags (Weigand, Preckel & Fischer, 2022). Begabungen umfassen demnach leistungsbezogene Entwicklungspotenziale „[...] als individuelle Konstellation aus Fähigkeiten (‚can do') und (dynamisch sich entwickelnden) Persönlichkeitsmerkmalen (‚will do')" (LemaS, 2018, S. 1). Begabung gilt als Voraussetzung für Leistung, die „[...] durch langfristige systematische Anregung, Begleitung und Förderung das Individuum in die Lage versetzt, sinnorientiert und verantwortungsvoll zu handeln [...]" (iPEGE, 2009, S. 17). Dieser entwicklungsbezogene Begabungsbegriff geht mit einem breiten und dynamischen Leistungsverständnis einher, welches ebenfalls in LemaS erarbeitet wurde. Demnach meint Leistung sowohl die Leistungshandlung selbst (Engagement, Investition, Performanz) als auch deren Ergebnis, und zwar in einer Vielzahl von Leistungsdomänen, welche letztlich auch den personalen Lebensentwurf und die gestaltende Teilhabe an der (Schul-)Gemeinschaft und Gesellschaft miteinschließen (LemaS, o. J.).[3]

3 Es gibt eine Vielzahl von Leistungsdomänen, d. h., dass Leistung in vielfältigen Kontexten und auf unterschiedliche Art erbracht werden kann. Überdurchschnittliche Leistungen werden zu-

Begabungsentfaltung ist mit einer Abkehr von den Defiziten der Kinder hin zu einer Stärkenorientierung verbunden, die *allen* Kindern zutraut, das eigene Begabungsprofil als Grundlage eines gelingenden Lebens zu entwickeln. Dem Handlungsfeld Schule kommt hierbei eine tragende Rolle zu – nicht zuletzt vor dem Hintergrund der neurowissenschaftlichen Erkenntnis, dass erst Lernen intelligent macht (Neubauer & Stern, 2007). Neuere Forschungen aus der kognitiven Neuropsychologie bestätigen: Begabung kann als Lernleistungsfähigkeit eines *jeden* Menschen betrachtet werden (Stadelmann, 2021).

Im Sinne von Artikel 29 Abs. 1a der UN-KRK (1989) folgt daraus ein inklusives Verständnis der Begabungsentfaltung, das *alle* Kinder, unabhängig von Geschlecht, Herkunft und sozialem Status und unter Ablehnung einer Unterscheidung nach (zugeschriebenen) Merkmalen, aber mit ihren vielfältigen Begabungsprofilen in den Blick nimmt. Dies verlangt ein inklusives Schulsystem und eine „Pädagogik der Vielfalt" (Prengel, 2019). Es fordert die Institution Schule sowie die darin handelnden Akteur*innen heraus, im Sinne einer advokatorischen Einstellung (Brumlik, 2017) für die Verwirklichung dieses Rechts der Kinder einzutreten und es in deren Interesse und Wohl zu realisieren. Dazu braucht es vielfältige Formen und Formate, die das Erkennen und Fördern im Rahmen eines breiten Begabungs- und Leistungsspektrums, das auch die Persönlichkeitsentwicklung der Kinder einschließt, ermöglichen.

3. Educational Leadership und Begabungsentfaltung in Forschung und Praxis

Die Realisierung von Begabungsentfaltung, die *alle* Kinder berücksichtigt, geht mit langfristigen und komplexen Veränderungs- und Gestaltungsprozessen in Schule und Unterricht einher (Maier-Röseler & Weigand, 2022). Aus zahlreichen Studien ist bekannt, dass Schulleitungen in solchen Prozessen eine wichtige Rolle einnehmen (Haenisch & Steffens, 2017; Marzano, Waters & McNulty, 2005) und damit indirekt auf das Lernen und die Leistung von Kindern, also deren Begabungsentfaltung, einwirken können (Liebowitz & Porter, 2019).

Die folgenden Ausführungen geben einen Einblick, in welchen konkreten Feldern Schulleitungen im Zusammenhang mit der Gestaltung einer begabenden Schule für *alle* Kinder agieren können. Dabei wird auf die Differenzierung zwischen *Management*[4] und *Educational Leadership* zurückgegriffen, die sich bei der Analyse von Schul-

---

meist in einer bestimmten Domäne erbracht; sie sind also oft domänenspezifisch. Leistung ist zudem dynamisch. So kann es längere oder kürzere Phasen besonderer Leistungsstärke und besonderen Engagements geben. Welche Domänen als Leistungsdomänen Beachtung finden, wird kulturell und sozial gesetzt bzw. ausgehandelt.

4 Management bezieht sich vorwiegend auf Prozesse, mit denen die organisatorischen und strukturellen Rahmenbedingungen der Schule angepasst werden, um Schule als pädagogische Institution funktionsfähig zu halten. In Zusammenhang mit der Förderung von Begabungen erstreckt sich das Management etwa auf organisatorische Fragen, wie die Verwaltung des Stundenbudgets für außerunterrichtliche Angebote, die Verankerung von Zeitressourcen für Coaching-/Mentoring-Gespräche oder die Restrukturierung der pädagogischen Praxis bei der Unterrichtstaktung oder der Neugestaltung von Lernräumen, um einige wenige Beispiele zu

leitungshandeln etabliert hat. Der Schwerpunkt des Beitrags liegt auf dem Educational Leadership, das sowohl Elemente der personalen Führung als auch den Bereich der pädagogischen Gestaltung und Weiterentwicklung von Schule umfasst (Schratz et al., 2019) und in der konkreten Praxis vielseitig ausgestaltet werden kann (Anderegg & Wilhelm, 2021). Dabei erscheinen Schulleitungen vor allem dann erfolgreich, wenn Führungsstile und -strategien flexibel und situativ ausgehandelt werden (Anderegg et al., 2023).

Wir greifen vier zentrale Felder heraus, in denen die Schulleitungen im Sinne von Educational Leadership die Entfaltung der Begabungen *aller* Kinder in Schule und Unterricht unterstützen können.

Aus Forschungsarbeiten zur Schulentwicklung ist bekannt, dass *erstens* die Verständigung auf gemeinsame Werte durch die schulischen Akteur*innen maßgeblich für die Qualität von Schulen (Rosenholtz, 1989) und das Gelingen von Veränderungsprozessen (Haenisch & Steffens, 2017) ist. Dies ist nicht trivial, aber im Zusammenhang mit Begabungsentfaltung insbesondere dann wichtig, wenn die schulischen Akteur*innen diverse und möglicherweise auch widerstreitende Begabungsverständnisse haben. Durch das Bewusstmachen eigener Vorstellungen und persönlicher sowie institutioneller Handlungsroutinen können mögliche Prozesse der Diskriminierung von Kindern im individuellen Handeln, aber auch in kollektiven Praktiken kritisch reflektiert und bearbeitet werden. Schulleitungen können eine solche Auseinandersetzung ermöglichen und dabei helfen, Visionen zu entwickeln. Ihre Haltung zur Begabungsvielfalt der Kinder und ihre Erwartung an die Ausgestaltung der Begabungsförderung kann Orientierung geben (Solzbacher & Kuhl, 2023).

Die Umsetzung der Begabungsentfaltung in der pädagogischen Praxis erfordert *zweitens* entsprechende Konzepte und Maßnahmen zur Begabungsförderung. Neben dem Erkennen der Begabungen im Sinne pädagogischer Diagnostik (Müller-Oppliger, 2021) kann Begabungsentfaltung durch entsprechende Lernanlässe und die Begleitung der Lernprozesse unterstützt werden. Darüber hinaus geht es darum, (Zeit-) Räume zu eröffnen, in denen vielfältige Leistungen von Kindern gezeigt und gewürdigt werden können. Ein besonderes Augenmerk liegt darauf, Angebote und Lernsettings *allen* Kindern zugänglich zu machen und vielfältige Begabungen anzusprechen. Kooperationen mit außerschulischen Partner*innen wie Kultureinrichtungen, Vereinen und Unternehmen sowie weiteren Fachstellen können zu einer adäquaten und vielfältigen Erweiterung begabungsfördernder Lernangebote beitragen. Schulleitungen im Sinne des Educational Leadership können bei diesen Vorhaben Maßstäbe setzen bzw. gemeinsam mit dem Kollegium entwickeln (Maier-Röseler, 2020) und Orientierung etwa bezüglich der Frage, welche Formate der Begabungsförderung in welchen Klassenstufen und Fächern oder im außerunterrichtlichen Bereich verwirklicht wer-

---

nennen. Management umfasst aber auch die Steuerung monetärer Ressourcen beispielsweise für die Finanzierung besonderer Lernangebote sowie die Verantwortung für die notwendige infrastrukturelle Ausstattung der Schule u. a. im Hinblick auf technologiegestütztes Lernen. Solche Managementprozesse flankieren und begleiteten das Educational Leadership, das im vorliegenden Beitrag bearbeitet wird. Für die Prozesse der Schulgestaltung und -entwicklung sind darüber hinaus etwa die Schaffung von Kooperations- oder Professionalisierungszeiten wichtig (Connolly, James & Fertig, 2017).

den sollen, bieten. Den Prozess hin zu einer begabungsfördernden Schule unterstützen Schulleitungen als Change Agents durch die Etablierung einer offenen Fehler- und Feedbackkultur, welche die Erprobung innovativer Ideen begünstigt (Kempfert & Ludwig, 2008). Educational Leadership vermag zudem dazu beizutragen, alle Akteur*innen im Prozess hin zu einem aufeinander abgestimmten Handeln und zu gemeinsamen Strategien zu unterstützen. Allerdings ist dieser Prozess komplex. Besondere Herausforderungen ergeben sich aus dem persönlichen Fokus einzelner auf individuelle Handlungsroutinen sowie der Erwartungshaltung, Schul- und Unterrichtsentwicklung könnte alleine aus der Summe des individuellen Handelns einzelner Personen entstehen (Maier-Röseler, 2023).

Vor diesem Hintergrund gilt *drittens* innerschulische Kooperation als weiteres Schlüsselmerkmal gelingender Begabungsentfaltung (Jurczok et al., 2022) und erfolgreicher Schulentwicklungsprozesse (Massenkeil & Rothland, 2016). Schulleitungen als Educational Leaders und Change Agents unterstützen hierbei insbesondere eine positive Kooperationskultur. Sie kooperieren im besten Fall selbst bzw. nutzen Kooperation und die Teilung von Verantwortlichkeiten gezielt für eine umfassende Schulgestaltung und betonen damit die Relevanz von Zusammenarbeit für die Umsetzung der Begabungsförderung. Das erscheint im Spiegel empirischer Ergebnisse zur Verbreitung und Nutzung von Kooperation (Nguyen & Ng, 2020) relevant. Zudem heben Studien zu erfolgreichem Schulleitungshandeln die Bedeutung geteilter Schulführung für die Gestaltung von Schule hervor (Schott, van Roekel & Tummers, 2020).

Viertens sind Professionalisierungsprozesse eine wichtige Säule bei der Realisierung der Begabungsentfaltung. Anforderungen ergeben sich hierbei aus der konkreten Gestaltung der Begabungsförderung sowie vor dem Hintergrund von Stigmatisierung, Rollenbildern und Diskriminierungstendenzen (Riefling & Koop, 2018). Die Funktion der Schulleitungen als Educational Leaders und Change Agents erstreckt sich von der generellen Aufgabe der Etablierung einer Professionalisierungskultur bis hin zur Unterstützung und Evaluation konkreter Professionalisierungsprozesse in Bezug auf Begabungsförderung (Maier-Röseler, 2021). Damit unterstreicht die Schulleitung die Bedeutung fachwissenschaftlicher, fachdidaktischer sowie pädagogischer Handlungskompetenzen, aber auch Haltungen und Einstellungen für die Umsetzung der Begabungsentfaltung als Element der Kinderrechte bzw. betont entsprechende Ansprüche an das professionelle Handeln der schulischen Akteur*innen. Auf Grundlage der zurückliegenden Ausführungen erscheinen kooperative Formate der Professionalisierung zielführend (Lipowsky & Rzejak, 2019), an denen die Schulleitung selbst partizipiert (Harris & Jones, 2017). Allerdings muss eine kooperative Professionalisierung an sich noch zu keiner gemeinsam verantworteten Schulgestaltung führen (Bergmüller-Hauptmann & Asbrand, 2020). Um das gemeinsame Handeln zu bestärken, kann Educational Leadership auf Grundlage von Professionalisierungsprozessen zwischen unterschiedlichen Perspektiven vermitteln, indem Begabungsentfaltung als Element der Kinderrechte zum gemeinsamen Verantwortungsbereich im Handlungsfeld Schule wird (Maier-Röseler, 2023).

4. Fazit

Wird die Entfaltung der Begabungen *aller* Kinder als ein Element des Kinderrechts auf Bildung und Förderung gemäß Artikel 29 Abs. 1a der UN-KRK (1989) betrachtet, sind damit Orientierungsrahmen und Handlungsfelder benannt, die es ermöglichen, Bildungsgleichheit zu unterstützen sowie gesellschaftliche Teilhabe und ein selbstbestimmtes Leben zu realisieren. Schulische Akteur*innen sind demnach herausgefordert, Schule und Unterricht begabungsfördernd zu gestalten und bestehende individuelle, aber auch kollektive Praktiken kritisch zu reflektieren und gegebenenfalls zu verändern. Damit die schulischen Gestaltungs- und Veränderungsprozesse gelingen, tragen Schulleitungen im Sinne von Educational Leadership als Visionär*innen und Change Agents eine große Verantwortung. Zur Verwirklichung einer Begabungsentfaltung für *alle* Kinder kommt es darüber hinaus aber auf alle Akteur*innen in der Schulgemeinschaft sowie letztlich auf die Verständigung in Politik, Kommunen und Zivilgesellschaft an – zum Wohl jedes einzelnen Kindes und eines gerechteren Zusammenlebens in der Zukunft.

Literatur

Anderegg, N., Knies, A., Jesacher-Rößler, L., & Breitschaft, J. (2023). Einleitung. In N. Anderegg, A. Knies, L. Jesacher-Rößler & J. Breitschaft (Hrsg.), *Leadership for Learning – gemeinsam Schulen lernwirksam gestalten. Führung von und in Bildungsorganisationen* (S. 10–22). Hep.

Anderegg, N., & Wilhelm, U. (2021). Begabungsfördernde Schulentwicklung und Schulführung. In G. Weigand & V. Müller-Oppliger (Hrsg.), *Handbuch Begabung* (S. 302–318). Beltz.

Bergmüller-Hauptmann, C., & Asbrand, B. (2020). Unterrichtsentwicklung und Lehrerprofessionalität. Dokumentarische Evaluationsforschung im Feld der Lehrerfortbildung. In R. Bohnsack & I. Nentwig-Gesemann (Hrsg.), *Dokumentarische Evaluationsforschung. Theoretische Grundlagen und Beispiele aus der Praxis* (2. Aufl., S. 103–120). Barbara Budrich.

Borland, J. H. (2010). Gifted Education Without Gifted Children. The Case for No Conceptions of Giftedness. In R. Sternberg & J. E. Davidson (Hrsg.), *Conceptions of Giftedness* (2. Aufl., S. 1–19). University Press.

Bremm, N. (2021). Anerkennungsgerechtigkeit in benachteiligten Sozialräumen. Defizitperspektiven und Möglichkeiten und Grenzen ihrer Bearbeitung im Rahmen eines Schulentwicklungsprojekts. In L. Brockmann, C. Hack, A. Pomykaj & W. Böttcher (Hrsg.), *Doing inequality. Soziale Ungleichheit im Sozial- und Bildungswesen. Reproduktion und Legitimierung* (S. 130–150). Beltz. https://doi.org/10.25656/01:21402

Brumlik, M. (2017). *Advokatorische Ethik. Zur Legitimation pädagogischer Eingriffe*. Cep.

Connolly, M., James, C., & Fertig, M. (2017). The difference between educational management and educational leadership and the importance of educational responsibility. *Educational Management Administration & Leadership*, *47*(4), 504–519. https://doi.org/10.1177/1741143217745880

Ditton, H., & Maaz, K. (2022). Sozioökonomischer Status, Bildungserfolg und Bildungsteilhabe. In H. Reinders, D. Bergs-Winkels, A. Prochnow & I. Post (Hrsg.), *Empirische Bildungsforschung* (S. 1083–1103). Springer.

Drucks, S., & Bremm, N. (2021). Funktionen von Defizitorientierungen von Lehrkräften im Kontext unterschiedlicher herausfordernder Lagen. In I. van Ackeren, H. G. Holtappels, N. Bremm & A. Hillebrand-Petri (Hrsg.), *Schulen in herausfordernden Lagen – Forschungsbefunde und Schulentwicklung in der Region Ruhr. Das Projekt „Potenziale entwickeln – Schulen stärken"* (S. 244–276). Beltz.

Ehmke, T., & Jude, N. (2010). Soziale Herkunft und Kompetenzerwerb. In E. Klieme, C. Artelt, J. Hartig, N. Jude, O. Köller, M. Prenzel & P. Stanat (Hrsg.), *PISA 2009: Bilanz nach einem Jahrzehnt* (S. 231–254). Waxmann.

Gardner, H. (1983). *Frames of mind. The theory of multiple intelligences.* Basic Books.

Haenisch, H., & Steffens, U. (2017). Schlüsselfaktoren für die Entwicklung von Schulen. In U. Steffens, K. Maag Merki & H. Fend (Hrsg.), *Schulgestaltung. Aktuelle Befunde und Perspektiven der Schulqualitäts- und Schulentwicklungsforschung* (S. 159–184). Waxmann.

Harris, A., & Jones, M. (2017). Leading professional learning: putting teachers at the center. *School Leadership & Management, 37*(4), 331–333.

Horvath, K. (2018). „Wir können fördern, wir können fordern, aber begaben können wir nicht." Pädagogische Begabungsunterscheidungen im Kontext sozialer Ungleichheiten. In A. Böker & K. Horvath (Hrsg.), *Begabung und Gesellschaft. Sozialwissenschaftliche Perspektiven auf Begabung und Begabtenförderung* (S. 239–261). Springer. https://doi.org/10.1007/978-3-658-21761-7_11

Hoyer, T., Weigand, G., & Müller-Oppliger, V. (2013). *Begabung. Eine Einführung.* WBG.

International Panel of Experts for Gifted Eucation. (iPEGE). (Hrsg.). (2009). *Professionelle Begabungsförderung. Empfehlung zur Qualifizierung von Fachkräften in der Begabtenförderung.* ÖZBF. https://www.oezbf.at/wp-content/uploads/2017/09/iPEGE_1_web.pdf.

Jurczok, A., Haase, A., Perleth, C., & Vock, M. (2022). Schul- und Unterrichtsentwicklung als Gemeinschaftsaufgabe von Teams und Netzwerken am Beispiel der Begabungs- und Leistungsförderung. In G. Weigand, M. Vock, F. Preckel, C. Fischer, C. Perleth, F. Käpnick & W. Wollersheim (Hrsg.), *Dimensionen der Begabungs- und Begabtenförderung in der Schule* (S. 99–114). wbv. https://doi.org/10.3278/9783763967858

Kempfert, G., & Ludwig, M. (2008). *Kollegiale Unterrichtsbesuche. Besser und leichter unterrichten durch Kollegen-Feedback.* Beltz.

Kultusministerkonferenz. (KMK). (2006). *Erklärung der Kultusministerkonferenz vom 3.3.2006 zur Umsetzung des Übereinkommens der Vereinten Nationen über die Rechte des Kindes. Beschluss der Kultusministerkonferenz vom 03.03.2006.* https://www.kmk.org/fileadmin/veroeffentlichungen_beschluesse/2006/2006_03_03-UN-Kinderrechte_.pdf.

Kultusministerkonferenz. (KMK). (2016). *Gemeinsame Initiative von Bund und Ländern zur Förderung leistungsstarker und potenziell besonders leistungsfähiger Schülerinnen und Schüler. Beschluss der Kultusministerkonferenz vom 10.11.2016.* https://www.kmk.org/fileadmin/Dateien/pdf/PresseUndAktuelles/2016/2016-11-28_Gem.Initiative_Leistungsstarke-Beschluss.pdf.

LemaS. (o. J.). *Welcher Begabungs- und Leistungsbegriff liegt „Leistung macht Schule" zugrunde?* https://www.leistung-macht-schule.de/files/230629-Leistung-macht-schule-Leistungsbegriff.pdf.

LemaS. (2018). *„Leistungsstarke" und „potenziell besonders leistungsfähige Schülerinnen und Schüler"*. https://phase1.lemas-forschung.de/themen/leistungs-und-begabungs-begriff.

Liebowitz, D. D., & Porter, L. (2019). The Effect of Principal Behaviors on Student, Teacher, and School Outcomes: A Systematic Review and Meta-Analysis of the Empirical Literature. *Review of Educational Research, 89*(5), 785–827. https://doi.org/10.3102/0034654319866133

Lipowsky, F., & Rzejak, D. (2019). Was macht Fortbildungen für Lehrkräfte erfolgreich? – Ein Update. In B. Groot-Wilken & R. Koerber (Hrsg.), *Nachhaltige Professionalisierung für Lehrerinnen und Lehrer. Ideen, Entwicklungen, Konzepte* (S. 15–56). Qualitäts- und UnterstützungsAgentur – Landesinstitut für Schule des Landes Nordrhein-Westfalen.

Macha, H. (2015). Besonders Begabte gendersensibel fördern. In C. Solzbacher, G. Weigand & P. Schreiber (Hrsg.), *Begabungsförderung kontrovers? Konzepte im Spiegel der Inklusion* (S. 60–68). Beltz.

Maier-Röseler, M. (2020). *Professionalisierung von Lehrpersonen an Einzelschulen. Theorie und Empirie im Dialog.* Barbara Budrich.

Maier-Röseler, M. (2021). Professionalisierung von Lehrpersonen: Wie können Schulleitungen das Lernen von Lehrerinnen und Lehrern unterstützen? In S. G. Huber (Hrsg.), *Jahrbuch Schulleitung 2021 – Impulse aus der Wissenschaft und Praxis* (S. 121–136). Carl Link.

Maier-Röseler, M. (2023). Kollegiale Professionalisierung und kooperative Professionalität im Kontext von Schulentwicklungsvorhaben. Chancen und Herausforderungen. In R. Porsch & P. Gollub (Hrsg.), *Professionalisierung von Lehrkräften im Beruf. Stand und Perspektiven der Lehrkräftebildung und Professionsforschung* (S. 199–214). Waxmann.

Maier-Röseler, M., & Weigand, G. (2022). Begabungs- und Leistungsförderung als Motiv schulischer Praxis. Leitbild- und Schulentwicklung an LemaS-Schulen. In G. Weigand, M. Vock, F. Preckel, C. Fischer, C. Perleth, F. Käpnick & W. Wollersheim (Hrsg.), *Dimensionen der Begabungs- und Begabtenförderung in der Schule* (S. 209–220). wbv. https://www.wbv.de/shop/openaccess-download/6004912w

Marzano, R. J., Waters, T., & McNulty, B. A. (2005). *School Leadership that Works. From Research to Results.* Association for Supervision and Curriculum Development.

Massenkeil, J., & Rothland, M. (2016). Kollegiale Kooperation im Lehrerberuf. Überblick und Systematisierung aktueller Forschung. *Schulpädagogik heute, 7*(13), 1–28.

Müller-Oppliger, S. (2021). Pädagogische Diagnostik – Potenzialerfassung und Förderdiagnostik. In V. Müller-Oppliger & G. Weigand (Hrsg.), *Handbuch Begabung* (S. 224–238). Beltz.

Neubauer, A., & Stern, E. (2007). *Lernen macht intelligent: warum Begabung gefördert werden muss.* Deutsche Verlags-Anstalt.

Nguyen, D., & Ng, D. (2020). Teacher collaboration for change: sharing, improving, and spreading. Professional Development in Education. *Professional Development in Education, 46*(4), 638–651. https://doi.org/10.1080/19415257.2020.1787206

Pflüger, R. (2022). Geschichte der Begabungsforschung. 100 Jahre, 5 Epochen, 2 Perspektiven. In H. Reinders, D. Bergs-Winkels, A. Prochnow & I. Post (Hrsg.), *Empirische Bildungsforschung* (S. 1151–1174). Springer. https://doi.org/10.1007/978-3-658-27277-7_60

Preckel, F. (2022). Hochbegabung unter einer Entwicklungsperspektive: Grundlagen und Implikationen für die Empirische Bildungsforschung. In H. Reinders, D. Bergs-Winkels, A. Prochnow & I. Post (Hrsg.), *Empirische Bildungsforschung* (S. 1199–1220). Springer. https://doi.org/10.1007/978-3-658-27277-7_62

Preckel, F., & Baudson, T. G. (2013). *Hochbegabung. Erkennen, Verstehen, Fördern.* C.H. Beck.

Prengel, A. (2019). *Pädagogik der Vielfalt. Verschiedenheit und Gleichberechtigung in Interkultureller, Feministischer und Integrativer Pädagogik* (4. Aufl.). Springer.

Riefling, M., & Koop, C. (2018). ‚Elitekind' und ‚Kopftuchmädchen' Perspektiven der Begabungsförderung im Lichte der Rationalen Pädagogik. In A. Böker & K. Horvath (Hrsg.), *Begabung und Gesellschaft. Sozialwissenschaftliche Perspektiven auf Begabung und Begabtenförderung* (S. 263–284). Springer. https://doi.org/10.1007/978-3-658-21761-7_12

Rosenholtz, S. J. (1989). *Teachers' Workplace. The social organization of schools.* Longman.

Roth, H. (1952). Begabung und Begaben. Über das Problem der Umwelt in der Begabungsentfaltung. *Die Sammlung, 7*, 395–407.

Schott, C., van Roekel, E., & Tummers, L. G. (2020). Teacher leadership: A systematic review, methodological quality assessment and conceptual framework. *Educational Research Review, 31*(100352). https://doi.org/10.1016/j.edurev.2020.100352

Schratz, M., Ammann, M., Anderegg, N., Bergmann, A., Gregorzewski, M., Mauersberg, W., & Möltner, V. (2019). Schulleitungshandeln an ausgezeichneten Schulen. *Zeitschrift für Bildungsforschung, 9*(1), 71–88. https://doi.org/10.1007/s35834-019-00243-5

Solzbacher, C., & Kuhl, J. (2023). Begabung – Begriffsvielfalt, Konstrukte, Modelle. In N. Miceli, (Hrsg.), *Praxisbuch Begabungsfördernde Schulentwicklung* (S. 26–45). Beltz.

Stadelmann, W. (2021). Begabungsentwicklung aus Sicht der Genetik und der kognitiven Neuropsychologie. In V. Müller-Oppliger & G. Weigand (Hrsg.), *Handbuch Begabung* (S. 133–148). Beltz.

Stamm, M. (2007). Begabtenförderung und soziale Herkunft. Befunde zu den verborgenen Mechanismen. *Zeitschrift für Soziologie der Erziehung und Sozialisation, 27*(3), 227–242.

UN-Kinderrechtskonvention. (1989). *Übereinkommen über die Rechte des Kindes.* https://www.unicef.de/informieren/ueber-uns/fuer-kinderrechte/un-kinderrechtskonvention.

Weiand, K., & Weigand, G. (2024). Begabung und Leistung – Zum wechselseitigen Verhältnis von öffentlichen Debatten, wissenschaftlichen und politischen Diskursen in historischer Perspektive. In J. Becker, M. Tribukait & A. Weich (Hrsg.), *Transformation der Leistung in Schule und Bildungsmedien* (S. 229–244). Unipress.

Weigand, G., Hackl, A., Müller-Oppliger, V., & Schmid, G. (Hrsg.). (2014). *Personorientierte Begabungsförderung. Eine Einführung in Theorie und Praxis.* Beltz.

Weigand, G., & Kaiser, M. (2021). Separativ oder integrativ? Inklusive Begabungs- und Begabtenförderung. In V. Müller-Oppliger & G. Weigand (Hrsg.), *Handbuch Begabung* (S. 290–301). Beltz.

Weigand, C., Preckel, F., & Fischer, C. (2022). Personorientierte Begabungsentwicklung in Lernumwelten als interdisziplinäre Grundlage von LemaS. In G. Weigand, M. Vock, F. Preckel, C. Fischer, C. Perleth, F. Käpnick & W. Wollersheim (Hrsg.), *Dimensionen der Begabungs- und Begabtenförderung in der Schule* (S. 19–37). wbv. https://www.wbv.de/shop/openaccess-download/6004912w.

Further Contributions in the Volume

For a deeper engagement with the implications of children's rights for pedagocical practice, we recommend reading the focus article by *Antonia Bongen* on diversity management as prevention for discrimination (pp. 79–86).

Another article focusing on leadership at the system level is authored by *Philipp Schubert*, *Melanie Hochmuth*, *Julia Hufnagl*, and *Silvia Annen* on recognition procedures in Germany as a leadership task (pp. 65–78).

Julia Hugo, Charlotte Assmann, Andreas Schmidt (Eds.)
Educational Leadership and Children's Rights?/
Kinderrechte als Führungsaufgabe?
 https://doi.org/10.31244/9783830998259_9

Margit Stein, Benjamin Möbus & Fabio Wensing

Das UNICEF-Kinderrechteschulenprogramm

Evaluation aus Perspektive von Lehrkräften, Schüler*innen und Eltern

Zusammenfassung
Das UNICEF-Kinderrechteschulenprogramm zielt darauf ab, die Rechte von Kindern und Jugendlichen als zentrale Akteur*innen in Schule und Unterricht zu stärken. Durch ein siebenstufiges Training, das sich an das gesamte Schulpersonal sowie an Vertreter*innen der Schülerschaft und der Eltern richtet, werden Schutz-, Förder- und Partizipationsrechte systematisch vermittelt und in der Schule verankert. Die vorliegende Studie greift das Forschungsdesiderat der bislang noch nicht erfolgten Evaluierung des Programms aus Sicht der beteiligten Akteur*innen auf. An einer zertifizierten UNICEF-Kinderrechtegrundschule wurden 25 Lehrkräfte, 39 Schüler*innen und 33 Eltern befragt. Erhoben wurden die Akzeptanz und Unterstützung des Programms, die Einschätzung der Umsetzung der Kinderrechte an der Schule sowie die wahrgenommenen Chancen und Herausforderungen bei der Implementierung aus Sicht der beteiligten Akteur*innen. Die Ergebnisse zeigen u. a., dass Lehrkräfte besser über die Implementierung informiert sind als Schüler*innen und Eltern; Schutzrechte, wie Anlaufstellen bei Mobbing und Diskriminierung, sind erfolgreich etabliert, während Förder- und Partizipationsrechte, etwa faire Bildungschancen und hohe Mitbestimmung, noch schwächer umgesetzt werden. Die Studie verdeutlicht die Notwendigkeit, Informations- und Ressourcenlücken zu schließen sowie verstärkt partizipative Strukturen zu fördern, um die Kinderrechte umfassend in der Schule zu verankern.

Schlüsselbegriffe
Kinderrechte, UNICEF-Kinderrechteschule, UN-Kinderrechtskonvention, Grundschule, Evaluation

The UNICEF Child Rights Schools Program

Evaluation from the Perspectives of Teachers, Pupils, and Parents

Abstract
The UNICEF Child Rights Schools Program seeks to empower the rights of children and adolescents as active participants in schools and educational settings. This initiative involves a seven-stage training program targeted at the entire school staff, as well as

representatives from the student body and parents, with the aim of systematically imparting and embedding protection, promotion, and participation rights within the school framework. This study addresses a research gap concerning the comprehensive evaluation of the program's effectiveness from the perspectives of the stakeholders involved. At a certified UNICEF Child Rights primary school, data were collected through surveys administered to 25 teachers, 39 students, and 33 parents. The survey focused on the acceptance and support of the program, the evaluation of the implementation of children's rights within the school, and the perceived opportunities and challenges in implementation from the stakeholders' viewpoints. The findings indicate that teachers possess a better understanding of the implementation process compared to students and parents. While protection rights, such as access points for addressing bullying and discrimination, have been successfully established, promotion and participation rights – including equitable educational opportunities and high rates of student participation – remain less effectively implemented. This study highlights the need to address information and resource gaps and to enhance participatory structures in order to fully integrate children's rights into the school environment.

Keywords
Children's Rights, UNICEF Child Rights Schools, UN Convention on the Rights of the Child, Elementary School, Evaluation

1. Die Umsetzung der UN-Kinderrechtskonvention in Schulen im Spiegel der Ziele des UNICEF-Kinderrechteschulenprogramms

Unter der Devise ‚Für jedes Kind' setzt sich das Kinderhilfswerk der Vereinten Nationen ‚UNICEF' (‚United Nations Children's Fund') heute in über 190 Staaten dafür ein, die in der UN-Kinderrechtskonvention (UN-KRK) 1989 kodifizierten Rechte von Kindern zu verwirklichen (UNICEF, 2023a). Sie enthält 54 Artikel und gewährleistet einklagbar umfassende Rechte für alle Kinder, d. h. Personen unter 18 Jahren, unabhängig von Geschlecht, Herkunft oder nationaler Zugehörigkeit. Die Kinderrechte werden dabei als eine Trias aus *Schutzrechten* (Art. 2, 8, 9, 16, 17, 22, 30, 32, 33, 34, 35, 36, 37, 38), *Förderrechten* (Art. 6, 10, 15, 17, 18, 23, 24, 27, 28, 30, 31, 39) und *Partizipationsrechten* (Art. 12, 13, 17) gelesen. Gefordert wird etwa ein umfassender Schutz vor physischer, sexualisierter und psychischer Gewalt (Schutzrechte), eine holistische Förderung der körperlichen, geistigen und seelischen Entwicklung (Förderrechte) sowie die altersgemäße Miteinbeziehung in alle schulischen, familiären oder politischen Angelegenheiten (Partizipationsrechte).

Anlässlich des 30. Jahrestages des Inkrafttretens der UN-KRK bilanziert UNICEF (2022a, S. 5), dass in Deutschland seit der Ratifizierung zwar erkennbare Fortschritte in Bezug auf die Umsetzung und Gewährleistung der Kinderrechte gemacht wurden, allerdings deutliche Nachholbedarfe für die in der Verantwortung der Bundesländer liegenden Bereiche Bildung und Kultus konstatiert werden, etwa in Bezug auf die Mitbestimmungsmöglichkeiten und Partizipationsrechte in der Schule (UNICEF, 2022a). Dabei stellt die Institution Schule, die aufgrund der Schulpflicht (potenziell) alle Kinder und Jugendlichen erreicht, einen besonders geeigneten Ort dar, um über Kinderrechte aufzuklären, Kinderrechtskompetenzen zu vermitteln und sie erfahrbar zu machen.

Auch die Kultusministerkonferenz (KMK) erkennt in ihrer Erklärung zur Umsetzung der UN-KRK „die altersgerechte Berücksichtigung der Rechte des Kindes auf Schutz und Fürsorge sowie auf Partizipation [als] essentiell für die Schulkultur" (KMK, 2006, S. 1); dies wird in dem Manifest ‚Kinderrechte, Demokratie und Schule' (Krappmann & Petry, 2016) konkretisiert, das auf die Erklärung aufbaut und darlegt, wie diese im Schulalltag umgesetzt werden kann, etwa im Rahmen von Service Learning und Engagementförderung.

Ein vielversprechendes „Instrument, um Kinderrechte in der Schule zu popularisieren und an der Schule strukturell zu verankern, stellt das UNICEF-Kinderrechteschulenprogramm dar, in welchem teilnehmende Schulen dabei unterstützt werden, Kinderrechte in das Curriculum der Schule aufzunehmen, im Unterricht explizit aufzugreifen sowie die Kinderrechte durch (vor allem) Partizipationsmöglichkeiten strukturell zu verankern" (Möbus & Stein, 2024, S. 123); allerdings wurden die UNICEF-Kinderrechteschulen sowie die Implementierung des Kinderrechteschulenprogramms bisher wissenschaftlich nicht umfassend evaluiert.

Die vorliegende Studie widmet sich daher der Evaluation des UNICEF-Kinderrechteschulenprogramms und untersucht dessen Akzeptanz sowie seine Umsetzung aus der Perspektive der beteiligten Akteur*innen (Lehrkräfte, Schüler*innen und Eltern). Dabei werden sowohl die Chancen als auch die Herausforderungen bei der Implementierung von Kinderrechten in deutschen Schulen beleuchtet. Ziel des Beitrags ist es, zentrale Erfolgsfaktoren und potenzielle Barrieren zu identifizieren, um eine fundierte Grundlage für die Weiterentwicklung des Programms zu schaffen.

2. Das UNICEF-Kinderrechteschulenprogramm im Überblick

Derzeit nehmen mit steigender Tendenz Schulen aus vier Bundesländern (Niedersachsen, Nordrhein-Westfalen, Sachsen und Schleswig-Holstein) am UNICEF-Kinderrechteschulenprogramm teil (Stand: Juni 2024; UNICEF, 2022b). Seit 2021 sind es primär Grundschulen – mit wenigen Ausnahmen auch Haupt- und Realschulen –, die etwa in Niedersachsen im Implementierungsprozess sind (Niedersächsisches Kultusministerium, 2023). Das UNICEF-Programm ist darauf ausgerichtet, Kindern nicht nur Wissen über ihre Rechte, sondern auch entsprechende Kompetenzen zu vermitteln, wie sie in der Institution Schule und ihrer Gemeinschaft für ihre Rechte aktiv eintreten können sowie Schule zu einem Setting umzugestalten, in welchem Schutz-, Förder- und Partizipationsrechte erfahrbar werden (UNICEF, 2022b; Möbus & Stein, 2024, S. 127).

Das diesbezügliche Training für die Schulen besteht aus sieben Stufen (Abb. 1), die in einem Zeitraum von rund zwölf Monaten konsekutiv bearbeitet werden (sollen). Konkret besteht das Training aus drei Präsenz- und vier E-Learning-Modulen: „Das Training beginnt mit einem pädagogischen Fachtag, an welchem das gesamte Schulpersonal eingeladen wird, sich, begleitet durch Trainer*innen von UNICEF, mit dem UNICEF-Kinderrechteschulenprogramm resp. mit Kinderrechten auseinanderzusetzen

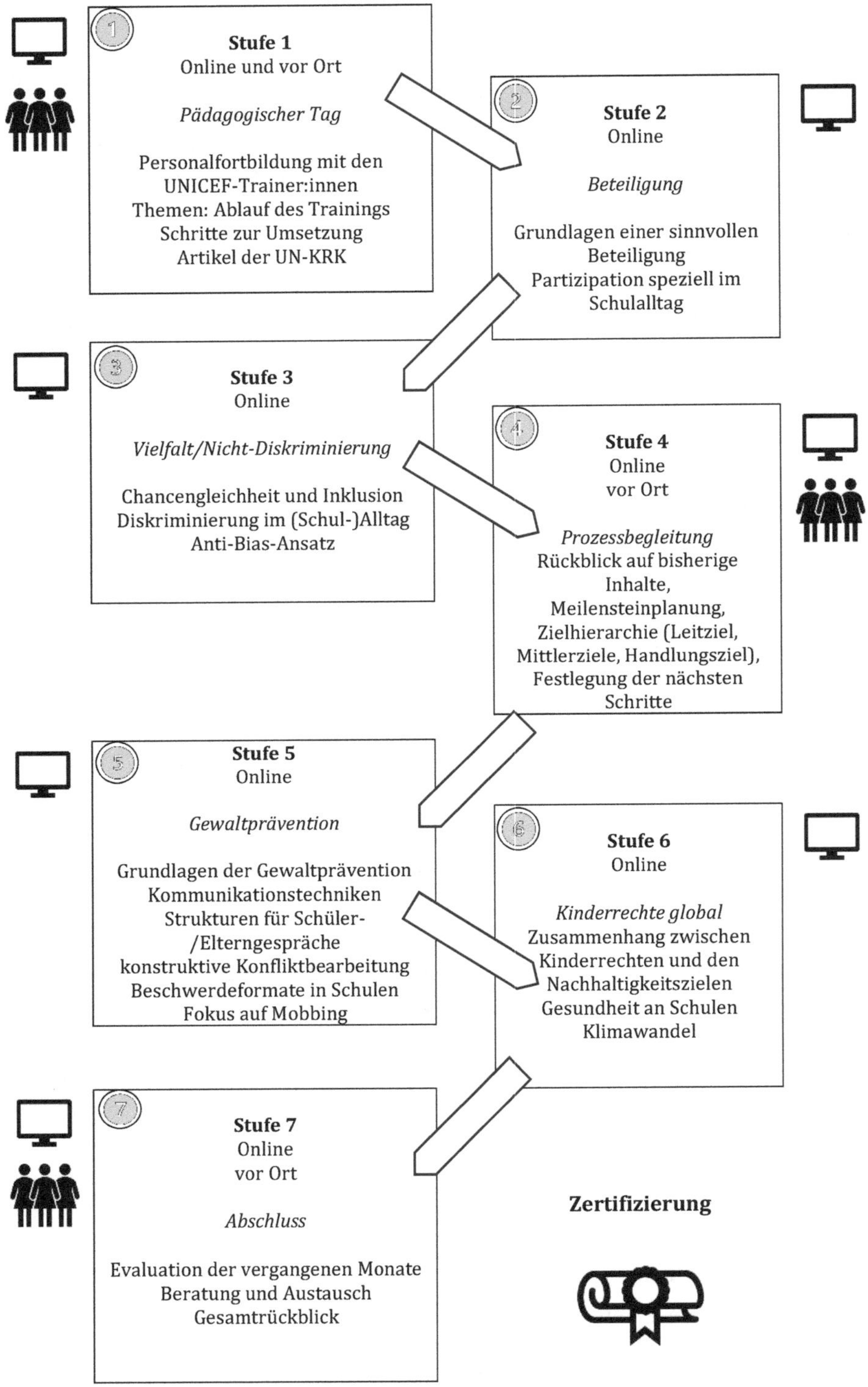

Abbildung 1: Siebenstufiges Kinderrechteschulentraining (nach UNICEF, 2022c).

(Stufe 1); anschließend erfolgen E-Learning-Module zu den Themenkomplexen *Beteiligung* (Stufe 2), *Vielfalt* und *Nicht-Diskriminierung* (Stufe 3), *Gewaltprävention* (Stufe 5) und *Kinderrechte global* (Stufe 6). Stufe 4 und 7 beinhalten – ebenfalls begleitet von den Trainer*innen – eine Reflexion des Umsetzungsprozesses und der weiteren Ziele des Programmes, an welchen die Verantwortlichen der Steuerungsgruppe teilnehmen sollen" (Möbus & Stein, 2024, S. 126).

Während des Trainings erhalten die Schulen die Möglichkeit, an regelmäßigen Netzwerktreffen zusammen mit den UNICEF-Trainer*innen sowie den Verantwortlichen anderer Kinderrechteschulen teilzunehmen.

Vor dem Start des Programms bilden Schulen eine aus drei bis acht Personen bestehende Steuergruppe (etwa Vertreter*innen des Schulpersonals, der Schülerschaft und der Eltern), welche den innerschulischen Entwicklungsprozess begleitet und die Schulgemeinschaft dabei unterstützt, das Programm, das Curriculum und das Leitbild entsprechend dieser Prozesse anzupassen und umzusetzen (UNICEF, 2023b).

3. Forschungsstand zur Implementierung von Kinderrechten an Schulen und zur Evaluation von kinderrechtsbasierten Schulentwicklungen

Sowohl im deutschsprachigen Raum als auch im internationalen Forschungskontext findet sich eine breite Studienlage zur Verankerung von Kinderrechten in Schulen. In Bezug auf das Recht auf eine gewaltfreie Erziehung wird in (inter-)nationalen Studien etwa die Verbreitung von Gewalt in Schulen thematisiert (*Schutzrechte*). Während das Recht auf Gewaltfreiheit in Schulen in Deutschland seit 1973 verbrieft ist, verbieten laut des UN-Reports ‚Toward a world free from violence – global survey on violence against children' (United Nations, 2016) nur 25 Prozent aller Länder Gewalt und Körperstrafen gegen Kinder in schulischen und familiären Kontexten. Auch in Deutschland wurden in einer Beobachtungsstudie mit 12.000 Fallvignetten von Prengel (2019) und Winklhofer und Prengel (2018) zur wertschätzenden bzw. herabwürdigenden Kommunikation von Lehrkräften u.a. in Schulen bei 25 Prozent der Interaktionen verletzende Aussagen oder Handlungen konstatiert, wobei 5 Prozent schwer verletzend waren.

Die Forschungen zu den *Förderrechten* im Schulkontext befassen sich häufig mit der Frage, ob es bzw. in welchem Umfang es bisher gelungen ist, den Grundsatz der Inklusion einzulösen, also inwiefern Kinder aller sozioökonomischen und soziokulturellen wie auch kognitiven Voraussetzungen gleichwertige Chancen auf Bildung erhalten (Sachverständigenrat deutscher Stiftungen für Integration und Migration, 2016; Bauer, Bittlingmayer & Scherr, 2023). Hier belegten u.a. die Studien und Expertisen der Autor:innengruppe Bildungsberichterstattung (2024) noch große Nachholbedarfe für Deutschland, da insbesondere strukturelle Hindernisse die vollumfängliche gleichwertige Beschulung aller Kinder erschweren und etwa Kinder mit Migrationshintergrund oder aus sozioökonomisch weniger potenten Familien sowohl bei der Schulwahl als auch der Kompetenzentwicklung schlechter gestellt sind.

Auch die Umsetzung der *Beteiligungsrechte* von Kindern wird kritisch betrachtet. Der 16. Kinder- und Jugendbericht beschreibt etwa ein „ziemlich erbärmliches Bild von schulischen demokratischen Beteiligungsmöglichkeiten" (BMFSFJ, 2020, S. 227), da Schüler*innen häufig die vorhandenen Partizipationsformen als „verordnete Autonomie" (ebd., S. 227) und „kontrollförmige Beteiligung" (ebd., S. 227) erleben.

Bisher wurden UNICEF-Kinderrechteschulen weltweit noch nicht umfassend wissenschaftlich evaluiert; eine wissenschaftliche Begleitung liegt jedoch für die DKHW-Kinderrechteschulen (Deutsches Kinderhilfswerk) vor. Hierzu fand eine quantitative Erhebung an 15 DKHW-Kinderrechteschulen mit standardisierten Befragungen von Schulleitungen, Lehrkräften, Schüler*innen und Eltern (74 Erwachsene und 84 Schüler*innen) sowie eine qualitative Befragung an drei Schulen (16 Erwachsene und sechs Schüler*innen) statt (DKHW, 2021). Erhoben wurden dabei ähnliche Dimensionen wie in der vorliegenden Untersuchung, insbesondere zu

- individuellen Bezügen zum Projekt (etwa Unterstützung und Engagement für das Projekt sowie Zugang zu Informationen und Materialien), zum
- Umgang miteinander (etwa Mobbing, Gewalt und Diskriminierung sowie aufgewandte Zeit und Unterstützung für Konfliktlösungen), zur
- Unterrichtsgestaltung (etwa demokratische Grundwerte, partizipative Methoden, nachvollziehbare Leistungsbeurteilung, Chancengleichheit), zur
- Ausstattung und Infrastruktur (etwa Räume, Mittagessen, Erholung/Spiel, Rückzugsmöglichkeiten) und zu
- Regeln und Mitgestaltung (etwa sinnvolle Regeln, transparente Abläufe, Leitbild).

Die Ergebnisse zeigten ein hohes Vertrauen darauf, dass aktiv gegen Gewalt, Mobbing und sexuelle Übergriffe vorgegangen wird (Schutzrechte), während Förder- und Beteiligungsmöglichkeiten geringer bewertet wurden, insbesondere aufgrund der infrastrukturellen Ausstattung (DKHW, 2021). Erwachsene sahen ein Verbesserungspotenzial im gegenseitigen Respekt; Schüler*innen kritisierten dagegen die geringe Partizipation im Unterricht und die mangelnde Thematisierung von Kinderrechten (DKHW, 2021, S. 33). Insofern zeigten sich unterschiedliche Haltungen innerhalb und zwischen den Gruppen. Als zentrale Gelingensbedingungen für die Verankerung von Kinderrechten in der Schule wurden „besonders engagierte Personen, eine Kultur der Offenheit und Partizipation sowie ein hohes Commitment gegenüber dem Projekt vonseiten aller Akteur*innen" (DKHW, 2021, S. 34) erkannt.

4. Methodik der Evaluation der UNICEF-Kinderrechteschulen

Die vorliegende Studie adressiert das Forschungsdesiderat, dass die UNICEF-Kinderrechteschulen aus Sicht der beteiligten Akteur*innen bislang noch nicht umfassend evaluiert wurden. Konkret werden, im Spiegel des Forschungsstandes, folgende Forschungsfragen zu beantworten versucht:

1. Wie wird das UNICEF-Kinderrechteschulenprogramm von den beteiligten Akteur*innen (Lehrkräfte, Schüler*innen und Eltern) hinsichtlich Akzeptanz und Unterstützung angenommen?
2. Wie schätzen sie die Umsetzung der Schutz-, Förder- und Beteiligungsrechte an der Schule ein?
3. Welche Chancen und Potenziale bietet die Einführung des UNICEF-Kinderrechteschulenprogramms für die Verbesserung der schulischen Praxis im Bereich der Kinderrechte?
4. Welche Herausforderungen und Probleme treten im Prozess der Einführung und Zertifizierung auf und wie können diese bewältigt werden?

Im Spiegel der Forschungsfragen wurde 2023 eine systematisierte Befragung durchgeführt. Das Sample umfasste 97 Personen (25 Lehrkräfte, 39 Schüler*innen der Jahrgänge drei und vier sowie 33 Eltern) einer seit drei Jahren zertifizierten Kinderrechtegrundschule in Niedersachsen. Für die Erhebung der Daten wurden insgesamt drei verschiedene Fragebögen für jeweils eine der drei Personengruppen eingesetzt: Die Fragebögen für das Schulpersonal und die Eltern wurden digital ausgegeben; die Schüler*innen der Klassenstufen drei und vier wurden im Klassenverband mit einem paper-and-pencil-Verfahren befragt. Im Vorfeld wurden jeweils datenschutzrechtliche Hinweise gegeben und die Zustimmungen (der Eltern) zur anonymisierten Befragung eingeholt.

Der Fragebogen setzt sich aus sechs Teilen zusammen (fünf quantitativen sowie einem qualitativen mit offenen Fragen; Abb. 2), die sich inhaltlich sowohl an der Struktur des siebenstufigen Kinderrechteschulentrainings von UNICEF als auch an dem Evaluationsbericht des DKHW (2021) orientieren. Alle Dimensionen wurden mit mehreren geschlossenen Items eingeleitet, die jeweils ein gemeinsames Merkmal messen. Auch die Antworten wurden geschlossen als – im Falle der Schüler*innen – vierstufige Likert-Skala gestaltet, um die bekannte Tendenz zur Mitte zu vermeiden, die sich insbesondere bei jüngeren Befragten zeigt (Porst, 2008). Diese Skala war zudem mit Piktogrammen zur visuellen Illustration unterlegt. Die Wahl einer fünfstufigen Skala für die erwachsenen Befragten beruht auf deren erhöhter Differenzierungsfähigkeit, die eine präzisere Erfassung von Meinungen und Einstellungen erlaubt. Als Ergänzung wurde den Befragten die Möglichkeit eingeräumt, eigene offene Antworten zu ergänzen, die allerdings nur die Lehrkräfte nutzten. Zur besseren Vergleichbarkeit waren die Fragebögen für alle Personengruppen ähnlich gestaltet und unterschieden sich hauptsächlich durch kindgerechte sprachliche Anpassungen.

Dimensionen	*Beispielitems (jeweils für Erwachsene und Kinder)*
Akzeptanz/ Engagement	*Erwachsene*: „Ich fühle mich über das Projekt Kinderrechteschulen gut informiert.“ *Kinder*: „Ich weiß, dass meine Schule eine Kinderrechteschule ist.“ *Erwachsene*: „Ich habe Zugriff auf Informationen und Materialien zum Thema Kinderrechte.“ *Kinder*: „Wir nutzen Material über Kinderrechte“.
Umsetzung Schutzrechte (Gewalt-prävention)	*Erwachsene*: „Die Kinder haben feste Ansprechpartner:innen, wenn sie Gewalterfahrungen machen.“ *Kinder*: „Wenn ich geärgert oder ausgeschlossen werde, weiß ich, bei wem ich mir Hilfe holen kann.“ *Erwachsene*: „Für die Bearbeitung von Konflikten stehen ausreichend Zeit und Unterstützung zur Verfügung.“ *Kinder*: „In meiner Klasse nehmen wir uns Zeit, um Probleme und Streit zu lösen.“
Umsetzung Förderrechte (Vielfalt/Nicht-diskriminierung)	*Erwachsene*: „Der Umgang miteinander ist an der Schule von gegenseitigem Respekt zwischen allen Beteiligten geprägt.“ *Kinder*: „Ich fühle mich in der Klasse ernst genommen.“ *Erwachsene*: „Jedes Kind hat gleiche Chancen, seine Potenziale voll zu entfalten.“ *Kinder*: „Im Unterricht wird kein Kind unfair behandelt.“
Umsetzung Partizipa-tionsrechte (Beteiligung)	*Erwachsene*: „Die Kinder kennen und nutzen die Beteiligungsmöglichkeiten an der Schule.“ *Kinder*: „Ich kann sagen, wenn mir etwas nicht gefällt.“ *Erwachsene*: „Die Interessen und Meinungen aller Kinder werden in die Unterrichtsgestaltung miteinbezogen.“ *Kinder*: „Ich kann mitbestimmen, wie wir im Unterricht arbeiten.“
Kinderrechte global	*Erwachsene*: „Die Inhalte der UN-Kinderrechtskonvention spielen im Unterricht eine Rolle.“ *Kinder*: „Im Unterricht sprechen wir über Kinderrechte.“ *Erwachsene*: „Die Kinder können das Wissen über Kinderrechte mit ihren eigenen lebensweltlichen Erfahrungen verknüpfen.“ *Kinder*: Ich kenne die UN-Kinderrechte.“

Abbildung 2: Quantitative Dimensionen der Fragebögen mit Beispielitems.

Die Daten wurden mithilfe der deskriptiven Statistik als Grundlage für die Darstellung und Auswertung analysiert. Aufgrund der trotz 97 Personen geringen Stichprobengröße wurde bei der Abschätzung möglicher unterschiedlicher Antwortmuster der Befragten auf eine inferenzstatistische Unterschiedlichkeitsabsicherung verzichtet; auch erfolgte bei den Skalen keine Indexbildung, da eine Analyse auf Itemniveau sinnvoller erscheint, um im Spiegel der Forschungsfragen zielgerichtet Aussagen treffen zu können. Zudem wurden jeweils die offenen Antworten in den Fragebögen nach Mayring und Fenzl (2019) mit Hilfe der Qualitativen Inhaltsanalyse ausgewertet, indem induktiv aus dem Material heraus im Sinne einer *zusammenfassenden Inhaltsanalyse* Kategorien gebildet wurden.

5. Ergebnisüberblick zur Befragung zu UNICEF-Kinderrechteschulen

5.1 Ergebnisüberblick

Insgesamt kristallisierten sich hinsichtlich der qualitativen Bestandteile des Fragebogens bei der Kategorienbildung zwei Hauptkategorien heraus, nämlich erstens die *Herausforderungen* mit den drei Unterkategorien *Zeitliche und finanzielle Ressourcenknappheit, Widerständigkeiten und Schwierigkeiten in der Elternarbeit* und *Erfordernis der integrierten Zusammenarbeit mit internen und externen Partner*innen* sowie zweitens die *Gelingensbedingungen*, wobei ein breites Feld unterschiedlichster Aktivitäten, anvisierter Zieldimensionen und Möglichkeiten der UNICEF-Kinderrechteschulen genannt wurde.

Nachfolgend werden zunächst im Sinne einer deskriptiven Überblicksdarstellung auf Basis der quantitativen Fragebogenanteile die Chancen und Herausforderungen bei der Umsetzung und Implementierung der Kinderrechte an der Schule aus Sicht der jeweils befragten Gruppen dargestellt. Hierbei kann jeweils nur eine Auswahl an Ergebnissen präsentiert werden, die anhand der Akzeptanz der Kinderrechteschule, der Einschätzungen zur schulischen Umsetzung der Schutz-, Förder- und Partizipationsrechte sowie einer allgemeinen bzw. globalen Bewertung der Kinderrechtssituation an der Schule strukturiert wurden. Es wurden hierbei jeweils insbesondere diejenigen Items genauer betrachtet, die allen Gruppen, wenn auch teilweise in sprachlich modifizierter Weise, gestellt werden konnten – einige der Items wie etwa zu finanziellen Ressourcen für die Umsetzung konnten nur an die Lehrkräfte gestellt werden – und/oder die sich als besonders implikationsreich für die Einführung der UNICEF-Kinderrechteschule erwiesen, da sie etwa einen Änderungsbedarf nahelegen.

Tabelle 1: Zustimmungen zu ausgewählten Dimensionen in Prozenten (‚trifft voll zu' und ‚trifft zu' bzw. ‚stimmt' und ‚stimmt teilweise'; in Klammern jeweils Prozentsatz höchster Zustimmung).[1]

Akzeptanz, Engagement und Wissen	**Lehrkräfte**	**Schüler*innen**	**Eltern**
Zustimmung zum Projekt UNICEF-Kinderrechteschule	100 (84)	98 (85)	85 (61)
Zugang zu/Nutzung von Material zum Thema Kinderrechte	92 (52)	67 (26)	33 (15)
Gutes Wissen um die Kinderrechte	92 (48)	64 (36)	45 (24)
Hoher Informationsstand zur UNICEF-Kinderrechteschule	80 (52)	/	42 (21)
Aktives Engagement für die UNICEF-Kinderrechteschule	44 (16)	/	21 (12)
Umsetzung Schutzrechte (Gewaltprävention)	**Lehrkräfte**	**Schüler*innen**	**Eltern**
Aktives Vorgehen gegen Mobbing, (sexualisierte) Gewalt	100 (84)	90 (64)	94 (76)
Verfahrensanweisungen und Hilfestellungen bei Gewalt	96 (72)	/	/
Feste Ansprechpartner*innen bei Gewalterfahrungen	92 (68)	98 (80)	85 (55)
Kommunikationstechniken als Gewaltprävention	84 (64)	/	15 (7)
Regelmäßige Schulungsprogramme für Lehrkräfte	52 (24)	/	12 (5)
Ausreichend Zeit/Unterstützung für Konfliktbearbeitung	24 (8)	36 (15)	24 (12)
Umsetzung Förderrechte (Vielfalt/Nichtdiskriminierung)	**Lehrkräfte**	**Schüler*innen**	**Eltern**
Kostenlose Leihe von Material und Lernmitteln	100 (48)	/	94 (55)
Feste Ansprechpartner*innen bei Diskriminierungen	92 (68)	98 (80)	85 (55)
Schulisches Engagement gegen Ungleichheit	84 (52)	/	75 (39)
Gegenseitiger Respekt in der Schule/Wohlfühlen	84 (32)	93 (72)	45 (18)
Chancengleichheit für alle Kinder	64 (28)	54 (23)	24 (9)
Umsetzung Partizipationsrechte (Beteiligung)	**Lehrkräfte**	**Schüler*innen**	**Eltern**
Kenntnis und Nutzung von kindlicher Beteiligung	96 (56)	/	54 (24)
Freie kindliche Meinungs- und Bedürfnisäußerung	88 (64)	89 (56)	36 (18)
Transparente Klassen- und Schülersprecher*innenwahlen	88 (60)	83 (44)	/
Entscheidungsbeteiligung für alle Gruppen	48 (28)	/	21 (12)
Einbezug der Interessen, Meinungen in den Unterricht	48 (20)	46 (18)	27 (15)
Kenntnis und Nutzung von Elternbeteiligung	44 (16)	/	39 (18)
Kinderrechte global	**Lehrkräfte**	**Schüler*innen**	**Eltern**
UN-Kinderrechte/UN-Kinderrechtskonvention als Unterrichtsthema	92 (76)	56 (31)	51 (18)
Verankerung von Kinderrechten im Schulleitbild	88 (72)	/	67 (52)
Sichtbarkeit der Kinderrechte als Fokus der Schule	80 (28)	/	66 (27)
Lebensweltliche Verknüpfung der Kinderrechte	60 (40)	/	45 (18)
Regionale Anerkennung der Schule für ihre Bemühungen	52 (24)	/	30 (12)

1 In Tabelle 1 werden ausschließlich die Zustimmungswerte („trifft voll zu" und „trifft zu" bzw. „stimmt" und „stimmt teilweise") dargestellt, um den Fokus auf die positiven Einschätzungen der Befragten zu legen. Dies ermöglicht eine kompaktere Darstellung der Ergebnisse sowie einen besseren Vergleich zwischen den verschiedenen Akteursgruppen. Die übrigen Antwortkategorien wurden zwar in der weiteren Analyse durchaus berücksichtigt, aber aus Gründen der Übersichtlichkeit nicht in der Tabelle aufgeführt.

Die hier überblickshaft dargestellten Ergebnisse werden nachfolgend deskriptiv erörtert und um offene Antworten, die seitens der Lehrkräfte gegeben wurden, ergänzt.

5.2 Detaillierter Ergebnisüberblick

Ad Forschungsfrage 1 (Akzeptanz und Unterstützung)
Das UNICEF-Kinderrechteschulenprogramm wird von allen Akteur*innen ideell unterstützt, wobei bis zu 100 Prozent der Befragten die Zertifizierung positiv bewerten. Über ein Drittel der Befragten erlebt die Kinderrechte als intern und extern sichtbar, sei es im Schulalltag oder im Unterricht. Dennoch zeigt sich eine deutliche Diskrepanz zwischen Akzeptanz und aktivem Engagement: Während die Einführung des Programms auf breite Zustimmung stößt, engagieren sich (nur) 44 Prozent der Lehrkräfte und 21 Prozent der Eltern aktiv. Als Gründe werden fehlende zeitliche und materielle Ressourcen genannt. Partizipation oder Engagement müsste auch durch die „Bereitstellung von unterstützenden Ressourcen“ (Lehrkraft 2) gewährleistet werden, etwa „in Form von Schulungen, Materialien oder Zeit“ (Lehrkraft 18).

Ad Forschungsfrage 2 (Umsetzung der Schutz-, Förder- und Beteiligungsrechte)
Die Schutzrechte, insbesondere der Schutz vor Gewalt und Diskriminierung, sind fest in der Schule und im Unterricht verankert, etwa durch gut kommunizierte Verfahrensanweisungen sowie feste Ansprechpartner*innen, wie auch die Evaluierung der Kinderrechteschulen des DKHW (2021) zeigt. Allerdings bestehen deutliche Unterschiede zwischen Lehrkräften, Schüler*innen und Eltern; so bewerten etwa Eltern die Wirksamkeit bestimmter Schulpraktiken, wie die Beteiligung von Kindern und das Schulklima, kritischer als das Schulpersonal. Diese Unterschiede verdeutlichen die Notwendigkeit einer offenen Dialogkultur, um die Schüler*innenbeteiligung und die Kooperation zwischen Schule und Elternhaus zu stärken.

Ad Forschungsfrage 3 (Chancen und Potenziale der Einführung)
Die Einführung des UNICEF-Kinderrechteschulenprogramms bietet bedeutende Chancen und Potenziale für die Verbesserung der schulischen Praxis im Bereich der Kinderrechte. Strukturell wurden aus Sicht der Akteur*innen erfolgreiche Beteiligungsmöglichkeiten implementiert, wie transparente Klassen- und Schülersprecher*innenwahlen sowie die Möglichkeit, im Unterricht frei Meinungen zu äußern und interessengeleitete Schwerpunkte zu setzen. Eine Lehrkraft betont: „Durch die praktische Erfahrung von Mitbestimmung lernen die Kinder früh die Grundprinzipien der Demokratie kennen“ (Lehrkraft 22); Schüler*innen könnten „demokratisch bei der Wahl der Ganztagsangebote […] wählen und [müssten lernen] auch mit ungünstigen Ergebnissen zu leben“ (Lehrkraft 6). Diese partizipativen Strukturen fördern nicht nur das demokratische Bewusstsein der Schüler*innen, sondern stärken auch ihre Selbstwirksamkeit und Verantwortungsübernahme. Zudem trägt das verbesserte Schulklima, das durch gegenseitigen Respekt und hochwertige Beziehungen zwischen Schüler*innen und Lehrkräften gekennzeichnet ist, wesentlich zur positiven Entwick-

lung der Kinderrechte bei. Dieses Schulklima wurde insbesondere von den Schüler*innen als sehr hoch eingeschätzt und von 85 Prozent der Lehrkräfte sowie etwa der Hälfte der Eltern bestätigt. Die Förderung eines respektvollen und unterstützenden Umfelds schafft somit optimale Bedingungen für die Umsetzung und Weiterentwicklung der Kinderrechte in der schulischen Praxis.

Ad Forschungsfrage 4 (Herausforderungen und Probleme der Einführung)
Die inhaltliche Verankerung der Partizipations- und Förderrechte ist im Gegensatz zu den Schutzrechten noch nicht umfassend in Schule und Unterricht umgesetzt, was auch eine zentrale Herausforderung der UN-KRK darstellt. Während Schutzrechte oft nach dem Verursacherprinzip durchsetzbar sind, sind Förder- und Beteiligungsrechte schwerer zu konkretisieren (UNICEF, 2022a; Bär, 2022). Ein Großteil der Eltern schätzt das Chancenpotenzial und die Mitbestimmungsmöglichkeiten der Schüler*innen zurückhaltender ein als Lehrkräfte und Schüler*innen selbst. Besonders die Kommunikation mit den Eltern sowie die enge Zusammenarbeit mit Schulsozialarbeiter*innen werden als zentrale, jedoch herausfordernde Aspekte wahrgenommen: „Die Kommunikation mit den Eltern spielt hier eine zentrale Rolle" (Lehrkraft 23) und „die Einbeziehung der Eltern in den Prozess der Konfliktbearbeitung kann herausfordernd sein" (Lehrkraft 25). Zudem zeigen offene Antworten der Lehrkräfte mehrfach Widerstände seitens der Eltern, was die Einbindung in den Beteiligungsprozess erschwert (Lehrkraft 14). Trotz einer hohen Sichtbarkeit des Kinderrechtefokus innerhalb der Schule fehlt es zudem an ausreichender Aufmerksamkeit und Unterstützung durch den umliegenden Sozialraum, insbesondere die Kommunalpolitik. Die Ergebnisse verdeutlichen die Notwendigkeit einer stärkeren Einbindung der Kommunen, um eine gesunde und sichere Entwicklung der Schüler*innen zu fördern (UNICEF, 2022a; Bär, 2022).

6. Diskussion und Ausblick

Zu konkludieren gilt, dass das UNICEF-Kinderrechteschulenprogramm ein vielversprechendes Instrument zur Förderung von Kinderrechten in Schulen darstellt. Dass Kinderrechte bedeutsam sind, steht außer Frage. Die mangelnde schulische Umsetzung wird etwa schon vom BMFSFJ (2020) im 16. Kinder- und Jugendbericht moniert; insbesondere die zu gering ausgeprägten Partizipationsmöglichkeiten für Kinder an schulischen Angelegenheiten. Durch die gezielte Überwindung der in der Befragung identifizierten individuellen und strukturellen Herausforderungen und Probleme sowie die ferner aufgezeigten Chancen und Potenziale kann das Programm allerdings weiter optimiert und dadurch erfolgreich wie nachhaltig in das deutsche Schulsystem integriert werden.

Ein besonderer Schwerpunkt liegt diesbezüglich auf der Rolle des ‚Educational Leadership', da dem Führungshandeln gerade von Schulleitungen eine entscheidende Bedeutung für die erfolgreiche Umsetzung der Kinderrechte sowie des UNICEF-Kinderrechteschulenprogramms in Schulen zukommt. Educational Leadership umfasst die „Qualität und Kompetenz, einen führenden Einfluss auf die Mitglieder der Bildungseinrichtung auszuüben [...] zur Erreichung von Bildungsvisionen und -zielen" (Yan & Han, 2018, o. S.). Um das Ziel der umfassenden Etablierung von Kinderrechten – etwa durch die Einführung von UNICEF-Kinderrechteschulen – voranzubringen, müssen allerdings nicht nur die Schulleitungen und Lehrkräfte an den Einzelschulen weitere Verantwortung übernehmen. Hier wären auch die Ständige Konferenz der Kultusminister der Länder (KMK) sowie die Schul- und Kultusministerien der Bundesländer mit ihren Unterabteilungen und Referaten gefordert, noch stärker prägend und fördernd (sowie fordernd) zugunsten der Einführung von UNICEF-Kinderrechteschulen aufzutreten und gegenüber Schulen dezidiert Einfluss auszuüben, um Kinderrechte umfänglich an Schulen zu gewährleisten und Kinder über ihre Rechte aufzuklären. Die Ministerien könnten etwa die Einführung der UNICEF-Kinderrechteschulen in Erlassen nahelegen oder aber finanziell oder ideell (noch) stärker unterstützen.

Es darf allerdings nicht dabei bleiben, nur Mängel festzustellen und an die Schulen zu appellieren, mehr für Kinderrechte zu tun. In Erklärungen oder Erlassen zu Kinderrechten wird oft sehr abstrakt beschrieben, welche Schritte die Einzelschulen unternehmen könnten oder sollten, um die Stärkung von Kinderrechten zu intensivieren. Dieses Defizit muss adressiert werden. Zudem zeigt die Befragung deutlich, dass es auf Landes- und Kommunalebene der Bereitstellung von materiellen, zeitlichen und finanziellen Ressourcen in Schulen und Kommunen als Schulträger bedarf. Damit eine erfolgreiche Umsetzung und Thematisierung von Kinderrechten an Schulen sowie die Implementierung von UNICEF-Kinderrechteschulen gelingt, müssen Verantwortliche auf schulischer Mikroebene (Schulleitungen, Lehrkräfte und Schüler*innen) und auf bildungspolitischer Makroebene (KMK, Schul- und Kultusministerien) aktiv Verantwortung übernehmen.

Allerdings gilt es auch auf die Limitationen der dem Beitrag zugrunde liegenden Befragung hinzuweisen: Eine Limitation ergibt sich aus dem vornehmlich quantitativen Vorgehen der Studie und der Tatsache, dass die Eltern und Schüler*innen auch bei den offenen Antwortmöglichkeiten im Fragebogen diese Option – anders als die Lehrkräfte – nicht ausschöpften. Durch das quantitative Vorgehen besteht somit möglicherweise die Problematik, dass weitere Chancen und Potenziale, aber auch Risiken und Konfliktlinien, die nicht vorab theoriegeleitet und deduktiv durch die Forschenden anvisiert wurden, nicht erfasst wurden. Dieser Problematik kann nur durch eine zusätzliche qualitative Vertiefung mit Hilfe problemzentrierter Interviews entgegengewirkt werden. Aus der Limitation leitet sich folgerichtig ein Forschungsdesiderat ab, das von den Autor*innen durch qualitativ vertiefende Befragungen von Schulleitungen, Lehrkräften und Schüler*innen an drei weiteren UNICEF-Kinderrechteschulen gegenwärtig geschlossen wird. Limitierend wirkt in Bezug auf die Aussagekraft der Ergebnisse zudem die geringe Stichprobengröße von nur 97 Personen, die zudem an nur einer Schule gewonnen wurden; herausgearbeitete Chancen, Potenziale sowie Risiken und Konflikte könnten somit Spezifika der befragten Schule darstellen und möglicherweise nicht generalisierbar auf andere UNICEF-Kinderrechteschulen übertragen werden. Hierzu müsste die Befragung sowohl quantitativ als auch qualitativ auf weitere

Schulen ausgeweitet werden, etwa im Sinne einer durch die Kultusministerien veranlassten umfänglichen Evaluierung der Einführung des Programms.

Literatur

Autor:innengruppe Bildungsberichterstattung. (Hrsg.). (2024). *Bildung in Deutschland 2024. Ein indikatorengestützter Bericht mit einer Analyse zu beruflicher Bildung*. wbv. https://www.bildungsbericht.de/de/bildungsberichte-seit-2006/bildungsbericht-2024/pdf-dateien-2024/bildungsbericht-2024.pdf.

Bär, D. (2022). Die Bedeutung der UN-Kinderrechtskonvention für Städte und Gemeinden. In Deutsches Komitee für UNICEF (Hrsg.), *30 Jahre UN-Kinderrechtskonvention. Eine Bilanz* (S. 29–35). Deutsches Komitee für UNICEF.

Bauer, U., Bittlingmayer, U. H., & Scherr, A. (Hrsg.). (2023). *Handbuch Bildungs- und Erziehungssoziologie. Bildung und Gesellschaft*. Springer VS. https://doi.org/10.1007/978-3-658-30903-9_66

Bundesministerium für Familie, Senioren, Frauen und Jugend. (BMFSFJ). (Hrsg.). (2020). *16. Kinder- und Jugendbericht. Förderung demokratischer Bildung im Kindes- und Jugendalter*. BMFSFJ. https://www.bmfsfj.de/resource/blob/162232/27ac76c3f5ca10b0e914700ee54060b2/16-kinder-und-jugendbericht-bundestagsdrucksache-data.pdf.

Deutsches Kinderhilfswerk e.V. (DKHW). (2021). *Evaluationsbericht Gelingensbedingungen einer nachhaltigen Verankerung von Kinderrechten in der Grundschule*. https://www.kinderrechte.de/fileadmin/Redaktion-Kinderrechte/2_Kinderrechtebildung/2.3_Kinderrechteschulen/2.3.1_Materialien/DESI_Evaluationsbericht_2021-09-17.pdf.

Krappmann, L., & Petry, C. (Hrsg.). (2016). *Worauf Kinder und Jugendliche ein Recht haben. Kinderrechte, Demokratie und Schule: Ein Manifest*. Debus Pädagogik.

Kultusministerkonferenz. (KMK). (2006). *Erklärung der Kultusministerkonferenz vom 03.03.2006 zur Umsetzung des Übereinkommens der Vereinten Nationen über die Rechte des Kindes*. https://www.kmk.org/fileadmin/veroeffentlichungen_beschluesse/2006/2006_03_03-UN-Kinderrechte_.pdf.

Mayring, P., & Fenzl, T. (2019). Qualitative Inhaltsanalyse. In N. Baur & J. Blasius (Hrsg.), *Handbuch Methoden der empirischen Sozialforschung* (2. Aufl., S. 633–648). Springer VS.

Möbus, B., & Stein, M. (2024). Kinderrechtbasierte Schulen als Realutopie. Entwicklungen und Herausforderungen bei der Implementierung des UNICEF-Kinderrechteschulen-Programms. In K. Sen, M. Staats, D. Wassermann, B. Friele, M. Kart, H. Knothe, J. Rieger & B. Schomers (Hrsg.), *Utopien Sozialer Arbeit* (S. 122–135). Beltz Juventa.

Niedersächsisches Kultusministerium. (2023). *Wo Kinderrechte sichtbar und fühlbar werden*. https://www.mk.niedersachsen.de/startseite/aktuelles/wo-kinderrechte-sichtbar-und-fuhlbar-werden-226074.html.

Porst, R. (2008). *Fragebogen. Ein Arbeitsbuch*. Springer VS.

Prengel, A. (2019). *Pädagogische Beziehungen zwischen Anerkennung, Verletzung und Ambivalenz* (2. überarb. und erw. Aufl.) Barbara Budrich.

Sachverständigenrat deutscher Stiftungen für Integration und Migration. (SVR). (2016). *Doppelt benachteiligt? Kinder und Jugendliche mit Migrationshintergrund im deutschen Bildungssystem*. Expertise I. SVR. https://www.svr-migration.de/wp-content/uploads/2023/01/SVR-FB_Doppelt_benachteiligt-8.pdf.

United Nations. (UN). (2016). *Toward a world free from violence – global survey on violence against children*. United Nations.
United Nations Children's Fund. (UNICEF). (2022a). *30 Jahre UN-Kinderrechtskonvention in Deutschland. Eine Bilanz.* Deutsches Komitee für UNICEF e.V. https://www.unicef.de/_cae/resource/blob/265970/dcde4969d59d8ef954a9e7e77149d540/download-30-jahre-kinderrechtskonvention-data.pdf.
United Nations Children's Fund. (UNICEF). (2022b). *Schulen leben Kinderrechte.* https://www.unicef.de/informieren/schulen/kinderrechteschulen.
United Nations Children's Fund. (UNICEF). (2022c). *Kinderrechteschulen Programm. Wir leben Kinderrechte.* https://www.unicef.de/_cae/resource/blob/239484/461947873a1db8583b43f3b590f91333/broschuere-kinderrechteschulen-programm-data.pdf.
United Nations Children's Fund. (UNICEF). (2023a). *Wo wir arbeiten.* https://www.unicef.org/where-we-work.
United Nations Children's Fund. (UNICEF). (2023b). *Ihr Weg zur Kinderrechteschule. Teilnahmevoraussetzungen.* https://www.unicef.de/_cae/resource/blob/235800/7fe9a47c737a43ec629cdf1ac6407610/pdf-teilnahmevoraussetzungen-data.pdf.
Winklhofer, U., & Prengel, A. (2018). Ethische Leitlinien für pädagogische Beziehungen. *Diskurs Kindheits- und Jugendforschung, 13*(1), 103–108.
Yan, W., & Han, Y. (2018). Educational Leadership. In A. Farazmand (Hrsg.), *Global Encyclopedia of Public Administration, Public Policy, and Governance* (S. 1581–1586). Springer.

Further Contributions in the Volume

For a case study on the realization of children's rights in educational practice, read the focus article by *Linn Behrendt*, that illustrates the concept of 'nursery democracy' for early childhood education as an answer to Art. 12 UN CRC (pp. 131–138).

Another article, that focuses on schools, is authored by *Mirjam Maier-Röseler, Enkeleta Shtërbani*, and *Gabriele Weigand*. They explore the implications of Article 29 Para. 1 of the UN CRC concerning children's rights to develop talents through school education (pp. 103–114).

Julia Hugo, Charlotte Assmann, Andreas Schmidt (Eds.)
Educational Leadership and Children's Rights?/
Kinderrechte als Führungsaufgabe?
 https://doi.org/10.31244/9783830998259_10

Linn Behrendt

Normative Forderungen des Art. 12 UN-KRK an pädagogische Institutionen und deren Leitungsakteure

Zusammenfassung
Art. 12 UN-KRK sichert Kindern das Recht auf Berücksichtigung des Kindeswillens zu. Kinder haben demnach das Recht, ihre Meinung in allen sie betreffenden Angelegenheiten frei zu äußern. Der Beitrag erörtert den konkreten Aussagegehalt dieses Kinderrechts, überführt ihn in ein normatives Leitbild für die pädagogisch-institutionelle Praxis frühkindlicher Bildung und konkretisiert dieses anhand des Konzepts ‚Die Kinderstube der Demokratie'. Es wird herausgearbeitet, dass pädagogische Fachkräfte eine partizipative Haltung einnehmen müssen. Darüber hinaus müssen geeignete Selbst- und Mitbestimmungsmöglichkeiten für Kinder geschaffen und strukturell verankert werden. Eine besondere Rolle bei der Etablierung einer kinderrechtsorientierten Arbeit können Leitungsakteure in pädagogischen Institutionen spielen, indem sie eine kinderrechtsorientierte Haltung im pädagogischen Team und nach außen vertreten.

Schlüsselbegriffe
Art. 12 UN-KRK, Kinderrechte, Partizipation, frühkindliche Bildung

Normative Demands of Art. 12 UN CRC on Educational Institutions and their Leaders

Abstract
Art. 12 of the UN CRC guarantees children the right to have their voices heard. Accordingly, children have the right to express their opinion freely in all matters concerning them. The article discusses the concrete content of this children's right, translates it into a normative model for the pedagogical-institutional practice of early childhood education and concretises this using the concept of 'Die Kinderstube der Demokratie' (engl.: 'The nursery of democracy'). It is emphasised that educational professionals must adopt a participatory attitude. In addition, suitable opportunities for children to participate and co-determine must be created and structurally anchored. Managers in educational institutions can play a special role in establishing child rights orientated work by representing a child rights orientated attitude within the educational team and externally.

Keywords
Art. 12 UN CRC, Children's Rights, Participation, Early Childhood Education

1. Einleitung

Das Übereinkommen über die Rechte des Kindes (UN-Kinderrechtskonvention, UN-KRK) sichert Kindern in Art. 12 UN-KRK das Recht auf Berücksichtigung des Kindeswillens zu. In diesem Beitrag wird der Begriff ‚Kind' im Sinne der UN-KRK verstanden. Demnach ist ein Kind jeder Mensch, der das achtzehnte Lebensjahr noch nicht vollendet hat, soweit die Volljährigkeit nach dem anzuwendenden Recht nicht früher eintritt.

> „Die Vertragsstaaten sichern dem Kind, das fähig ist, sich eine eigene Meinung zu bilden, das Recht zu, diese Meinung in allen das Kind berührenden Angelegenheiten frei zu äußern, und berücksichtigen die Meinung des Kindes angemessen und entsprechend seinem Alter und seiner Reife." (Art. 12 Abs. 1 UN-KRK)

Die UN-KRK ist ein völkerrechtlicher Vertrag und hat in Deutschland den Rang eines Bundesgesetzes (Art. 59 Abs. 2 GG). Mit der Ratifizierung der UN-KRK haben sich die Vertragsstaaten (Deutschland am 5. April 1992) verpflichtet, dieses Recht auf nationaler Ebene entsprechend umzusetzen. Pädagogische Institutionen sind somit aufgefordert, Kinder als Träger von Rechten anzuerkennen und ihre Arbeit an Kinderrechten auszurichten (Maywald, 2023).

Mit Blick auf die pädagogische Praxis stellen sich vor diesem Hintergrund für pädagogische Institutionen und ihre Leitungsakteure die Fragen, welche konkreten Forderungen sich aus Art. 12 Abs. 1 UN-KRK ableiten lassen und welche Umsetzungen das Recht in der pädagogisch-institutionellen Praxis verlangt. Diesen Fragen soll im Folgenden nachgegangen werden. Ausgehend von einer erläuternden Auseinandersetzung mit Art. 12 Abs. 1 UN-KRK (*Kapitel 2*) soll ein normatives Leitbild für den Umgang mit diesem Recht im pädagogisch-institutionellen Setting abgeleitet werden (*Kapitel 3*). Anschließend wird das Konzept ‚Die Kinderstube der Demokratie' als Praxisbeispiel vorgestellt, das den Implikationen des Art. 12 Abs. 1 UN-KRK Rechnung trägt (*Kapitel 4*). Abschließend wird ein Resümee gezogen (*Kapitel 5*). Aufgrund der Fokussierung auf die Entwicklung eines normativen Leitbildes für die pädagogisch-institutionelle Praxis wird nur auf den ersten Absatz von Art. 12 UN-KRK eingegangen. Der zweite Absatz des Artikels bezieht sich auf Kinder betreffende Gerichts- und Verwaltungsverfahren, was für diesen Beitrag nicht relevant erscheint.

2. Art. 12 Abs. 1 UN-KRK – Berücksichtigung des Kindeswillens

Art. 12 Abs. 1 UN-KRK, das Recht auf Berücksichtigung des Kindeswillens, gehört zu den vier allgemeinen Grundprinzipien, die der UN-Ausschuss für die Rechte des Kindes aufgestellt hat und auf denen die UN-KRK basiert.

> „Kinder und Jugendliche sollen die Möglichkeit erhalten, gehört zu werden. Sie dürfen ihre Anliegen und Beschwerden äußern. Bei staatlichen Entscheidungen, die das Kind oder den Jugendlichen betreffen, sind sie zu beteiligen, ihre Meinung muss dem Alter und der Reife entsprechend berücksichtigt werden." (BMFSFJ, 2018)

Entsprechend handelt es sich bei Art. 12 Abs. 1 UN-KRK um ein Beteiligungsrecht. Diese Einordnung verdeutlicht, dass es sich bei diesem Kinderrecht nicht nur um eine singuläre subjektive Rechtsposition handelt. Vielmehr kommt der darin verankerten Beteiligungsdimension eine besondere Bedeutung für die Umsetzung weiterer Rechte der UN-KRK zu (Deutsches Institut für Menschenrechte, 2019). Art. 12 Abs. 1 UN-KRK umfasst dabei mehrere Dimensionen:

Fähigkeit zur Meinungsbildung: Art. 12 Abs. 1 UN-KRK sichert „dem Kind, das fähig ist, sich eine eigene Meinung zu bilden", das Recht zu, diese Meinung frei zu äußern. Die Fähigkeit, sich eine eigene Meinung zu bilden, ist nicht an einen bestimmten Entwicklungsstand oder ein bestimmtes Alter gebunden. Verschiedene Faktoren tragen dazu bei, dass sich ein Kind eine eigene Meinung bilden kann (z. B. Informationen und Erfahrungen) (Cremer, 2012). Die allgemeine Bemerkung des UN-Ausschusses zu Art. 12 UN-KRK fordert an dieser Stelle, „die Fähigkeit eines Kindes, sich eine unabhängige Meinung zu bilden, so hoch, wie möglich einzuschätzen" (Deutsches Institut für Menschenrechte, 2019, S. 8).

Kinder betreffende Angelegenheiten: Kinder, die sich eine eigene Meinung bilden können, haben das Recht, diese Meinung „in allen das Kind berührenden Angelegenheiten" (Art. 12 Abs. 1 UN-KRK) frei zu äußern. Sobald eine Angelegenheit das Kind betrifft, hat es also das Recht, gehört und beteiligt zu werden. Der UN-Ausschuss zu Art. 12 UN-KRK betont an dieser Stelle die Bedeutung einer „weiten Auslegung" (Deutsches Institut für Menschenrechte, 2019, S. 10).

Berücksichtigung der Meinung des Kindes: „Die Vertragsstaaten [...] berücksichtigen die Meinung des Kindes angemessen und entsprechend seinem Alter und seiner Reife" (Art. 12 Abs. 1 UN-KRK). Das biologische *Alter* allein kann also nicht darüber entscheiden, welches Gewicht der Meinung des Kindes zukommt. Entscheidend ist auch die *Reife* im Sinne der Fähigkeit, bestimmte Umstände einer Angelegenheit verstehen und beurteilen zu können (Deutsches Institut für Menschenrechte, 2019).

3. Normatives Leitbild des Art. 12 Abs. 1 UN-KRK für pädagogisch-institutionelle Settings

Die in Kapitel 2 formulierten Anforderungen aus Art. 12 Abs. 1 UN-KRK lassen sich in ein normatives Leitbild für pädagogisch-institutionelle Settings überführen: Übergeordnet ist eine *partizipative Grundhaltung* der pädagogischen Fachkräfte und der Leitungsakteure pädagogischer Institutionen erforderlich (Schubert-Suffrian & Regner,

2018). Nach Schröder[1] (1995) bedeutet Partizipation, „Entscheidungen, die das eigene Leben und das Leben der Gemeinschaft betreffen, zu teilen und gemeinsam Lösungen für Probleme zu finden" (S. 14). Partizipation umfasst also drei Bereiche: Selbstbestimmung, Mitbestimmung und Problemlösung. Die pädagogischen Fachkräfte, zu denen auch die Leitungsakteure einer Institution gehören, müssen eine Haltung entwickeln, die diese drei Bereiche der Partizipation anerkennt und fördert. Bei der Etablierung einer solchen Haltung in der Institution kommt den Leitungsakteuren eine besondere Rolle zu. Sie müssen den Kinderrechten und einer kinderrechtsorientierten Pädagogik allgemein positiv gegenüberstehen, damit sich partizipative Strukturen etablieren können (Schäfer, 2023).

Neben der Grundhaltung bedarf es *geeigneter Partizipationsmöglichkeiten* für Kinder in pädagogischen Institutionen. Nach dem Verständnis von Schröder (1995) sind dabei entsprechend Selbstbestimmungs-, Mitbestimmungs- und Problemlösungsmöglichkeiten für Kinder zu berücksichtigen. Jede Institution kann eigene Konzepte entwickeln, die diese drei Partizipationsbereiche abdecken und zu den Rahmenbedingungen und den Kindern der Institution passen. Schäfer (2023) empfiehlt dabei, die Größe der Einrichtung, das Alter und die Vorerfahrungen der Kinder zu berücksichtigen. Darüber hinaus sollten unterschiedliche Beteiligungsformen (z. B. formal-repräsentativ, offen-basisdemokratisch, projektbezogen, problemlösend-partizipativ) geschaffen werden. Kinder benötigen zudem die Möglichkeit zur Beschwerde. Sie müssen sich an interne oder externe Vertrauenspersonen wenden können, wenn sie sich unwohl, missachtet, unverstanden oder falsch behandelt fühlen (Wolff, 2022).

„Die Freiheit des jungen Menschen ergibt sich nicht von selbst; sie muss gewollt, beschlossen und gestaltet werden" (Kupffer, 1980, S. 19). Damit Kinder ihre Beteiligungsrechte in der pädagogisch-institutionellen Praxis verbindlich zugestanden werden, müssen die Selbst- und Mitbestimmungsrechte von Kindern sowie Beschwerdeverfahren schließlich *strukturell verankert* werden, z. B. in der pädagogischen Konzeption (Hansen & Knauer, 2016b). Pädagogische Fachkräfte tragen dabei die Verantwortung, Kindern ihre Rechte aktiv zukommen zu lassen (Maywald, 2016). Je jünger die Kinder sind, desto schwieriger ist es für sie, ihre Beteiligungsrechte selbst einzufordern (Hildebrandt & Pergande, 2022). Das folgend vorgestellte Praxisbeispiel ‚Die Kinderstube der Demokratie' trägt diesem Umstand Rechnung.

4. Praxisbeispiel ‚Die Kinderstube der Demokratie'

‚Die Kinderstube der Demokratie' ist ein Beispiel für die praktische Umsetzung von Art. 12 Abs. 1 UN-KRK in der institutionellen frühkindlichen Bildung. Das Konzept wurde ab 2001 von Rüdiger Hansen, Raingard Knauer und Bianca Friedrich entwickelt (MJFJF, 2004) und zunächst als Modellversuch in einzelnen Kindertageseinrichtungen erprobt. Anschließend wurde ‚Die Kinderstube der Demokratie' theoretisch,

1 Es wird sich an dem Verständnis von Schröder (1995) orientiert, da es sich in den Bildungsleitlinien für Kindertageseinrichtungen des Landes Schleswig-Holstein (MSGJFS, 2020) wiederfindet, in dem auch das folgende Praxiskonzept entwickelt wurde.

didaktisch und methodisch weiterentwickelt, sodass inzwischen bundesweit verschiedene Träger mit dem Konzept arbeiten (Sturzenhecker, Richter & Lehmann, 2016).

'Die Kinderstube der Demokratie' sieht zunächst vor, dass sich die pädagogischen Fachkräfte darüber verständigen, welche Selbst- und Mitbestimmungsrechte sie den Kindern im institutionellen Alltag einräumen wollen und können (Hansen, Knauer & Sturzenhecker, 2009). Die Zusammensetzung des pädagogischen Teams variiert je nach Bundesland und Träger der Einrichtung. In der Regel besteht es aus einer Einrichtungsleitung, einer Stellvertretung, Gruppenleitungen und Gruppenkräften mit jeweils unterschiedlichen pädagogischen Qualifikationen (Autorengruppe Fachkräftebarometer, 2023). Die pädagogischen Fachkräfte legen die Inhalte und Grenzen der Beteiligung fest. Dabei können alle Entscheidungen, die in der Kindertageseinrichtung anstehen, diskutiert werden, vom Speiseplan und der Vereinbarung von Essensregeln bis hin zu Finanz- und Personalangelegenheiten (Hansen & Knauer, 2015).

Haben sich die pädagogischen Fachkräfte darüber verständigt, welche Beteiligungsrechte sie den Kindern in der Institution einräumen wollen, muss festgelegt werden, wie die Kinder ihre Rechte wahrnehmen können. Dazu werden Beteiligungsstrukturen und -gremien eingeführt (Hansen & Knauer, 2015). Dies können z. B. Kinderräte und Kita-Konferenzen sein, in die jede Kita- oder Stammgruppe demokratisch gewählte Kinder entsendet. Darüber hinaus sollte es ein Gremium geben, an dem grundsätzlich alle Kinder teilnehmen können. In der Regel sind dies Stamm- oder Gruppenversammlungen oder offene Kinderkonferenzen (Sturzenhecker et al., 2016). Zur strukturellen Verankerung der Beteiligungsrechte und -gremien sieht 'Die Kinderstube der Demokratie' die Erarbeitung einer *Kita-Verfassung* vor. Ein Auszug aus einer solchen Verfassung dient als Beispiel:

> „§ 10 Mahlzeiten
>
> (1) Jedes Kind hat das Recht, selbst zu entscheiden, ob, was und wie viel es isst und trinkt, sofern keine medizinische Indikation und keine familiäre religiös oder ethisch begründete Einschränkung vorliegen und für alle Kinder genug da ist. Dieses Recht umfasst auch das Recht des Kindes selbst zu bestimmen, ob und was es probieren möchte.
>
> (2) Die Kinder haben das Recht, unter Einbeziehung der Hauswirtschaftskräfte über die Auswahl und die Gestaltung des Mittagessens mitzuentscheiden. Die pädagogischen Mitarbeiterinnen und Mitarbeiter behalten sich das Recht vor zu bestimmen, dass bestimmte Nahrungsmittel nicht zum Frühstück mitgebracht werden dürfen." (Hansen & Knauer, 2015, S. 248)

Die Kita-Verfassung soll die Beteiligungsrechte und -verfahren in der pädagogischen Institution dauerhaft und verlässlich regeln (Sturzenhecker et al., 2016).

Begibt sich eine Kindertageseinrichtung erstmals auf den Weg der Partizipation, bietet sich zunächst die Durchführung eines *Partizipationsprojektes* an. Partizipationsprojekte sind ebenfalls ein Strang des Konzeptes 'Die Kinderstube der Demokratie' und können zu unterschiedlichen Themen geplant werden. Ein Beispiel wäre die Neugestaltung eines Spielgerätes auf dem Außengelände. Es wird beschlossen, die Kinder aktiv an diesem Prozess zu beteiligen. Dazu wird dann ein Projektplan geschrieben (siehe Tab. 1). Dieser enthält ein konkretes Ziel. Außerdem werden in dem Plan die einzelnen Projektschritte festgehalten und festgelegt, in welchen Formen die Kinder mitbestimmen und mitwirken können (Hansen & Knauer, 2015). Partizipationsprojekte haben den Vorteil, dass sie zeitlich begrenzt sind und genau festgelegt ist, in welchen Projektschritten die Kinder wieviel Mitbestimmung und Beteiligung erhalten (Hansen & Knauer, 2016a).

Tabelle 1: Beispiel-Projektplan für die Neugestaltung eines Spielgerätes (nach Hansen & Knauer, 2015).

Projektschritt	**Wer entscheidet/handelt?**		**Anmerkungen**
	Fachkräfte	**Kinder**	
Ideen sammeln	x	x	Kataloge, Bücher, gemalte Bilder
Neues Spielgerät aussuchen		x	Besprechung im Morgenkreis, Abstimmen mit Klebepunkten
Finanzen klären	x		
Aufbau planen	x	x	
Vorschriften prüfen	x		
Altes Spielgerät abreißen	x		Hausmeister*in
Material besorgen	x		Hausmeister*in
Neues Spielgerät aufbauen	x	x	Kinder dürfen unter Anleitung der/des Hausmeister*in helfen

Kindertageseinrichtungen, die mit dem Konzept ‚Die Kinderstube der Demokratie' arbeiten, erfüllen die geforderten Kernelemente des normativen Leitbildes: Sie nehmen eine partizipative Grundhaltung ein, schaffen geeignete Partizipationsmöglichkeiten durch die Vereinbarung von Selbstbestimmungsrechten der Kinder und die Etablierung von Beteiligungsgremien und/oder Partizipationsprojekten. Sie verankern diese Selbst-, Mitbestimmungs- und Problemlösungsmöglichkeiten strukturell in der Kita-Verfassung.

5. Resümee

Dieser Beitrag illustriert exemplarisch, wie ein abstraktes Kinderrecht in die pädagogisch-institutionelle Praxis überführt werden kann. Pädagogische Fachkräfte und insbesondere Leitungskräfte tragen die Verantwortung dafür, dass Kinderrechte in der Praxis umgesetzt und gefördert werden. Dieser Beitrag soll Mut machen, sich der Verantwortung bewusst zu stellen, die abstrakt anmutenden Kinderrechte in der konkreten Praxis umzusetzen.

Literatur

Autorengruppe Fachkräftebarometer. (2023). *Fachkräftebarometer Frühe Bildung 2023. Weiterbildungsinitiative Frühpädagogische Fachkräfte.* https://doi.org/10.3278/9783763976287

Bundesministerium für Familie, Senioren, Frauen und Jugend. (BMFSFJ). (2018). *VN-Kinderrechtskonvention.* https://www.bmfsfj.de/bmfsfj/themen/kinder-und-jugend/kinderrechte/vn-kinderrechtskonvention#:~:text=Das%2520Übereinkommen%2520über%2520die%2520Rechte%2520des%2520Kindes%2520besteht,und%2520persönliche%2520Entwicklung%252C%2520dem%2520Beteiligungsrecht%2520und%2520dem%2520Kindeswohlvorrang.

Cremer, H. (2012). Kinderrechte und der Vorrang des Kindeswohls. *Anwaltsblatt, 62*(4), 327–329.

Deutsches Institut für Menschenrechte. (Hrsg.). (2019). *Allgemeine Bemerkung Nr. 12: Das Recht des Kindes auf Gehör.* https://www.institut-fuer-menschenrechte.de/publikationen/detail/allgemeine-bemerkung-nr-12-2009.

Hansen, R., & Knauer, R. (2015). *Das Praxisbuch: Mitentscheiden und Mithandeln in der Kita* (9. Aufl.). Bertelsmann Stiftung.

Hansen, R., & Knauer, R. (2016a). „Die Kinderstube der Demokratie". Eckpunkte eines Konzepts zur Eröffnung von Demokratiebildung von Kindern in Kindertageseinrichtungen. In B. Sturzenhecker, E. Richter & T. Lehmann (Hrsg.), *So machen Kitas Demokratiebildung* (S. 15–27). Beltz.

Hansen, R., & Knauer, R. (2016b). Kinderschutz braucht eine „konstitutionelle Pädagogik". *KiTa aktuell, 9*, 176–178.

Hansen, R., Knauer, R., & Sturzenhecker, B. (2009). Die Kinderstube der Demokratie. Partizipation von Kindern in Kindertageseinrichtungen. *Theorie und Praxis der Sozialpädagogik, 12*(2), 46–50.

Hildebrandt, F., & Pergande, B. (2022). Beteiligung von Kindern im Kita-Alltag: Theoretische Überlegungen und empirische Erkenntnisse aus der BiKA-Studie zu Partizipation in Krippen. In R. Knauer & B. Sturzenhecker (Hrsg.), *Demokratische Partizipation und Inklusion in Kindertageseinrichtungen* (S. 290–307). Beltz Juventa.

Kupffer, H. (1980). *Erziehung. Angriff auf die Freiheit.* Beltz.

Maywald, J. (2016). 25 Jahre UN-Kinderrechtskonvention. In L. Krappmann & C. Petry (Hrsg.), *Worauf Kinder und Jugendliche ein Recht haben: Kinderrechte, Demokratie und Schule: Ein Manifest* (S. 57–69). Debus Pädagogik.

Maywald, J. (2023). Der Kinderrechtsansatz im Ganztag. Beteiligung – Förderung – Schutz. In J. Maywald, L. Pesch & K. Dohle (Hrsg.), *Ganztag im besten Interesse der Kinder* (S. 31–97). Herder.

Ministerium für Justiz, Frauen, Jugend und Familie des Landes Schleswig-Holstein. (MJFJF). (Hrsg.). (2004). *Die Kinderstube der Demokratie. Partizipation in Kindertagesstätten.* https://www.partizipation-und-bildung.de/pdf/Hansen%20et%20al_Die%20Kinderstube%20der%20Demokratie.pdf.

Ministerium für Soziales, Gesundheit, Jugend, Familie und Senioren des Landes Schleswig-Holstein. (MSGJFS). (Hrsg.). (2020). *Leitlinien zum Bildungsauftrag in Kindertagesstätten.* https://www.schleswig-holstein.de/DE/landesregierung/ministerien-behoerden/VIII/Service/Broschueren/Broschueren_VIII/Kita/BildungsleitlinienDeutsch.pdf?__blob=publicationFile&v=2.

Schäfer, C. D. (2023). Partizipation als Qualitätsdimension im Ganztag. Denn ohne Kinder geht es nicht (gut). In J. Maywald, L. Pesch & K. Dohle (Hrsg.), *Ganztag im besten Interesse der Kinder* (S. 79–88). Herder.

Schröder, R. (1995). *Kinder reden mit!* Beltz.
Schubert-Suffrian, F., & Regner, M. (2018). *Partizipation in der Kita*. Herder.
Sturzenhecker, B., Richter, E., & Lehmann, T. (2016). *So machen Kitas Demokratiebildung.* Beltz.
Wolff, M. (2022). Beteiligung und Machtreflexion als Grundprinzipien pädagogischen Handelns. In J.-F. Huffmann, L. Pesch & A. Scheffler (Hrsg.), *Gelingende Partizipation* (S. 33–43). UTB.

Further Contributions in the Volume

Another practical example for implementing children's rights is provided by *Margit Stein, Benjamin Möbus,* and *Fabio Wensing* on the UNICEF Child Rights Schools Program (pp. 115–129).

The focus article by *Antonia Bongen* on diversity management as a prevention for discrimination offers another perspective on the practical implications of children's rights (pp. 79–86).

Julia Hugo, Charlotte Assmann, Andreas Schmidt (Eds.)
Educational Leadership and Children's Rights?/
Kinderrechte als Führungsaufgabe?
 https://doi.org/10.31244/9783830998259_11

Thea Jenner

Kinderrechtssensibler Ganztag

Implikationen der Kinderrechtskonvention für die Gestaltung ganztägiger Bildungs- und Betreuungsangebote

Zusammenfassung
Dieser Beitrag untersucht die Implikationen der UN-Kinderrechtskonvention (UN-KRK) vor dem Hintergrund der geteilten Verantwortung von Schule und Kinder- und Jugendhilfe für die Gestaltung ganztägiger Bildungs- und Betreuungsangebote im Sinne des Ganztagsförderungsgesetzes (GaFöG). Die These lautet, dass es einer zeitgemäßen Übersetzung der abstrakt formulierten Kinderrechte anhand der vier Dimensionen *Schutz, Versorgung, Förderung* und *Partizipation* in konkrete Handlungsempfehlungen bedarf, um die Qualität im Ganztag zu stärken.

Schlüsselbegriffe
Ganztag, Rechtsanspruch, Kinderrechte, Ganztagsförderungsgesetz, UN-Kinderrechtskonvention

A Children's Rights Approach to All-day Schooling

Implications of the Convention on the Rights of the Child for All-day Education and Care Programs

Abstract
This article examines the implications of the UN Convention on the Rights of the Child (UN CRC) given the shared responsibility of the school system and the child welfare system regarding the organization of all-day education and care programs according to the German *Ganztagsförderungsgesetz (GaFöG)*. It states that the abstractly formulated children's rights in their four dimensions of protection, care, academic support and participation need to be translated into concrete recommendations to strengthen the quality of all-day programs.

Keywords
All-day schooling, Legal Entitlement, Children's Rights, German Ganztagsförderungsgesetz, UN CRC

1. Einleitung

Ab dem 1. August 2026 tritt der Rechtsanspruch auf ganztägige Bildungs- und Betreuungsangebote für Kinder im Grundschulalter (GaFöG) stufenweise in Kraft. Damit gewinnt der Diskurs um die Verwirklichung von Kinderrechten im Ganztag an Bedeutung. Das in der Fachliteratur angeführte Argument leuchtet ein: Wenn Kinder mehr Zeit in Institutionen verbringen, wie die steigenden Nutzungszahlen von Ganztagsschulen und Hortangeboten verdeutlichen (Autor:innengruppe Bildungsberichterstattung, 2024, S. 142), dann müssen „diese Bildungsorte […] jenseits ihres speziellen Bildungsauftrags die alterstypischen Bedürfnisse und Entwicklungsaufgaben […] berücksichtigen" (Arnoldt, 2023, S. 201) und damit kinderrechtssensibel gestaltet werden (Wichmann, 2011, S. 363). Auch aus familienpolitischen Überlegungen ist die Umsetzung von Kinderrechten im Ganztag dringend geboten: Zum einen verändern sich Familienstrukturen, und damit fällt es Institutionen zu, mehr Funktionen zu übernehmen, die früher bei der Familie lagen (El-Mafaalani, 2024; Wichmann, 2011; BT-Drucksache 19/27200). Zum anderen können ganztägige Angebote Erziehungsberechtigten einen Vollzeit- oder vollzeitäquivalentem Beschäftigungsumfang ermöglichen, und so zur besseren Versorgung von Kindern beitragen, deren Familien in Armut leben.

Grundsätzlich sind Überlegungen zur Frage, was gute und kinderrechtssensible Ganztagsangebote ausmachen, die zur Verwirklichung von Kinderrechten beitragen, nicht neu. Enderlein und Krappmann (2006) entwickelten schon vor knapp 20 Jahren die „Thesen für eine ‚Gute Ganztagsschule'" (Enderlein & Krappmann, 2006, S. 79). Neu ist die gesetzliche Regelung durch das GaFöG und die geteilte Verantwortung von Schule und Kinder- und Jugendhilfe. Der Rechtsanspruch kann an verschiedenen Orten realisiert werden: In der Schule, in Horten und anderen Einrichtungen (mit Betriebserlaubnis) der Kinder- und Jugendhilfe und – mit Hilfe von Kooperationsvereinbarungen – auch in Zusammenarbeit mit außerschulischen Partnern. Zentral ist vor dem Hintergrund der Konstruktion des Rechtsanspruchs damit, dass institutionenübergreifende bzw. ganzheitliche Ansätze verfolgt werden (Arnoldt, 2023, S. 203) und diese kinderrechtssensibel gestaltet werden.

2. Implikationen der Dimensionen der Kinderrechtskonvention

Die Einführung des Rechtsanspruchs und der vom Bund geförderte Ganztagsausbau[1] verfolgt relevante gesellschaftliche Ziele: Bildungs- und Teilhabechancen für Kinder, eine bessere Vereinbarkeit von Familie und Beruf (insbesondere hinsichtlich der Stärkung von Müttererwerbstätigkeit) und damit verbunden eine Abfederung des aktuellen Fachkräftebedarfs (BT-Drucksache 19/29764, S. 1). Auch die Umsetzung von

1 Der Bund unterstützt den Ganztagsausbau mit Finanzhilfen in Höhe von bis zu 3,5 Milliarden Euro für Investitionen in die kommunale Bildungsinfrastruktur. Auch an den Betriebskosten wird sich der Bund beteiligen (ab 2026 aufsteigend und dann ab 2030 mit bis zu 1,3 Milliarden Euro pro Jahr).

Kinderrechten ist ein formuliertes Ziel im Sinne der Gesetzesbegründung „Die Einführung des Anspruchs und die Gewährung von Finanzhilfen zum quantitativen und qualitativen Ausbau von ganztägigen Bildungs- und Betreuungsangeboten dienen auch der Umsetzung der VN-Kinderrechtskonvention“ (ebd., S. 17). Bislang fehlt aber – sowohl im wissenschaftlichen Diskurs als auch auf den Steuerungsebenen von Bund, Ländern und Kommunen – eine spezifische Perspektive auf die Verwirklichung von Kinderrechten in der Praxis des Ganztags (Bendig, 2023). Als positive Beispiele werden in der Fachliteratur Maßnahmen genannt, die überwiegend auf der Ebene der Einrichtung und im Sinne von Selbstverpflichtungen und -reflexionen umgesetzt werden: UNESCO-Kinderrechteschulen (Bendig, 2023), Praxisleitfäden und Checklisten (Dohle, 2023) oder Reflexionsimpulse, wie z. B. die Reckahner Reflexionen zur Gestaltung pädagogischer Beziehungen (Deutsches Institut für Menschenrechte et al., 2017). Zu prüfen wäre, ob die Bedingungen in ganztägigen Bildungs- und Betreuungsangeboten „[...] der kinderrechtlichen Prüfung standhalten [und ob] [...] Schutz-, Förder- und Partizipationsrechte“ (Bendig, 2023, S. 170) auf Bundes-, Landes-, kommunaler Ebene und Ebene der einzelnen Einrichtungen beachtet werden. Im Folgenden wird diesbezüglich eine grobe Skizzierung entlang der Kinderrechtsdimensionen *Schutz, Versorgung, Förderung* und *Partizipation* vorgenommen.

2.1 Schutz

Den Einrichtungen und Angeboten des Ganztags obliegt eine besondere Verantwortung, den Schutz der Kinder vor Gewalt (Art. 19), vor sexuellem Missbrauch (Art. 34) sowie den Schutz der Privatsphäre (Art. 16) sicherzustellen. Bildungsinstitutionen können zwar einerseits „eine schützende Gegenwelt zu bedrohlichen Situationen in der Familie oder im sozialen Umfeld“ (Wichmann, 2011, S. 363) darstellen; andererseits bergen sie das Risiko, selbst ein Umfeld zu bilden, das den Schutz von Kindern nicht sicherstellen kann oder sogar missachtet. Nach dem Offenlegen von Missbrauchsfällen an der Odenwaldschule und in der katholischen wie evangelischen Kirche ist die Risikolage, der Kinder und Jugendliche in ihrem Alltag ausgesetzt sind, verstärkt ins Augenmerk der Öffentlichkeit gelangt.[2] Zudem rückt das Thema des psychischen und seelischen Wohlbefindens in den Fokus von Forschung (Piezunka, 2023); und seit Entstehen der KRK im Jahr 1989 ist das Thema des Schutzes von Kindern *in* bzw. ihrer Teilhabe *an* der digitalen Welt hinzugekommen.

Notwendig sind ausformulierte Schutzkonzepte und Notfallpläne für den Ganztag. Für betriebserlaubnispflichtige Einrichtungen der Kinder- und Jugendhilfe (z. B. Horte) sind verbindliche Schutzkonzepte seit 10. Juni 2021 vorzuhalten, für den Bereich Schule gibt es solche Regelungen bisher nicht. Schutzkonzepte müssen zudem auch von den Beteiligten umgesetzt und in der räumlich-sächlichen Gestaltung realisiert

---

2 In diesem Zusammenhang ist auch auf die bestehende, übergreifende Datenlücke hinzuweisen: Rauschenbach und Kindler (2022) fordern eine empirische Wende im Kinderschutz und das regelmäßige Erheben von Indikatoren. Bisher ungeklärt ist, welche Indikatoren das für einen institutionenübergreifenden Ganztag sein könnten, und in welchem Rahmen diese regelmäßig erhoben werden könnten.

werden (bspw. bei der Gestaltung von sanitären Einrichtungen, Umkleidebereichen, Rückzugsorten etc.).

2.2 Versorgung

Die Versorgungsdimension (Art. 24 und Art. 31) adressiert die Erfüllung menschlicher Grundbedürfnisse: Essen und Trinken, Bewegung, Freizeit, Spiel, Ruhe und auch Schlaf (Wapler, 2020, S. 17). Kinder haben das Recht auf eine gute Versorgung – gerade im Ganztag. Die zunehmende Zahl von knapp 2,1 Millionen Kindern und Jugendlichen unter 18 Jahren, die in Deutschland unterhalb der EU-offiziellen Armuts(gefährdungs)grenze leben, verleiht der Dimension zusätzliche Bedeutung (Destatis, 2024; Butterwege, 2019). Am Beispiel der Verpflegung wird deutlich, dass der Ganztag eine verantwortungsvolle Position einnimmt: wenn Kinder weniger Mahlzeiten zu Hause einnehmen, dann müssen die in Institutionen angebotenen Mahlzeiten zwei grundlegende Anforderungen erfüllen: einerseits in ausreichender Menge, andererseits in Qualität und Attraktivität angeboten werden.

Während die Deutsche Gesellschaft für Ernährung e.V. (DGE) für die Gemeinschaftsverpflegung wissenschaftlich basierte Qualitätsstandards formuliert hat, fehlen Standards und kinderrechtsensible Handlungsempfehlungen für die übrigen Aspekte der Versorgungsdimension. Offen ist u. a. wie die Gestaltung von Räumen (auch sanitären Einrichtungen, Ruhezonen etc.) aussehen muss, damit sie dem Kinderrecht auf Bewegung und Ruhe entspricht.

2.3 Förderung

Grundsätzlich entspricht die Rechtslage in Deutschland dem in der KRK festgeschriebenen Recht auf Bildung (Art. 28 und 29) im Sinne eines Zugangs zu Bildungsinstitutionen und dem Recht des Kindes entsprechend seiner Bedürfnisse und Fähigkeiten gefördert zu werden (Füssel, 2020). Jedoch stellt sich in Hinblick auf die Ausgestaltung des Rechtsanspruchs auf ganztägige Bildung und Betreuung die Frage der Reichweite von Artikel 28 und 29 gegenüber Artikel 18. Die KRK unterscheidet Kindertagesbetreuung und Schule; das GaFöG bringt diese unterschiedlichen Bereiche zusammen. In der Folge müsste ein von Schule, Kinder- und Jugendhilfe und ggf. auch außerschulischen Akteuren formuliertes gemeinsames Bildungsverständnis auf Ebene der Länder entwickelt werden, wie es in einigen Ländern bereits geschehen ist (z. B. Thüringer Bildungsplan bis 18 Jahre; Bildungsgrundsätze in Nordrhein-Westfalen).

Zweitens wird hinsichtlich der Qualitätsaspekte des Ganztags deutlich, dass sich das in der KRK verankerte umfassende Recht auf Bildung auf Angebotsebene widerspiegeln muss. Neben der Förderung basaler Kompetenzen ist im Sinne der KRK auch an Förderung in vielfältigen Bereichen zu denken: Sprache und Kommunikation; soziales Miteinander; Umgang mit Emotionen/Konfliktfähigkeit; Bewegung; Umwelt/

Nachhaltigkeit; MINT; kulturelle Bildung, Gesundheit, Gleichstellung und Sexualpädagogik etc.

Und drittens ergibt sich aus dem Zusammenwirken von KRK und UN-Behindertenrechtskonvention, dass der Ganztag inklusiv zu gestalten ist, sodass allen Kindern im Grundschulalter durch die Förderung in ganztägigen Bildungs- und Betreuungsangeboten Teilhabe ermöglicht wird.

2.4 Partizipation

Partizipation (Art. 12 und Art. 13) wird in der pädagogischen Praxis teilweise verengt gedacht: nämlich als Demokratieerziehung, z. B. durch Einführung eines Klassenrats oder der Bearbeitung von Kinderrechten im Unterricht. Beides ist wichtig[3], im Sinne des Vorrangs des Kindeswohls (Art. 3) muss Partizipation jedoch breiter gedacht werden – nämlich über den unmittelbaren Kontext von Schule und Unterricht hinaus (Gerarts, 2024).

Für die Weiterentwicklung des Ganztags im Sinne des GaFöGs und der KRK müssten Kinder an der Ausgestaltung des Ganztags auf kommunaler Ebene beteiligt werden. In vielen Kommunen existieren bereits Institutionen zur Beteiligung/Anhörung von Kindern: Kinder- und Jugendbeteiligungsbüros, -parlamente, -beauftragte oder Ombudsstellen. Darüber hinaus sind Kinderrechte bei allen Maßnahmen und Verwaltungsentscheidungen der Kommunen zu beachten, die ein Kind oder mehrere Kinder betreffen, in dem kinderrechtsrelevante Umstände eruiert werden und eine Anhörung/Berücksichtigung der Kinder durchgeführt wird (Donath, 2019). Für den Ganztag bedeutet dies, dass Kommunen etwa bei der u. a. auch baulichen Planung und Gestaltung des Ganztagsausbaus die Interessen von Kindern in formalen Beteiligungsverfahren anhören müssen – wenn z. B. eine Mensa gebaut, eine Sporthalle saniert oder ein Schulhof neugestaltet wird.

3. Ausblick

Dieser Beitrag versucht zu skizzieren, dass die Integration von Kinderrechten im Ganztag bisher nur defizitär vollzogen wird. Dabei zeigt sich ein heterogenes Bild: Während Einrichtungen der Kinder- und Jugendhilfe aufgrund der Bedingungen für die Betriebserlaubnis insbesondere hinsichtlich der Schutz- und Versorgungsdimension der Kinderrechte etwas besser aufgestellt sind, müssten diese Dimensionen im Bereich Schule stärker verankert werden, d. h., sie müssten Eingang in Schulgesetze

3 Eine wesentliche Voraussetzung für die Umsetzung von Partizipation ist eine „positive Grundhaltung" der Lehr- und Fachkräfte gegenüber der Beteiligung von Kindern (Schäfer, 2022, S. 82). Problematisch ist für alle Dimensionen der KRK, aber insbesondere für die Dimension der Partizipation, dass Kinderrechte kaum in Aus- und Weiterbildungen gelehrt werden, sodass nicht grundsätzlich davon ausgegangen werden kann, dass dem im Ganztag beschäftigten Personal die Inhalte der Kinderrechte und Möglichkeiten ihrer Umsetzung in die Praxis ausreichend bekannt sind (Krappmann, 2022, S. 28).

finden und von den Schulträgern und Schulen umgesetzt werden. Für die Förderungsdimension stellen gemeinsame Bildungspläne von Schule und Kinder- und Jugendhilfe auf Landesebene einen Lösungsansatz dar. Für die Dimension der Partizipation müssen Kommunen ihrer Verpflichtung, Kinder beim Ganztagsausbau zu beteiligen, nachkommen. Zudem stellt sich die noch offene Forschungsfrage, wie die Umsetzung von Kinderrechten im Ganztag vor dem Hintergrund des Zusammenwirkens von Schule und Kinder- und Jugendhilfe gelingen kann.

Literatur

Arnoldt, B. (2023). Ganztagsschule durch Kooperationen kind- und jugendgerecht gestalten. Warum tragen außerschulische Akteur:innen zur Qualität bei und wie gelingt die Zusammenarbeit? *SchulVerwaltung spezial: Zeitschrift für Schulgestaltung und Schulentwicklung, 25*(5), 201–204. https://doi.org/10.25656/01:27862

Autor:innengruppe Bildungsberichterstattung. (2024). *Bildung in Deutschland 2024. Ein indikatorengestützter Bericht mit einer Analyse zu beruflicher Bildung.* wbv. https://doi.org/10.3278/6001820iw

Bendig, R. (2023). ‚Ich habe Rechte und kann darauf vertrauen, dass sie umgesetzt werden' Kinderrechtsansatz und Kinderperspektive als Qualitätsmerkmal. In L. Pesch, K. Dohle & J. Maywald (Hrsg.), *Ganztag im besten Interesse der Kinder. Kinderrechte für Große Kinder verwirklichen* (S. 160–173). Herder.

Butterwege, C. (2019). Bildung – ein probates Mittel zur Bekämpfung von (Kinder-)Armut in Deutschland? In G. Quenzel & K. Hurrelmann (Hrsg.), *Handbuch Bildungsarmut* (S. 743–767). Springer. https://doi.org/10.1007/978-3-658-19573-1_30

Destatis – Statistisches Bundesamt. (2024, 1. Juli). *Jedes siebte Kind in Deutschland armutsgefährdet* [Pressemitteilung]. https://www.destatis.de/DE/Presse/Pressemitteilungen/2024/07/PD24_N033_63.html.

Deutsche Gesellschaft für Ernährung e.V. (2023). *DGE-Qualitätsstandard für die Verpflegung in Schulen* (5. Aufl.). DGE.

Deutscher Bundestag. (2021). *Drucksache 19/29764: Gesetzentwurf der Fraktionen der CDU/CSU und SPD. Entwurf eines Gesetzes zur ganztägigen Förderung von Kindern im Grundschulalter (Ganztagsförderungsgesetz – GaFöG), 18.05.2021.* https://dserver.bundestag.de/btd/19/297/1929764.pdf.

Deutscher Bundestag. (2021). *Drucksache 19/27200: Neunter Familienbericht. Eltern sein in Deutschland – Ansprüche, Anforderungen und Angebote bei wachsender Vielfalt, 03.03.2021.* https://dserver.bundestag.de/btd/19/272/1927200.pdf.

Deutsches Institut für Menschenrechte Berlin/Deutsches Jugendinstitut München/MenschenRechtsZentrum an der Universität Potsdam/Rochow Museum und Akademie für bildungsgeschichtliche und zeitdiagnostische Forschung an der Universität Potsdam. (Hrsg.). (2017). *Reckahner Reflexionen zur Ethik pädagogischer Beziehungen.* Rochow-Edition. https://paedagogische-beziehungen.eu/.

Dohle, K. (2023). Checkliste: Bildungseinrichtungen im besten Interesse der Kinder gestalten. In L. Pesch, K. Dohle & J. Maywald (Hrsg.), *Ganztag im besten Interesse der Kinder. Kinderrechte für Große Kinder verwirklichen* (S. 174–177). Herder.

Donath, P. (2019). *Gutachten: Kinderrechte im kommunalen Verwaltungshandeln.* Deutsches Kinderhilfswerk e.V. https://shop.dkhw.de/de/fachpublikationen/165-gutachten-kinderrechte-im-kommunalen-verwaltungshandeln.html.

El-Mafaalani, A. (2024). *Bildungsgerechtigkeit im Ganztag durch Multidimensionalität erreichen* [Video]. BMFSFJ. https://www.recht-auf-ganztag.de/gb/videomitschnitt-keynote-prof-el-mafaalani-238454.

Enderlein, O., & Krappmann, L. (2006). Thesen für eine ‚Gute Ganztagsschule'. In S. Knauer & A. Durdel (Hrsg.), *Die neue Ganztagsschule. Gute Lernbedingungen gestalten* (S. 79–84). Beltz.

Füssel, H.-P. (2020). Recht auf Bildung. In I. Richter, L. Krappmann & F. Wapler (Hrsg.), *Kinderrechte. Handbuch des deutschen und internationalen Kinder- und Jugendrechts* (S. 223–246). Nomos.

Gerarts, K. (2024). *Die UN-Kinderrechte als Grundlage pädagogischen Handelns. Ein Blick auf Möglichkeiten und Grenzen.* https://katharina-gerarts.de/Media.

Krappmann, L. (2022). Die UN-Kinderrechtskonvention in Deutschland. Wie weit sind wir gekommen? In Deutsches Kinderhilfswerk (Hrsg.), *Kinderrechte in Deutschland. Interdisziplinäre Perspektiven auf Errungenschaften und Herausforderungen kinderrechtlicher Arbeit in Deutschland* (S. 19–32). Kopaed.

Ministerium für Kinder, Familie, Flüchtlinge und Integration des Landes Nordrhein-Westfalen & Ministerium für Schule und Bildung des Landes Nordrhein-Westfalen. (Hrsg.). (2018). *Bildungsgrundsätze. Mehr Chancen durch Bildung von Anfang an.* Herder.

Piezunka, A. (2023). Seelische Verletzungen in der Gestaltung pädagogischer Beziehungen. In N. Leonhardt, A. Goldbach, L. Staib & S. Schuppener (Hrsg.), *Macht in der Schule. Wissen – Sichtweisen – Erfahrungen. Texte in Leichter Sprache, Einfacher Sprache und Fachsprache* (S. 218–230). Klinkhardt. https://doi.org/10.35468/5980-13

Rauschenbach, T., & Kindler, H. (2022). Auf dem Weg zu Qualitätsindikatoren für das Kinderschutzsystem in Deutschland. In Deutsches Kinderhilfswerk (Hrsg.), *Kinderrechte in Deutschland. Interdisziplinäre Perspektiven auf Errungenschaften und Herausforderungen kinderrechtlicher Arbeit in Deutschland* (S. 91–103). Kopaed.

Schäfer, C. D. (2022). Partizipation als Qualitätsdimension im Ganztag: Denn ohne Kinder geht es nicht (gut). In L. Pesch, K. Dohle & J. Maywald (Hrsg.), *Ganztag im besten Interesse der Kinder. Kinderrechte für Große Kinder verwirklichen* (S. 79–88). Herder.

Thüringer Ministerium für Bildung, Jugend und Sport. (Hrsg.). (2019). *Thüringer Bildungsplan bis 18 Jahre.* MBJS. https://bildung.thueringen.de/bildung/bildungsplan.

Wapler, F. (2020). *Chancen für guten Ganztag für Kinder im Grundschulalter: menschenrechtliche Perspektiven.* Bertelsmann. https://www.bertelsmann-stiftung.de/de/publikationen/publikation/did/chancen-guten-ganztags-fuer-kinder-im-grundschulalter-menschenrechtliche-perspektiven-all.

Wichmann, M. (2011). Kinderrechte und Kinderschutz in der Ganztagsschule. In J. Fischer, T. Buchholz & R. Merten (Hrsg.), *Kinderschutz in gemeinsamer Verantwortung von Jugendhilfe und Schule* (S. 361–372). Springer VS.

Further Contributions in the Volume

A focus on a specific leadership is offered by *Hanna Luise Bronnert-Härle* and *Esther Dominique Klein* who empirically explore transformational leadership as an answer for issues of schools in marginalized communities (pp. 23–39).

Another practical example for implementing children's rights is provided by *Margit Stein*, *Benjamin Möbus,* and *Fabio Wensing* on the UNICEF Child Rights Schools Program (pp. 115–129).

Editors

Herausgeberinnen und Herausgeber

Charlotte Assmann (M.Ed.) is a PhD scholar, funded by the Foundation of German Economy (Stiftung der Deutschen Wirtschaft) and works as research assistant at the Chair of School Pedagogy with a focus on Educational Governance and Educational Change at Friedrich-Alexander-University (FAU) Erlangen-Nuremberg. In her research she is concerned with the interface of school system development, namely school supervision and law.

Julia Hugo, Dr., works as a research assistant at the Chair of School Pedagogy with a focus on Educational Governance and Educational Change at Friedrich-Alexander-University (FAU) Erlangen-Nuremberg. Her research focusses on the interface between school system development and educational administration/law.

Andreas Schmidt is a PhD candidate at the Institute of Educational Science at the Eberhard Karls University of Tübingen. His current research focus is the empirical assessment of the professional theory of meta-reflexivity in teacher education. In a transnational research project, his newly developed scale on meta-reflexive principles is linked to other concepts, like empirical beliefs, to better understand teacher professionalization.

Authors

Autorinnen und Autoren

Silvia Annen, Prof. Dr., is a professor at the Professorship of Business Education at the University of Bamberg. Her research interests include recognition of qualifications and competencies, labour market usability of qualifications and returns to education, international comparative (vocational) education research, and governance of the education and employment system.

Linn Behrendt is a fellow of the Foundation of German Economy (Stiftung der Deutschen Wirtschaft) and is currently pursuing a master's degree in educational science at the University of Cologne. She specializes in early childhood and children's rights.

Antonia Bongen, fellow of the Foundation of German Economy (Stiftung der Deutschen Wirtschaft), works as pedagogy and qualitiy specialist for early childhood education in Wuppertal and as a lecturer at the University of Applied Sciences Düsseldorf. In her work she focusses on diversity in childhood and adolescence.

Hanna Luise Bronnert-Härle works as a research assistant at the Institute of General Didactics and School Pedagogy at TU Dortmund University. In her dissertation she investigates the relationship between leadership, school culture and parental involvement in schools serving marginalized communities.

Colin Cramer, Prof. Dr., is a professor of Educational Science at the University of Konstanz and the Thurgau University of Teacher Education. His current research focuses on teachers and teacher education, basic educational theory, and educational leadership.

Carolina Dahle, PhD, research fellow at the Faculty of Humanities, Sports and Educational Science at the University of South-Eastern Norway (USN). Her doctoral research focuses on the autonomy of school leaders in the implementation of inclusive education in Norway and Germany.

Melanie Hochmuth is a research associate and PhD candidate at the Professorship of Business Education at the University of Bamberg. Her research focuses on vocational orientation and guidance, transitions from school to vocational education and training, and the satisfaction and quality of vocational training.

Julia Hufnagl, an alumna of the sdw scholarship program, is a research associate and PhD candidate at the Professorship of Business Education at the University of Bamberg. Her research interests include Education for Sustainable Development (ESD), intersectional disadvantages and discriminatory processes in vocational education and training, and international comparative (vocational) education research.

Thea Jenner, Dr., works at the Federal Ministry of Education and Research in Germany. Her work in the division "Funding of School Infrastructure" focuses on issues relating to all-day schooling, open educational resources and games/esports.

Esther Dominique Klein, Prof. Dr., is a professor at the Institute of General Didactics and School Pedagogy at TU Dortmund University. Her current research focuses on educational leadership, the improvement of schools serving marginalized communities and the collaboration between schools and school authorities.

Ruth Luzmore is a research fellow at the University of Southampton and a lecturer at the National Institute of Teaching and Education. Her research interests include educational leadership and professional development of teachers.

Mirjam Maier-Röseler, Dr., is a research associate at Department of Humanities and Social Sciences at the University of Education Karlsruhe. Her research interests include the development and design of schools, the continuous professional development of teachers and educational leadership. As part of the gifted education project and research association "Leistung macht Schule" (LemaS), she deals with issues relating to the collaboration and cooperative professionalization of actors and schools in networks.

Benjamin Möbus works as a research assistant and teaching coordinator in the subject of educational science at the University of Vechta. In his teaching and research, he focusses on the opportunities and challenges of digitalization (in inclusive settings) and the implementation of children's and human rights in schools and lessons.

Dong Nguyen, Dr., is an associate professor of Educational Leadership at Durham University, UK. He has conducted research across many education systems and is editor in chief of International Journal of Educational Management – one of the core journals in the field of educational leadership and management.

Robert Pham Xuan, Dr., is a senior scientist at the University of Continuing Education Krems, Department of Continuing Education and Educational Technologies. He holds a PhD in Educational Science. His research focuses on inequality, inclusion and school development in multi-track school systems.

Tine Sophie Prøitz, Prof. Dr., is vice dean for research at the Faculty of Humanities, Sports and Educational Science at the University of South-Eastern Norway (USN). Prøitz is currently principal investigator for the research project CLASS-Comparisons of Leadership Autonomy in School districts and Schools funded by the Research Council of Norway.

Andreas Schmidt is a PhD candidate at the Institute of Educational Science at the Eberhard Karls University of Tübingen. His current research focuses on the empirical investigation of meta-reflexive principles in teacher education and their relation to other theoretically aligned concepts.

Philipp Schubert is an instructional designer at the Media Didactics Service Center at the University of Bamberg. He advises and supports universities developing and implementing cross-university digital teaching and learning opportunities.

David Sehmisch is studying to become a secondary school teacher at Friedrich-Alexander-University Erlangen-Nuremberg. He also works as a student assistant at the Chair of School Pedagogy with a focus on educational governance and educational change as part of a research project.

Enkeleta Shtërbani is a research associate at the Department of Humanities and Social Sciences at the University of Education Karlsruhe. Her research interests include the development of school and teaching, team teaching, teacher collaboration within school and in school networks. As part of the gifted education project and research association "Leistung macht Schule" (LemaS), she deals with issues relating to the structures and collaboration processes between actors and schools in school networks, network research, and support.

Margit Stein, Prof. Dr., is professor of general education at the University of Vechta, Germany. Her teaching, research and work focuses primarily on the area of value-based and democratic coexistence in a heterogeneous society.

Gabriele Weigand, Prof. Dr., is a professor of education at the Department of Humanities at the University of Education, Karlsruhe. She is the coordinator of the gifted education project and research association "Leistung macht Schule" (LemaS). Her research interests include anthropology and biographical studies, gifted education and school development research, institutional and intercultural education.

Fabio Wensing is a trainee teacher at the Tweel elementary school in Garrel. As part of his studies to become an elementary school teacher with the subjects of mathematics and sport, he studied the linking of children's rights in schools in depth.

Reviewers
Gutachterinnen und Gutachter

Christopher Brown, Prof. Dr., is professor of education at the University of Southampton, Head of the Southampton Education School and distinguished visiting professor at the University of Tübingen. In his work he focuses on the question of how people go about harnessing great ideas to improve the human condition.

Sonja Ertl, Prof. Dr., is professor of primary school research with a focus on inclusive teaching and learning at the University of Augsburg. Her research interests include student-teacher-conferences and the topic of children's rights and co-determination.

Richard Göllner, Prof. Dr., is a professor of process-oriented classroom research at the University of Potsdam. His research focuses on teaching quality, teacher effects, and their assessment, as well as on examining the impact on students' learning and personality development in educational settings, such as schools or universities.

Johannes Gutbrod, Dr., is research assistant at the Institute for School Pedagogy and Didactics (ISD) at the Karlsruhe Institute of Technology, (KIT). In his work, he is interested in pedagogical theory of action, school theory, and school development, among other things.

Theresia Höynck, Prof. Dr., is a professor for child and juvenile law at the University of Kassel. Her main research interests are juvenile delinquency and child protection. She is president of the German Juvenile Court Association (DVJJ).

Barbara Lenzgeiger, Jun.-Prof. Dr., is a professor of primary school pedagogy and primary school didactics at the Catholic University of Eichstätt-Ingolstadt (KU). Her research focuses on teacher professionalism, teaching and learning in the digital world, and basic education, among other things.

Claudia Lohrenscheit, Prof. Dr., is professor of international social work and human rights at the Coburg University of Applied Sciences. She is also a member of the National Coalition and of the Scientific Advisory Board of the Network for the Implementation of the UN Convention on the Rights of the Child in Germany. Her research focuses on international social work and human rights, education against racism, sexism, and anti-semitism as well as social movements.

Andreas Paschon, Mag. Dr., is a senior lecturer in empirical teaching and learning research at the Paris Lodron University Salzburg. His research and teaching focuses on school development and children's rights.

Stefanie Rinaldi, Prof. Dr., is professor at the PH Luzern and head of Institute for Education in Social Sciences. Her main areas of work include global issues in the classroom, political education, global citizenship education, and children's rights/human rights and education.

David Rott, Dr., is teacher in higher education at the Institute of Educational Science at the University of Münster. His research interests include issues relating to diversity-sensitive school and teaching development, particularly with regard to children's rights.

Felix Schreiber, Dr., is a research associate at the Institute of Education Science, Department of School Education, at the University of Tübingen. His research interests include the professionalization of teachers, systematic approaches in educational science, and the development of methods for clarifying ambiguous concepts and topics in educational sciences for teacher education.

Johanna E. Schwarz, Prof. Dr., is professor and head of the Center for Leadership-Culture, coordinator and head of the university course for school development consulting at the PH Niederösterreich. Her research focuses on school management, school leadership, and school development as well as school development consulting.

Marcus Syring, Prof. Dr., is professor of educational science in the working group Educational Science with a Focus on School Pedagogy. His research interests include heterogeneity, interculturality and inclusion at grammar schools, teacher professionalization and professionalism.

Ulrich Trautwein, Prof. Dr., is a professor of empirical educational research and director of the Hector Research Institute of Education Sciences and Psychology. His research interests include educational effectiveness, teaching quality, digital education, student motivation, and talent development.

Joshua Weidlich, Dr., is assistant professor of digital higher education at the University of Zurich. Before that, he was a postdoctoral researcher in the Educational Technologies Group at the DIPF. His current research interests are in learning analytics, AI-supported feedback, and feedback literacy.

Index

Sachwortregister